AN ABSENT PRESENCE

NEW AMERICANISTS *A Series Edited by Donald E. Pease*

AN ABSENT PRESENCE

Japanese Americans in Postwar American

Culture, 1945–1960

CAROLINE CHUNG SIMPSON

Duke University Press   *Durham & London*   2001

© 2001 Duke University Press

All rights reserved

Printed in the United States of

America on acid-free paper ∞

Designed by Amy Ruth Buchanan

Typeset in Scala by Wilsted & Taylor

Publishing Services

Library of Congress Cataloging-

in-Publication Data appear on

the last printed page of this book.

For my mother,

Ann Marie Simpson,

with love for the past

and the daily struggles

and

In memory of my father,

Edward Glynn Simpson,

whose struggles were not

in vain

. . .

"Homemade, homemade!

But aren't we all?"

—ELIZABETH BISHOP,

"Crusoe in England"

CONTENTS

ACKNOWLEDGMENTS

The enormous wealth of good will and intelligence needed to complete a book comes from many sources, some of them far removed from the author herself. I begin by thanking my earliest supporters, without whom I would never have thought to venture this far. They include my graduate school colleagues at the University of Texas at Austin, Lisa L. Moore and Neil Nehring, who persevered in the face of much conservative political resistance to this project within my own department. I am indebted to the initial advice and encouragement of Susan Glenn, who remains a respected colleague and friend and an exemplar of feminist teaching and scholarship. The early years of my thinking about this project were also enabled by the friendship and love of a worthy group of women, including members and fans of the "Yam Queens" women's softball team: Kathryn Baker, Kate Adams, Kim Emery, Shelly Booth Fowler, Denise Majorca, and Gail McDonald.

Many friends and scholars took the time to comment on or offer much needed criticism of this book as I was completing it. I am especially grateful to members of my feminist writing group, including Priscilla Wald, Susan Glenn, Christine di Stefano, Shirley Yee, and Angela Ginorio, for reading every draft of every chapter that appears here, and then some. I am warmed by their company and instructed by their conversation. Very special thanks go to Priscilla Wald, who more than anyone else promoted my work on this topic and remains a valued colleague. Carolyn Allen was peerless in her unwavering support of me as both friend and colleague. I will never forget her tireless support of and commitment to untenured feminist scholars at the University of Washington, and I will certainly never be able to express properly just how grateful I am for her example.

Tom Lockwood, the chairperson of the department when I was hired, unequivocally and steadfastly extended both his official and personal support to my career, through all the highs and lows. He also had the uncanny potential for reviving my memories of the early years in Texas and Louisiana, and he is solely responsible for all comments made by "the Colonel." My University of Washington colleague and chairperson Shawn Wong, whose friendship was much needed in those first few years, has encouraged this work as well. As an early pioneer in Asian American studies, his influence is undeniable.

I regularly depended on my good friend Traise Yamamoto for her intellectual insights, her honesty, and her commitment to building an admirable life of good work and good friends. I looked for daily doses of humor and high wit from my "collaborator" Joycelyn Moody; for consultation on all matters of fashion and culture, Shelly Eversley; for a comforting talk or two, which may have more to do with that "ringing" in his ear than we know, Juan Guerra; for early friendship, vigorous debates, and Tony Roma ribs, France Winndance Twine; and for opportunities that proved invaluable and instructive, Johnnella Butler.

Several other individuals deserve thanks for taking the time to offer comments, encourage my project or, in some cases, point out when I was wrong in my reasoning. This group includes Richard Handler, who as a reader of the chapter on camp anthropology offered vital historical advice; Tak Fujitani, who would be surprised to know how much his brief comments and conversation with me during my one-day visit at the University of California at San Diego helped to refocus my attention; Amy Ling, who heard an early version of chapter 5, expressed interest in it, and encouraged its completion; Reynolds Smith, my editor at Duke, whose enthusiasm and support for this book is the factor most responsible for bringing it to press; and Elaine Kim, whose work and activism regularly inspires us all. I must also acknowledge my students at the University of Washington, both past and present, whose generous insights and probing questions in seminars helped me to work through several significant questions. These individuals are Gregory Choy, Karen Kuo, Michael Oishi, Jim Cheung Chin, Tamiko Nimura, Peter Kvidera, Ann Hiramine, Maureen Boyd, Monique Allewaert, Patrick Linder, Leigh Ann Berte, Christine Mower, and Bryn Gribben.

All of my work is, of course, grounded in my relationship to my family, both born and made. My mother's and father's sacrifices over the years hardly need recognition, but I remain humbled by their efforts and thankful for their lives, even when we did not always agree. I can say now that I love them completely, without complete understanding. My sister, Anita Rehm, remains my much needed touchstone to the past. My love and admiration for her is deep and unshakable, and, as my older sister, she remains for me, despite her protests and embarrassment, the measure of courage and strength of will. To Rick, Brannon, and Alyssa, my thanks for the summer visits, the good times, and the love while I took a break from the solitary job of writing this book to play soccer, ride bikes, and watch *Wallace and Gromit* videos. In my adopted immediate family thanks go to Kafka the wonder schnauzer for showing me the joy of simply being, which she has done so well for the past ten years; to my adopted in-laws, Wanda, Jack, Jack Wayne, and Kevin Hensley and Grant Petersen, thanks for the wild "family" stories; to the Keiths and Jamesons—Amy, John, Derry, and Quentin—my gratitude for taking me into your family that first summer and for coming back for more. But none of this would mean much without my partner, Lendy V. Hensley. How lucky I feel to have your love and share your life and the wonderful times to come.

Chapter five appeared in a slightly abbreviated form in *differences* 10.3 (1998) as "Out of an Obscure Place. Japanese War Brides and Cultural Pluralism in the 1950's." Grateful acknowledgment is made for permission to reprint here.

INTRODUCTION

This book has what may at first appear a paradoxical ambition. It argues for the historical absence of an event that is perhaps the most widely reported and studied single episode in Asian American history: the internment of Japanese Americans during World War II. For decades the debacle and devastation of internment have been known and written about by many scholars, who acknowledge that the internment of Japanese Americans remains an unparalleled act in the history of the nation. It was an act that involved the forced removal and imprisonment of almost 120,000 people of Japanese ancestry in the United States, two-thirds of whom were American citizens by birth, under nothing more than a suspicion of what the U.S. government deemed "disloyalty." What's more, the record of the enduring interest in Japanese American internment crosses almost every imaginable disciplinary and genre boundary throughout the last fifty years of American culture.

Social scientists, both then and now, have remained intrigued by the so-called problem of Japanese American identity that became the dubious rationalization for internment. Many, although not all, of the social scientists who studied the effects of internment in the 1940s were white anthropologists who had never worked in Japanese or Japanese American cultures before taking part in the government analysis projects installed in the camps. Still, their numerous governmental reports and their scholarly articles based on observations of internment continue to offer a wealth of archival information for scholars. In response to residual public interest in the event, two major memoirs of the internment experience were published in the years immediately following the interment: Mine Okubo's *Citizen 13660* in 1946, and Monica

Sone's *Nisei Daughter* in 1953. John Okada's *No-No Boy*, the most famous novel about the psychological aftermath of the internment, was published posthumously in 1959. During the same period, short story writer Hisaye Yamamoto emerged as a major young literary voice, one whose stories of intraracial conflict and women's struggles greatly complicated the portrait of Japanese Americans' experiences of the prewar, wartime, and postwar years. The result of all this examination and retelling was that the mass removal and internment of Japanese Americans quickly went from being solely a topic of governmental and social scientific interest to becoming the most discussed area of Asian American history and culture. The much-lauded fictional accounts of Hisaye Yamamoto in the 1950s in effect completed the narrative circulation of the national or public chronicle of internment, and in just slightly more than ten years after the camps had been closed.

What is more, with the advent of the civil rights movement in the 1960s and the liberation movements that followed it, legions of American intellectuals from subsequent generations who were developing the burgeoning field of Asian American studies began to try to go beyond analyses of the political and economic reasons for wartime internment to reveal its deeper socio-psychological ramifications for Japanese Americans.[1] In the 1970s and 1980s, while Asian American literary scholars retrieved and took note of the work of Sone, Okubo, Okada, and Yamamoto, historians Michi Weglyn, Roger Daniels, Peter Irons, Yuji Ichioka, and social scientists Peter Suzuki and Richard Nishimoto contributed even more to outlining the impact of internment. In short, the collective corpus of work on the internment in the past fifty years seems to argue for the exhaustion of the political and cultural analyses of Japanese American internment.[2]

Yet the frequent visibility of the subject of internment in intellectual and cultural discourses, especially in the decade that followed the closure of the internment camps, along with the resulting sense of national reflection and recovery, belies a surprising lack of discussion of the function of the national remembering of that event, one that clearly reproves the Foucauldian concept of discourse and historicity. My purpose here to explore the historical permutations in postwar national discourses about Japanese American internment obviously owes much to Michel Foucault's legendary thesis from the first volume of *The History of Sexuality*. There he outlines his intention to analyze "the way in which sex is put into discourse":

To account for the fact that it [sex] is spoken about, to discover who does the speaking, the positions and viewpoints from which they speak, the institutions which prompt people to speak about it and which store and distribute the things that are said . . . to search . . . for instances of discursive production (which also administer silences, to be sure), of the production of power (which sometimes have the function of prohibiting), of the propagation of knowledge (which often cause mistaken beliefs or systematic misconceptions to circulate); *I would like to write the history of these instances and their transformations.*[3] (emphasis added)

Foucault's pivotal argument regarding the "silencing" effects of some discourses (and national or official histories are prime examples of these) applies to popular American discourses on the internment, where the proliferation of information in the immediate postwar years ironically furthered the nation's avoidance of the deeper challenge of the role of internment in our understanding of postwar and cold war national history.[4]

In an important essay, media critic Marita Sturken argues that "the forced internment of mainland Japanese American citizens after the bombing of Pearl Harbor in 1941 is an event for which history provides images primarily through their absence."[5] The internment exists everywhere in the immediate postwar as a vacated history, which Sturken likens to the "traces of events for which there have been no camera images" or narratives, because "the cultural mediation of memory" (693) that the event entailed was too disruptive to be borne by conventional historical accounts of the nation. The historical process of remembering by forgetting, of discursive inclusion that works to evade or displace, which Foucault enshrined as a peculiarly Western and modern defense, also characterizes the American recognition of the Japanese American experience in the 1940s and 1950s. In effect, Japanese American internment history is articulated within a simultaneous containment of its meaning, as an "absent presence," to cite Sturken's compelling term, which remains irretrievable. Although the present volume takes its title from Sturken's observations about the neglect of the memory of internment in histories of the national experience of the 1940s and 1950s, and admittedly builds on the by now familiar or, in some cases, disputed Foucauldian framework for approaching the study of historical discourses, it goes still further to try to understand more precisely how these elusive processes of history and memory have allowed the internment and Japanese American identity to be remembered or reconstituted as an "absent presence" in successive national discourses. This book, then, attempts to "brush history against the grain," to be compelled by Walter Benjamin's famous observations on the need to "blast a specific life out of the era or a specific work out of the lifework" in order to see how the event is compelled by the conflicting and uneven interests of history and nation.[6]

Wary of simply viewing the generation of historical or public discourses about the internment as sufficient to define its full meaning or function, and equally cautious of assuming that the apparent "absence" of an event in historical narratives or visual media marks its irrelevance or denial, this study approaches the analysis of Japanese American internment as a project in understanding how history and memory are negotiated when the need to remember an event challenges the ideals of democratic nationalism and the narrative unity of nation that historical discourses ostensibly provide. Put another way, I do not ask what happened, which we know all too well as testified by the litany of published works mentioned above. Nor do I simply follow without question Sturken's compelling assertion that to remember the internment we must do so "in the absence of history" about it, although it is true, as Sturken points out, that we have barely perceived the underlying ideological significance of the historical and cultural narratives we weave about the internment or about Japanese American identity. Instead, I attempt to draw on a series of discursive "instances" when the specter of internment became implicated, either by displacement or engagement, in the articulation of nationhood in the tumultuous postwar and cold war years. Thus, I ask equally how the centrality of internment in some discourses "screens" it from view and how the dismissal or diminution of internment's importance in other cases may sometimes merely underscore its significance.

Although this project is certainly informed by Foucault's genealogical method of attempting to disrupt the linearity and unity of historical discourses by conceiving of the past as a series of singular, incommensurable, and suspended events, I am ultimately seeking to reinvest the genealogical approach with a concern for the specific conditions of material struggle against dominant forces, keeping in mind that no events are truly "lost" to national or "statist" history, and that the means by which events are reincorporated is never stable or uniform. Perhaps the only generalization to be drawn from a genealogical approach is that the disruptive events, or counter-histories, of any period are vital to the production and perpetuation of dominant national history, as Michel de Certeau observes in his essays on historiography. He points out that in the writing of national history "nothing must be lost in the process (exploitation by means of new methods)," a statement that aptly describes the national remembrance or recording of internment, which has been subtly—almost imperceptibly at times—and repeatedly recapitulated in important postwar national discourses.[7] Possibly the boldest claim of this book is that the U.S. postwar and later cold war nation is, in large measure, reproduced and renewed through the narrativity of the internment discourses, a narrativity that only *seems* to exclude what is "too disruptive to be borne by conventional historical narratives": "Alphonse Dupront has said, 'The sole quest for "meaning" remains indeed a quest for the Other,' but, however contradictory it may be, this project aims at 'understanding' and, through 'meaning,' at hiding the alterity of this foreigner; or, in what amounts to the same thing, it aims at calming the dead who still haunt the present, and at offering them *scriptural tombs*" (emphasis added) (2).

The "absent presence" of Japanese American internment in the postwar era, and the political and representational struggles that internment has created for Japanese Americans even today, may be another way of flagging the vicissitudes of maintaining such "scriptural tombs," whether in the faint imprints of past moments or the salvaged personal memories of survivors. All of these, it must be acknowledged, share an unreliability inherent to representation, and as a consequence all resurface in a myriad of forms in the wide-ranging national debate about Japanese American identity and internment. In short, I do not wish to pose either ethnic memory or genealogy as the antithesis or corrective of national history, because to do so is to disregard the dynamic and mutable relationship between them and to replicate the binary of public/private. Any critique of the discursive networks producing national history is inevitably also a critique of the mediation of even the internees' memories of their incarceration, a critique of that which is understood as the realm of personal or private recollection. These realms of personal memory must also be examined as vital areas in the construction of the history and, particularly in the tense years of the cold war, the urgent need to maintain the boundaries of the national. In the immediate postwar years the historical remembering of the relocation and incarceration of Japanese Americans quickly became one of the most troubling accounts of wartime America, for it revealed "the fissure that opened up between experiencing an event and remembering it in representation," as national exigencies set about manipulating the "instability" of the collective memory of the internment to mark a new phase in the life of a nation's history.[8]

The manipulation of the United States' internment of Japanese Americans was, while frequently blatantly racist, by no means uncomplicated by other issues. Although theorists of the nation have long conceded the pervasive connection between nationalism and racism, they are also quick to point out that the inflection of race in nation is, in the words of Etienne Balibar, "a question of historical articulation" that hinges on the recognition of the "polymorphism of racism." A primary illustration of this polymorphism is the fact that "racism and sexism function together" and that "racism always presupposes the existence of sexism."[9] Certainly the historical renarrativizations of the internment, or sometimes simply the casual references to it in the nervous decade (1945–1955) that followed, illustrate the "polymorphism" of the racial discourse about Japanese American internment, as the nation's articulation of its meaning was simultaneously and unevenly affected by gender and class questions that loomed in the postwar or cold war nation and rendered the memory of the internment, if nothing else, "contingent and subject to change."[10] As a form of remembrance, the internment was often reconstituted by its articulation through other sites of crises in which the memories of nationally sanctioned racial violence or women's oppression threatened to overwhelm the nation's need to inaugurate a renewed postwar or cold war present: the history of antiblack racism in the United States; the immediate postwar backlash against women's visible economic independence during the war; the anxiety about middle-class white heteronormativity; the liberal dilemma of the U.S. decision to use the atomic bomb; and the paranoia of a fifth-column Japanese influence in the nation that forecast the coming excesses of McCarthyism. The inexhaustible reenactments and retellings of the internment have prolonged its suspension as an unfinished story; in the postwar era especially it hovers as an event at once safely postponed and dangerously mutable. In some instances, the merest allusion to internment, especially one that purported to deny its significance as a trauma, might be simultaneously threatened by the unanswered question of what it tries to exclude.[11]

Despite the complexity of internment narratives and their promise for revealing much about the processes of the making of postwar national history, only isolated attempts have been made to parse the formative effects of the politics of internment on the development of historical representations the postwar or cold war nation. The representation of the memory of that event in the 1950s has been obscured in both nostalgic constructions of and scholarly work on cold war America. Although the internment of Japanese Americans is widely known, the several superb accounts of the internment cited above have been generally passed over by historians and scholars of the period, who often fail even to mention it as a watershed event in America's wartime history. This is true even in the case of the historical critiques of the nostalgia of collective memories of the 1940s and 1950s that emerged first from revisionist historians and, in more recent years, from feminist historians as well.[12] Although the work of feminist scholars such as Elaine Tyler May, Joanne Meyerowitz, and Wendy Kozol has often been most successful in exposing the contradictions and foibles of cold war nationalism (offering in the process some of the most compelling interdisciplinary criticisms of U.S. postwar culture), their analyses of how gender politics informed concepts of the nation have focused, until very recently, on the dilemmas of white middle-class women. Elaine Tyler May's pioneering study of gender and U.S. nationalism, *Homeward Bound: American Families in the Cold War Era*, primarily addresses the popular perception and shaping of white middle-class domesticity. Although Joanne Meyerowitz and Wendy Kozol have since expanded the terms of May's influential approach to include the early postwar years, interjecting an important new focus on black femininity and national differences, respectively, nothing has yet emerged from feminist scholars to take up the central dilemma posed by Japanese American experience in the postwar and cold war periods.[13] This neglect has both typified and reinforced the neglect of internment as a factor in the shaping of the nation in the 1940s and 1950s.

This book calls for more attention with sharper focus on the circulation of the internment as a key part of the project of a critical historicism, as a vital opportunity for critiquing history as a deeply troubled exercise in both remembering and forgetting, particularly when the memory of internment emerges in narratives of postwar and cold war America. Given the general disregard for investigating the complex politics of remembering and writing the history of internment, both then and now, what remains for most students of the postwar era is the merest vestige of the significance of the event. In the occasional allusion to or the footnoted reference on the internment that appear in most general histories of the period, we witness the scholarly reflection of the broader ongoing national struggle to come to terms with the meaning and function of Japanese American identity in the postwar years.

By trying to imagine a postwar America from the remembered realms of Japanese American experience and politics, the following analyses of key "instances" of discourse about the internment attempt to shed light on the mutually constitutive relationship of postwar national history to Japanese American memory. Inasmuch as internment apparently has been effaced from prominence in a variety of histories and depictions of the 1940s and 1950s, I argue that the national and historical experience and effects of internment remain considerable nonetheless. As the chapters to follow reveal, the processes of remembering any aspect of internment history are also often acts designed to demarcate the boundaries of the postwar nation. Clearly, Japanese Americans, and sometimes merely the emerging notion of Japanese American identity, were vital to the terms of the cultural politics of cold war America because of, as well as in spite of, our collective ignorance of the internment process and its subsequent fallout. The unaccounted, unstable presence of the memory of Japanese American internment in postwar history in fact provides for its formative function in the development of major debates and events of the period.

In recapturing and recasting a series of events and controversies in postwar culture, this volume attempts to fill a critical and historical void, both in postwar or cold war cultural studies and in Asian American cultural studies, by investigating the means by which the social and political disenfranchisement of Japanese Americans during the late 1940s and early 1950s shaped the expression of national identity and postwar history. A closer examination of the broad themes of most conventional histories of early postwar America—whether they include debates about the atomic bomb, the rages of McCarthyism, the crises of racial integration, or the widespread anxiety over middle-class gender roles—reveals that mainstream representations of and discourses about Japanese Americans' place in the national order were pivotal to the nation's attempts to negotiate these emergencies, even while the shifting representations of Japanese American internment tended to obscure this fact.

During the remarkable period of internment, and despite the public's obvious awareness of internment and the major social scientific interest in it, little was written in the popular press about the mass movement of mainland Japanese Americans, primarily because it conflicted with the focus on the more positive and inspirational deeds and causes of the war. The war against the tyranny and oppression of Nazi Germany and Imperial Japan often necessitated portraying the United States as a virtual paragon of democratic virtues. But when the internment did emerge as a topic of discussion it threatened to undermine the reputation of U.S. democracy because the internment exposed the arbitrariness of the very enterprise of national history and the myth of exceptionalism that history sustains. One of the few feature articles on the internment appeared toward the end of the war period in a March 1944 edition of *Life* magazine, and in it the emphasis was on the functional, normative aspects of camp life and the celebration of the spirit of many Japanese Americans' loyalty to the nation. Yet, as the inaugural moment of postwar visibility for Japanese Americans argues, even this article in *Life* inevitably could not avoid recognizing the contradictions and incommensurabilities of Japanese American internment; the article was perhaps a harbinger of the disturbing effects of the nation's engagement with the question of Japanese American identity that were to come in the decade ahead.

Although the varied dimensions of popular postwar discourse on Japanese American identity often shared the common purpose of denying the significance of the struggle to define Japanese Americans, the dilemma of what it meant to be Japanese American in an era marked by suspicion of citizens' loyalty, fears about national security, and violent reactions to the dismantling of racial privilege clearly touched a chord in the national psyche. Indeed, as I argue in chapter 2, the difficulty of Japanese American incarceration and relocation as a vital part of the war abroad ultimately left its mark on the formation of postwar policy in occupied Japan. Liberal anthropologists stationed in the internment camps to observe Japanese Americans were also instructed to use the opportunity to develop policies for administering the Japanese after the war. Because of their conflicted efforts both to help Japanese Americans and to use them to learn how to reform the Japanese after the war, the U.S. postwar view of Japan was significantly affected by the administration of internment. Although there is now little evidence of this influence, it remains an important element of the politics of the U.S. occupation of Japan and, as a close examination reveals, of the politics of Japanese American postwar culture.

Indeed, the entanglement of concepts of Japanese and Japanese American identity was a constant part of the problem posed by the presence of Japanese Americans. Their lifelong ties to Japan and, in the case of the Issei and even certain Nisei individuals, their ambivalent national and cultural statuses often continued to exceed the bounds of national imagination during the years of the Red scare. Despite her contemporary erasure from the history of McCarthyism, Iva Toguri d'Aquino, a Nisei from Los Angeles, was, during the late 1940s, the most notorious target of anti-Communist hunters. She was tried, convicted, and imprisoned for being the legendary Tokyo Rose in the most expensive treason trial of the period, a trial that far exceeded the costs of the trials of either the Rosenbergs or Alger Hiss. While the Rosenberg and Hiss trials are certainly no less important than that of Tokyo Rose in the annals of McCarthyism, my analysis of the Tokyo Rose trial reveals the significance of a residual fear of a Japanese fifth column in the United States to the success of the hysteria of the midcentury Red scares. D'Aquino's story adds still another level of ethnic and gender anxiety to the complex cultural motivations and appeals of McCarthyism. She was punished for a range of political transgressions and feminine excesses, including her allegedly provocative radio transmissions, which provoked anxieties about women's roles and sexualities (both of which were rooted in fears about the subversiveness of popular culture and consumerism), as well as her elusive geopolitical placement, which fueled growing suspicions about national security. In both senses, d'Aquino disturbed ideological boundaries, whether between Japan and America or between traitor and patriot.

So, too, the presence of Japanese American women in the debates about the atomic bomb bothered the distinctions between the United States as a benevolent democracy and the world of the Japanese victims of the bomb. When liberal factions in the United States organized the Hiroshima Maidens Project to bring young, female victims of the atomic bombings to America for corrective surgery, they hoped for a mission of peace that would enshrine the nation as a force for moral good despite the overwhelming threat of the bomb's past use and future hazards. In an era marked by increasing anxieties about American motherhood and femininity, attributing the recovery of the "maidens" to the influence of the numerous "white American mommies" who boarded them after their surgeries offered a means to restore faith both in the state of the nation and its domestic hierarchies. But the participation of Helen Yokoyama and Mary Kochiyama—two Japanese American women who had been forced from their homes and had seen them turned into political battlefronts—in the Hiroshima Maidens Project clearly upset the notion of American domesticity as a privileged arena of national life. By highlighting Yokoyama and Kochiyama's participation and subsequent political activism, chapter 4 reveals how the myth of American exceptionalism depended on and was serviced by the management of the postwar concept of middle-class white domesticity.

In the final chapter, I confront the little-discussed relevance of Japanese war brides to the transformations in the popular representations of Japanese American identity. Although prestigious cultural critics such as Horace Kallen debated the crisis posed by the Brown decision in 1954, Japanese war brides experienced a brief and intense "instant" of cultural visibility. As white Americans tried to contain the threat posed by black integration and, less obvious, to overlook the failed terms of Japanese American resettlement, they turned to the story of the Japanese war bride married to the white soldier as the site of the regeneration of belief in cultural pluralism. In doing so, white liberals provided an "obscure place" out of which the illusion of white innocence and democratic ideals could be safely revived. Almost overnight, the coverage of Japanese war brides transformed what were viewed as opportunistic aliens into gracious and hard-working traditional housewives fully accepted by white America. The radical shift in their representation signaled the need of white Americans for a story of racial harmony and domestic success that was obviously difficult to extract from the national histories of either African Americans or Japanese Americans.

Throughout the postwar years, the potential of interned Japanese Americans' presence in the body politic to disturb the problems of American identity remained a perpetual threat, an irrepressible part of the negotiation between the needs of national history and the "incommensurabilities" of racial memory. What follows, then, is an accounting of the Japanese American presence through its absence, for it is ironically that very absent presence—unseen but nonetheless felt—that made Japanese American experience and identity a powerful force in postwar American history and culture.

ONE

"That Faint and Elusive Insinuation": Remembering Internment and the Dawn of the Postwar

He walked along, thinking, searching, thinking and probing, and, in the darkness of the alley of the community that was a tiny bit of America, he chased that faint and elusive insinuation of promise as it continued to take shape in mind and in heart.—John Okada, *No-No Boy*

This epigraph, the closing line of John Okada's 1957 novel *No-No Boy*, may ironically serve as an apt beginning for the exploration of the discursive production of internment in the postwar period, asserting as it does the uncertain or transitional status of Japanese Americans in those years. The story of Ichiro Yamada, a Nisei whose desperate efforts to avoid the oblivion of history, to keep merely the "faint insinuation" of an American promise in his ken, expresses faith in the dream of America even as it indicts the miserable terms of a dream viewed from "the darkness of the alley." Yamada, the main character of the novel, returns home to Seattle and a bleak and hopeless situation from a federal prison where he has served out the last years of the war as a "no-no boy"; that is, as one who answered "no" and "no" to questions 27 and 28 on a loyalty questionnaire administered to Japanese Americans in the internment camps. The questionnaire, no less than the initial act of relocation, was a watershed event in the wartime experience of all Japanese Americans. More importantly, however, its use and the responses to it reveal the ambiguous terms and, for Japanese Americans answering the questionnaire, potentially dangerous stakes of the government's attempts to regulate and redefine what it perceived as the "problem" of Japanese American identity.

Required of all internees seventeen years and older, the question-naire delivered in 1943 dared a population already forcibly incarcerated merely on suspicion of a potential for "disloyalty" to answer in the affirmative to the following charged questions: "Are you willing to serve in the armed forces of the United States on combat duty wherever ordered?" and "Will you swear unqualified allegiance to the United States of America and faithfully defend the United States from any or all attack by foreign and domestic forces, and forswear any form of alle-giance or obedience to the Japanese Emperor, and to any other foreign government, power or organization?"[1] Although officials administer-ing the internment intended the questionnaire to assess the feelings of internees regarding possible release and draft induction, for many Japanese Americans questions 27 and 28 amounted to a catch-22. If they answered "yes-yes" then they were placing themselves wholly in the hands of a government that viewed them as second-class citizens with few if any constitutional rights. If they answered "no-no," as Ichiro does, then they irrevocably sealed their fates as disloyal subjects who were open to punishment. The loyalty oath thus worded was an-other example of the nation's ignorance of the predicament of Japanese Americans; many wanted to declare full loyalty "but only after the res-toration of citizenship rights" stripped from them without due pro-cess.[2] It seemed the only alternatives offered by the government were to submit completely to one's second-class status or to engage an active resistance that placed one on the margins of society. Those such as Ichiro who chose to answer "no-no" paid the price accorded to suspect domestic elements in times of war. In the novel his situation mirrors that of his fellow "no-no boys" who exist on the periphery of a periph-ery, so-called disloyals from an already dubious group.

As the novel ends, Ichiro's futile search for a place in America has barely improved; he is quite literally on the borders of American visibil-ity, walking "in the darkness of the alley of the community that was a tiny bit of America." Ichiro Yamada's vigil, his "thinking, searching, thinking and probing" for "that faint and elusive insinuation of prom-ise" (251) challenges the noble memory of the nation's war efforts by suggesting how the injustices perpetuated at home during the war nec-essarily arraign the ultimate meaning of victory after the war. But per-haps most fundamental is the way in which the final sentence of No-No Boy, as the last word in Okada's chronicle of the immediate postwar predicament of Japanese American resisters, opens up the possibility of reconstituting the crucial moment in national history of the period of weeks following the announcement of final victory, whether the first hours or the first days, which also declared the heroic ascension of the United States to super-nation status.

When magazines and newspapers covered the spontaneous V-J or "victory over Japan" parties on August 15, 1945, the mood was reported as undeniably upbeat and the nation appeared utterly united in celebration. In major cities such as New York and Chicago, American GIS and civilians were depicted flooding the streets and, in a tumult of raucous cheer, blocking traffic, chanting, setting off firecrackers, honking their horns, and "singing, shrieking and shouting" in what *Life* magazine called "an orgy of frenzy and fun."[3] Decades later, when the nation observed the fiftieth anniversary of V-J Day in 1995, all three major television networks and CNN replayed the same scenes from *Life*, including the now legendary Alfred Eisenstaedt photograph of the young white sailor capturing a white nurse in an impromptu victory embrace. If anyone doubts the persistence of the initial nostalgic renderings of the postwar period, the fiftieth-anniversary recycling of the familiar cliches of national history reveals that they were apparently intact a full half century later. This entrenched, familiar context of a nation's overwhelming triumph seems to leave little room for the defeated and depressed mood of *No-No Boy*, with its contrasting portrait of Japanese American disaffection and dispossession as an "American" condition unfolding outside the umbrella of national jubilation. For Ichiro, there are no happy homecomings, no victory parades. As emblems of the postwar antiheroic, both Ichiro's story and the memory of the historical event of internment that defines his American postwar future are, in the words of Marita Sturken, "absent from the litany of World War II images." *No-No Boy* offers a picture of Japanese Americans after internment that logically "presents an image both too disruptive and too domestic to conform to the war's narratives" of the nation as a symbol of individual liberty at home and of freedom abroad.[4]

In light of *No-No Boy's* potential for fracturing the nostalgic or official remembrance of postwar jubilation, George Lipsitz characterizes Okada's narrative of male Nisei experience during the 1940s and 1950s as a prime generator of "counter-memories," alternative processes of memorializing the past that he deems essential to the progressive renegotiation of national history and identity. Emerging from such narratives, "counter-memory is a way of remembering and forgetting that starts with the local, the immediate, and the personal. Unlike historical

narratives that begin with the totality of human existence and then locate specific actions and events within that totality, counter-memory
starts with the particular and the specific and then builds outward toward *a total story"* (emphasis added).[5] For Lipsitz, the ethnic American
novel in particular is not only a source of counter-memories, but it
often offers these alternative narratives of nation and history in order
to question the "use of the past" in a manner that "speaks to present
day intellectual concerns with time, history, subjectivity, and fragmentation" (215). Although Lipsitz acknowledges the importance of poststructuralist theories of the fragmentation of narrative and subjectivity
to his argument for the ethnic novel as counter-memory, he is also
quick to distinguish his concept of counter-memory from Michel Foucault's famous definition of "counter-history" as a process of "recording the singularity of events *outside of any monotonous finality"* (emphasis added).[6] Lipsitz contends that Foucault's refusal to admit any
coherence in historical events "could just as easily obscure real connections, causes and relationships—atomizing common experiences into
accidents and endlessly repeated play." "Events matter," Lipsitz concludes, "and describing them as accurately as possible (although never
with certain finality) can, at the very least, show us whose foot has been
on whose neck" (214).

David Palumbo-Liu indirectly endorses Lipsitz's misgivings about
the poststructuralist embrace of historical and subjective indeterminacy, which he suggests encourages us to overlook the material conditions that lead to an awareness of racism. Palumbo-Liu argues that
postmodernity in general consistently "harbors within it a particular
anxiety with regard to race and culture" that often motivates its celebration of disunity and ambiguity as a paradoxical means of avoiding recognition of social injustices and political hierarchies. Seen in this light,
Foucault's theory of the unlimited potential of counter-history may
appear "haunted by the loss" of the unified or dominant subject, a
loss that Palumbo-Liu specifically links to the proliferation of late-
twentieth-century critiques of racial and sexual privilege and, more
concretely, the increasing presence of the voices of people of color and
women in national debates. Thus, although poststructuralist theorists
may commend the cultural potential of this loss of subjective coherence, their fascination is ultimately dubious "since the loss is not
mourned" and thus not identified as the ironic symptom of a pervasive
social anxiety over the passing of a certain mode of white male privi-

lege.[7] In their separate analyses of such postmodern theories, both Lipsitz and Palumbo-Liu contribute to a healthy skepticism of poststructuralist perspectives of history and narrative. They expose its tendency to broadly proclaim the condition of postmodern fragmentation in vaguely universal or strictly aesthetic terms, and thus its potential to efface the continuing effects of political struggles emanating from racial violence or economic disenfranchisement.

Yet despite these considerable limitations, Foucault's critiques of history and subjectivity continue to offer some very useful, even if provisional, strategies for complicating the operations and functions of power and language, of history and memory or counter-history. In addition to his skepticism, Lipsitz's "concern with time, history, subjectivity and fragmentation" indirectly affirms poststructuralism's insistence on exploring the complexity of subjectivity and narrativity. Even as he rejects Foucault's concept of counter-history, he remains open to the need for critical deployment of its insights, primarily by reconnecting its project with the historical terms of material and social struggle, however shifting or contradictory these terms may also prove to be.[8] As Ann Stoler argues, we need not follow Foucault's controversial prescriptions "with exegetical care" in order "to explore how his insights might inform our own" analyses of popular discourses and national histories that are clearly affected by increasingly abstruse conditions of dislocation and alienation.[9] Put another way, understanding "whose foot is on whose neck" does not preclude the importance of recognizing the instability of forms of domination and discrimination, as Foucault no doubt did.[10] In fact, a reconsideration of Foucault's critiques of history and language in light of recent revelations may offer vital directives for approaching the ambivalence in discourses that emerged to redefine and remember Japanese American subjectivity in the wake of internment and for considering the potentially powerful impact of these discourses on the emerging concept of postwar national identity.

In her groundbreaking reconsideration of Foucault's theories of race and racism, Stoler argues that his late College de France lectures on "racisms of the state" reveal his concept of counter-history as "not simply a search for the discontinuities of history as so many commentators have claimed, but a more challenging analytic concern with the tension between rupture and reinscription, between break and recuperation in discursive formations."[11] She deems "one of the hallmark features of his work" his concern with "the discursive *bricolage* whereby an older discourse of race is 'recovered,' modified, 'encased,' and 'encrusted' in new forms" (61). Foucault opened his lectures, which represent his most extensive and final commentary on the functions of racism in national or "statist" discourse, with an elaboration of his understanding of the oppositional histories that grew out of the "historical knowledge of struggles." In it Foucault "rejects the notion of power as repression" of these counter-histories in order to understand the shifting function of counter-histories within a discourse of national identity. Foucault argues instead that: "in fact, those unitary discourses which first disqualified and then ignored them [counter-histories] when they made their appearance, are, it seems quite ready now to annex them, to take them back within the fold of their own discourse and to invest them with everything this implies in terms of their effects of knowledge and power".[12] Foucault's evolving interest in the ambiguous historical and discursive functioning of counter-histories was ultimately connected to his interest in how the state, or the modern nation, reclaims or "annexes" such histories. The discovery of links between Foucault's concept of counter-history and critiques of national racism makes his theories of counter-history particularly relevant to comprehending the ways in which popular discourses about Japanese American internment tried to reclaim that event as an unstable counter-historical narrative "within the very unitary discourses [it] opposed" (206).

Thus, the conflict between race and nationality that often framed the narrative of Japanese American internment was coincident with the then current anxieties about gender and class, including in particular anxieties about American manhood. The primacy of the situation of the "no-no boys" indicates, for instance, that the historical narratives of Japanese American men's resistance was often cohered as part of more visible fears about the state of national masculinity in the postwar period. The concern with white masculinity in particular has been remarked by a number of cultural critics of the period, who point predominantly to the cinematic exploration of the instability of white masculinity in major films from the late 1940s and early 1950s. Kaja Silverman was among the first to examine the masculine crises in *The Best Years of Our Lives* (1946), a story of returning white war heroes from different social and economic backgrounds who struggle to find their function in a postwar nation that seems devoid of the gallant opportunities and ideals that defined the war effort.[13] Marita Sturken's argument about the disturbing effects of the Japanese American presence in the 1955 film *Bad Day at Black Rock*, in which Spencer Tracy plays an investigator who stumbles across the murder of a male Japanese farmer in a western town, similarly builds on the recognition of doubts about the state of white masculinity in these years. Although the farmer, Komoko, is never seen in the film (he remains "an absent presence"), the dilemma of Japanese American persecution that his name evokes initiates the film's questioning of the myth of noble masculinity so often associated with the American West and the white cowboys who are ultimately found guilty of Komoko's murder.[14]

Evidence exists that even the gleeful victory parades, arguably the penultimate image of America on the verge of peace and prosperity, were fraught with fear and uncertainty about masculinity, because the same sources that on August 15, 1945, celebrated the V-J Day parties as a whirlwind of giddy exuberance and optimism also acknowledged that these parties often ended hours later in chaos and confusion. In city after city, American soldiers on leave destroyed businesses and public works, openly expressing their pent-up frustrations and perhaps their trepidation about peace. And what began as a playful rush to steal a victory kiss from any nearby woman could sometimes turn into violent sexual assault as well. The violence in general reached such a fever pitch in San Francisco that civilians were warned off the streets at night until gangs of drunken soldiers could be contained.[15] Like the detonation of the first atomic bomb two weeks before, V-J Day reflected the twinned senses of national victory and defeat. The scripting of a hopeful national experience was, in one way, a necessary means of repressing the violence of white masculine dissatisfaction and division that split the experience of national time in a manner that could not be effectively contained by any single narrative focus.

Annexed by the almost immediate national nostalgia for the dawning of a new postwar era in American history, the events constituting the counter-historical memories of *No-No Boy* and the violence of V-J Day celebrations were effectively contained and reconfigured by the forms of their retelling. Still, they remind us that the continued ignorance of the fissures and contradictions in the negotiation of national and historical postwar memory merit more sustained analysis. As counters to the nostalgic memory of the nation in victory, and cutting as they seem "against the grain" of postwar history, the largely forgotten experiences of Japanese Americans on the eve of the postwar period must be, in the words of Walter Benjamin, "blasted out of the continuum of history" where the story of their internment and release is remembered as, at worst, a stumbling block on the road to freedom, a temporary setback.[16] To comprehend the complex functioning of Japanese American memory we must examine how it was "annexed," how its power as a collective memory was uneasily reclaimed in the interests of the national celebration of the war and of postwar Americanism. The effort of reclamation, however, was not unequivocal. The historical management or containment of Japanese American internment and resettlement as a national wartime and postwar experience simultaneously threatened and enabled the continuing nostalgia for this era as a golden time in national history. As an almost ghostly "absent presence" in postwar America, the narrative or discursive representation of Japanese American internment encompasses the paradoxical authority of counter-histories or ethnic/racial memories, which serve as the *necessary occlusions* of national history. As the nation's unstable attempts to remember Japanese American interment in the immediate postwar period suggests, even the faintest sense of what is forgotten or excluded may prove as vital to ensuring the meaning and unity of national history as the event that is centrally remembered and endlessly repeated.

Of course, this argument is exclusive neither to Japanese American experience nor to the early postwar years. As Lisa Lowe has famously defined it, Asian American identity in general has been a repository for "the contradictions of immigrant marginality" that have consistently characterized the nation's comprehension of Asian Americans, whether actual immigrants or native born.[17] For Lowe, these contradictions are best illustrated by the historical necessity of Asian labor to the building of the United States, which is in turn repeatedly defined by the maintenance of Asian exclusion and unassimilability. Lowe's emphasis on how the "forgetting" or repression of histories of Asian American labor and cultural participation has been integral to the regulation of the nation as a liberal democracy provides a vital link between the contradictory uses of Japanese American marginalization and trauma in the discursive production of the postwar nation and the broader studies of Asian American culture, history, and identity. As studies of "alien-ated" citizens, popular discourses about Japanese Americans no less than many other Asian American groups often became the disavowed means to regenerate and reimagine a postwar national collective. As a result of the denial of the significance of Asian

Americans to the shaping of national histories, few scholars of American culture grasp the complexities of the politics of Asian American identity, which has never been a simple matter of citizenship versus alien status.

Although the boundary distinguishing "immigrant" (and therefore "alien") and "native" or "citizen" became increasingly porous rather than stable for Japanese Americans, and although many Nisei felt they faced a choice between an avowal of faith in the "faint" promise of citizenship or a bold resistance to an unjust national agenda, in truth the seeming opposition between the nation's need for Japanese Americans' loyal submission to second-class citizenship and the resistance embraced by the "no-no boys" was never so clear or absolute. The survival of the nation was instead, as Lowe so powerfully asserts, dependent on maintaining the indeterminate social, political, and economic position of Japanese Americans.[18] In fact, the discursive potential of Japanese American internment, the complicated means by which Japanese American experience exposes "the uses of the past," may be seen in the ways in which the most visible coverage of the meaning of Japanese American wartime experience grappled with them as *both* citizens and aliens. This recognition forces us to acknowledge the contradictions informing the assertion that the Asian American subject always "has a historically 'alie-nated' relation to the category of citizenship" (12). For even in the best cases, where Asians are permitted "to become U.S. citizens as exceptions to the whites-only barrier," their inclusion as "aliens ineligible to citizenship" may merely highlight "the historical racialization of Asian Americans" and "rearticulate the processes of legal enfranchisement and the ostensive lifting of legal discriminations in the 1950s" (20). In the early postwar period, more than a few of the most visible national discourses about internment utilized the perpetually "alien-ated" citizen status of Japanese Americans—arguably the subversive power of the internment remembering—to renew or redefine the possibilities of the postwar American nation.

The Nisei, the largest group in the camps and the focus of most studies of Japanese American identity in the wartime and postwar years, existed both as citizens in fact and as aliens in treatment. Although observers and government officials at the time often viewed the so-called loyal and disloyal designations as mutually exclusive and opposing categories or types of Japanese American identity, popular discourses on internment instead expose the frequent blurring and mutability of these categories and, as a result, the precariousness of the nation that would frequently build its survival on the arbitrary logic of loyalty or disloyalty in the McCarthy years yet to come. As a narrative suggesting the dimensions of Japanese American internment in the making of the postwar nation, John Okada's *No-No Boy* introduces us to the discursive uncertainty of Japanese Americans' relationship to national categories in the 1950s. Is it any wonder, then, that as a Nisei Ichiro Yamada's intellectual and political agency is deemed at once "faint" and "elusive" *and* "continuing to take shape"?

"Killing Time" in the Camps:
Embodying and Reclaiming Internment

Although it is perhaps true that the ongoing struggles of Japanese Americans were largely obscured during and certainly after the war, the power of their presence and the impact of their relationship to the nation, are, in retrospect, apparent. The popular media, far from simply burying the news of Japanese American internment as the war ended, sometimes actively engaged the concept of Japanese Americanness both as a discomfiting challenge to national ideologies and histories and as a means of recasting national boundaries. Although certainly different in the terms of their engagement from *No-No Boy*, popular journalistic discourses of internment, including especially photojournalistic representations, were forced to acknowledge the persistence of Japanese Americans' national alienation as part of the process of reclaiming the event and deploying it to revive the meaning and importance of national identity. On the eve of postwar victory, indeed just before Okada completed *No-No Boy*, Japanese Americans *were* expressly recognized as the bearers of a powerful national memory. In some instances, the internment was overtly discussed as a historical event that necessitated no less than the thorough critique and revision of American boundaries and democratic principles. The unprecedented modern American trauma of massive Japanese American relocation and internment so clearly threatened the ideal of the American nation that it created an undeniable uncanny effect by seeming to dissolve the difference between America as a symbol of democratic freedom and the tyranny of a police state represented by the Axis powers.[19] Although the need to confront legal and institutional racism would not occur for another decade, precipitated in large measure by the fight against communism and the recognition that, in the words of Robert Lee, "racial attitudes are critical to the way in which the conduct of Americans" is judged, Japanese American internment, as an unstable source of national memory of the war, emerged as early as 1944 as an equally precarious source for the reconsideration of the meaning and future of American identity in an agitated new postwar era.[20] The remembering of the internment, far from being an area of avoidance, sporadically dotted the popular scene in a manner that made it as difficult to ignore as to define. Although it might not have been a major news story, the question of Japanese American internment was still newsworthy despite the risks entailed in broaching the subject of civil rights violations.

In its March 20, 1944, edition, on the very eve of the postwar period, *Life* magazine, the most popular magazine in America at the time, presented its readers with the first feature article on Japanese American internment to appear in a major publication.[21] Many West Coast Americans had, of course, read about the internment in their local papers when it was initiated in early 1942, but the rest of the country remained relatively uninformed about, as well as unconcerned with, the politics of internment. Other than a passing knowledge of the relocation and incarceration of Japanese Americans, most Americans knew and heard few details of camp life. Once Japanese Americans had been removed to the internment camps, even West Coast news reports on their existence abated. But after two years of Japanese American imprisonment in the camps, and with the end of war in Europe at hand, *Life* determined it was time to reacquaint its readers with the condition of interned Japanese Americans. This aim was met by an article that focused solely on the infamous Tule Lake camp, the most notorious of the internment sites used to house the most ardent resisters to the relocation order. The camp had also witnessed a series of the most explosive riots and protests to occur in any of the ten internment camps located in the West. In part, *Life*'s decision to limit its coverage to a camp reserved for "trouble makers" merely capitalized on the intrigue behind the otherwise dreary story of Japanese American detention during World War II.[22] In their introduction to the article, the magazine's editors hail the camp's concentration of so many "pressure boys," another term for "no-no boys," as "responsible for Tule Lake's reputation as worst of all civilian detention camps in U.S." (25). *Life* elected to frame its pictorial report of Japanese American internment, which the editors proclaimed as "the first of its kind," and certainly one of the very few to reach such a large national audience, as a privileged glimpse into the lives of "18,000 Japanese considered disloyal to U.S." (25). The disturbing conflation of "disloyal" with Japanese American echoes throughout the body of the article, which was written by Carl Mydans.

Yet Mydans also clearly views the nation's suspicions about Japanese Americans as unfounded and, at least in the case of certain subjects, perhaps irreparable. The author seems to struggle between the fact of many of the Tule Lake internees' expressed "disloyalty" to the United States and the equally damning mitigating fact of the government's violation of the civil rights of an entire domestic or citizen population. As a result of its negotiation of these apparently opposing perspectives, *Life*'s article on Tule Lake may be read as a defining moment, when the confrontation with the specific situation of internment as a form of Japanese American memory of the war almost unavoidably turned to a critique of the terms and conditions of American democracy in the postwar period. Mydans's article is neither a celebration of Japanese Americans' struggle to prove their loyalty nor a ringing endorsement of America's handling of the internment. Instead, the report mixes his personal reflection on the cruelties of his own incarceration in a Japanese POW camp with his muted liberal critique of the denial of citizens' rights in a manner that seems to mourn the internment as marking the death of "an American way." Mydans indirectly inaugurates the upcoming postwar period as one in which Americans may have to confront the loss of their innocence and their distinction. But even more than this, the *Life* article is among the first to demonstrate the discursive instability of the internment as a memory of the nation at war that held the simultaneous potential both to defamiliarize notions of the national body (and thus the meaning of America itself) and to reassert the overwhelming power of national identity to bestow a final legitimacy.

The photograph that accompanies the *Life* article (fig. 1) on Tule Lake provides an indication of the isolated concern of both the magazine's editors and the article's author. The photo, which shows the collective, brooding reserve of the "pressure" or "no-no" boys, seems to incarnate the seditious sentiments that the government worried might reside unchecked in Japanese American communities. The photograph was actually taken by Mydans, who, as a staff photographer for *Life* as well as a sometime correspondent, embodied the magazine's innovative mix of photos and reports that pioneered the field of photojournalism in the 1930s and 1940s.[23] The photo depicts five male figures lined up and looking down on the photographer, who seems almost to be encircled by them. The caption reinforces the photographer's casting of these Japanese American men as threatening: "These five Japs are among 155 trouble makers imprisoned in the stockade within the Tule Lake Segregation Center. Here they are answering roll call" (25). The men's personal appearance, dress, and posturing further the impression of defiance and distrust. Although an apparently congenial older man appears at the center of the group, sporting short, graying hair and a beard and clutching a pipe, like the others his clothes are both rumpled and slightly ill fitting. The older man's grandfatherly gaze is overshadowed by the presence to his right of a much younger man with a full, dark beard, pointed mustache, and longer hair flowing back behind his ears. In the posture and garb of a "greaser," he wears a leather bomber jacket and his hands are stuffed in his pockets as he acknowledges the camera's presence with the barest hint of amusement. Difficult to read, his expression may just as easily represent an invitation to approval or a wry smile of disdain. The young man to the left of the older man also has his hands lodged in his trouser pockets, as he, too, stares down at Mydans in strained indifference. Together, these two figures act to frame the potential gentility of the older man, who is almost lost within the photograph's presentation of male delinquency. The two younger men at the far end of the camera's frame merely complete the scene; their hands are crossed in front of their chests and they also have beards and stern, strangely unreadable expressions. This is the portrait of Japanese American "trouble makers" that immediately explains and validates the reasons for internment and begs the question of Japanese Americans' incomprehensible difference. Although in hindsight the impassive gaze of the men in the photograph might be understood as a shield against the intrusive and irrational surveillance of the nation, in 1944, with the war in the Pacific quickly becoming the focal point of Allied efforts, these were still the familiar faces of a potential Japanese treachery.

The apparent braggadocio of these stand-ins for the thousands of other interned Japanese Americans clearly locates the community's menace to the nation in the development of a strain of insurgent racialized masculinity that eludes even as it conjures distinct cultural

Fig. 1 "Troublemakers" at Tule Lake (*Life*, March 20, 1944).

categories. These Japanese American "trouble makers" combine a number of the stereotypical signs of the delinquent or criminal—the leather jacket, the defiant stance, and the almost hip, indifferent gaze of the working-class urban tough occupying his corner of the street— but they also conjure broadly racialized images of fanatical oriental ty- rants in the Fu Manchu mustache and the longer hair of the one cen- trally placed figure. Although Mydans's staging of the photograph at- tempts to present these men as a looming domestic danger contained by the dreary routine of an official "roll call," his subjects nonetheless ultimately remain hard to grasp as alien masculine threats. Although some readers no doubt understood their staged inscrutability as indica- tions of a defunct Japanese rigidity, the clothes and the postures of these men evoke at once an attitude so peculiarly "Western" and "mod- ern" in their unkempt disregard and casual poses that they trouble any singular interpretation.

In many ways, this photograph's elusive power merely reflects the representational problems that Marianne Hirsch argues are inherent in all visual representations of traumatic events.[24] Inescapably both documentary and aesthetic, both committed to recapturing the physical facts of the moment and subtly restructuring those facts to affect emotions, photographs "introduce agency, control, structure, and therefore distance from the real, a distance which could leave space for doubt" (10). According to Hirsch, it is the "doubt" that remains in all photographic images that produces "a more permeable and multiple text" (11). Although photojournalistic essays such as Mydans's *Life* article became critical to documenting the major events of the twentieth century, they also inevitably manipulated points of ambiguity that left them in many ways open to the unintentional expression of counter-historical elements. Here, the memory of internment is literally written on the bodies of the "pressure boys," who, despite the editors' efforts to distinguish them as foreign threats to the nation, disturb the divide between the alien Japanese and the familiar Western masculine threat. This opening photograph also reveals the importance of the construction of the body, especially as a national symbol, in the functioning of internment as an unstable site of national memory.

Because the photographic image of Japanese American men works against the text ("these five Japs are among 155 trouble makers") by drawing attention to the impossibility of the "pressure boys" as either an exclusively alien or a national masculine threat, it suggests the ways in which the configuration of the Japanese American male body "manifests the stigmata of past experience and also gives rise to desires, failings and errors" that Foucault located in historical bodies.[25] As a primary element of the counter-history that emerges from the story of Japanese American internment, the maligned Japanese American male body subtly reveals itself as "a body totally imprinted by history and the process of history's destruction of the body" (150). But more important, the indeterminacy of the "pressure boys" as bearers of a Japanese masculine threat reveals how domination "engraves memories" on bodies that it cannot completely contain. Thus the ambivalence disturbing the presentation of the "pressure boys" in *Life*'s 1944 article anticipates the significance of the instability of cultural categories of gender more broadly in early postwar representations of the Japanese American experience of internment.

In 1946, approximately two years after the publication of Mydans's article, the wartime artist and illustrator Mine Okubo, a Nisei who had been interned along with her brother at Topaz relocation center in Utah, published *Citizen 13660*, the first memoir or eyewitness account of the experience of internment.[26] Conceived as an illustrated text organized around the bold line drawings that Okubo completed while in camp, the graphic memoir is her attempt "to tell the story of camp life for my many friends who faithfully sent letters and packages to let us know we were not forgotten" (ix). *Citizen 13660* offers a bleak visual portrait of the physical and psychological conditions of camp life. Although the geographical displacement of the Japanese American body is clearly an emblem in her story of the legal and political jeopardy in which the community was placed, Okubo's illustrated text relies on the literal physical bodies of Japanese Americans to demonstrate the means by which they came, by virtue of their containment, to incarnate the hidden power of a memory that once experienced never could be completely effaced even if it is rendered unrecognizable through subsequent acts of remembrance.

Like *Life*'s article, Okubo's text highlights the contradiction of the difference and familiarity of the Japanese American male body as a national presence. But the effect of her focus is even more disturbing because of its disaffected presentation. At first ensconced in the Tanforan relocation center, the first stop en route to Topaz, Okubo grimly records the alienation and despair of the Issei, whom she represents as marginal figures who are one step away from total obliteration. In an early drawing in the memoir, she depicts two forlorn and elderly Issei men ascending the steps of the clapboard hospital that served the Tanforan center, while in the background a group of stoop-shouldered other Issei men watch "a rickety hearse" parked outside. Okubo observes that the "old men sitting in front of the hospital would watch and wonder 'when will my turn come?' " (58). This early scene illustrates how her portrayal of the Issei men brutally links the unavoidable facts of their bodies' degeneration to their racial difference and, on a more subtle level, to their social alienation amid the harsh conditions of the camps. Still later, Okubo represents the "bachelor" quarters as a cramped, row upon row scene of Issei men in various stages of waiting, living a kind of death as they "slept and snored, dressed and undressed, in one continuous public performance" (63) of their now empty existences. Although her concentration on capturing the physical or literal details of camp life locates the "public performance" of the internees' lives at the center of the story, the insistence on getting the physical experience of incarceration "right" has the unavoidable effect of obscuring the deeper story of, in this example, the Issei men portrayed. The repressed network of feelings and experiences that are cleverly and ironically invoked by Okubo's deceptively simple descriptions of Issei men's daily lives culminates in the reader's awareness of the glaring absence of the body of Okubo's own Issei father.

As the story begins, Okubo's mother dies and Okubo returns from Europe, where she has been studying art. She describes her life in America as one lived with her only remaining family, a brother. When they are relocated, she and her brother naturally list themselves as "a family," and they work hard to remain together with Okubo "as head of the family" (32). Later in the narrative, however, Okubo casually informs us that her father is still alive; but we are told only that he sends "infrequent letters . . . always posted from a new camp in a different state" (61). The informed reader may conclude that, like other Issei men suspected of so-called disloyalty, Okubo's father was probably separated from his family and sent to a series of camps for rounds of interrogation and review. Remarkably, the father is not accorded any other mention; Okubo's "family" story ends with her restrained emotional departure from the camp that "fades away in the distance" (209). Still, the absence of her father from the story of the Okubo "family," like the too apparent boredom of the Issei men's daily life, lingers as a powerful reminder of both the irretrievable and undeniable dimensions of history and memory for Japanese Americans. Here, in the first autobiographical account of internment produced by Japanese Americans, we find that the power of Issei male bodies resides in their varying stages of decline or disappearance, which shadow the community's future and ensure the force of the emerging memory of Japanese American internment in the postwar years. The silence that circumscribes the father's absence suggests that the historical trauma of internment is, at least in part, written in the absence of bodily evidence of harm or injury, revealing a loss beyond words or representation, and thus beyond complete memorialization.

As a compelling memory of the war, *Citizen 13660* is retrieved as an absence, one that draws its power from its repeated foreclosure of representation. The early depictions of the flatness and liminality of the Issei men and the dawning awareness of the "missing" body of Mr. Okubo are critical to shattering our narrative expectations, as the death of the patriarchal order at once marks a loss *and* an opportunity. It in-

augurates *Citizen 13660* as a remembered historical text and creates
the narrative's central dilemma: the problem of declaring subjectivity
against the loss of the male body and the patriarchal domestic order on
which history depends for its intelligibility. The force and fragility of
Japanese American memory of the war are at once figured in the sub-
tlety and nuance of Okubo's combined textual and visual narration of
this quandary.

Not just the body of her text but also Okubo's own body is subjected
to the transfiguring narrative demands of historical representation. In
many of the framed scenes, in fact, her body seems to bear the most
visible and troubling representational effects of the divestiture of traditional kinship and communal connections for Japanese Americans.
She exists at the periphery of many illustrations, either expressionless
or downcast, her body often stiffly removed from or crowded into the
frame of the scene she illustrates. As the title *Citizen 13660* suggests,
Okubo's account focuses on how the government's enforcement of relocation and internment affected the reconstitution of Japanese Americans through a process of depersonalization; she ceases to be Mine
Okubo and becomes merely an integer in a larger equation. Both
Okubo and her brother find their existence reduced to the narrow
spaces of camp life or, more specifically, the dusty confines of a horse
stall that has been turned into a crude living space. Unlike subsequent
memoirs of camp life that emerged in the early 1970s to detail the psychological and emotional experience of the internment, such as Jeanne
Wakatsuki Houston's *Farewell to Manzanar* and John Okimoto's *American in Disguise*, Okubo's 1946 narrative is eerily removed and lacking
in earnest optimism.[27] Instead, she dispassionately details the bureaucratic, physical regulation of the thousands of Japanese American bodies herded into the isolated desert camp: the medical exams administered en masse; the endless waiting for meals in lines that snaked for
blocks through the camps; and the restricted contact with the world beyond the barbed wire. The bodies represented in Okubo's story bear
silent or "absent" witness to the alienating effects of the rigid segregation and classification of Japanese Americans.

In the face of the diminished function of Issei men and fathers as
the bearers of a properly patriarchal history, the bodies that come to
predominate in Okubo's illustrations are those of women whose loss
of individuality and liberty is figured in the obsession with the loss
of their femininity. To survive the rugged physical conditions of the

camp, "women, from grandmothers to toddlers, wore slacks or jeans" (52), we are told in a scene that Okubo represents as a faceless line of women viewed from the rear, an anonymous conglomeration of form-less bodies whose only conventional gender marker is the hair neatly knotted in a bun at the back of the head. A variation on the "absent presence" defining Okubo's inclusion of male or paternal bodies, this illustration seems to extend the portrait of the trauma of internment to include not simply the erasure but also the irreparable damage done to traditional social bodies, including the "heads" of households and the habiliments of femininity. The combined erosion of gender differ-ences and of paternal, heteronormative hierarchies is repeatedly in-voked in references to the fact that "mothers had lost all control over their children" and "family life was lacking" (89). The lack of these so-cial relations quickly becomes synonymous with Japanese Americans' loss of national identity and political rights. In a world where "everyone was dressed alike" (153), "all residential blocks looked alike" and "peo-ple were lost all the time" (136), the absence of heteronormative family arrangements in particular seems to be a source of anxiety and resigna-tion, the ultimate sign of the loss of democratic individualism.

Okubo's suggestion that there is a connection between heteronor-mative domesticity and national identity or belonging calls attention to "the reciprocal relation between the bourgeois family and a society which takes the nation form," in the words of Eitienne Balibar.[28] The sense of a national kinship typically validates the family and is in turn naturalized by its substitution for the family itself and its prescriptions of an almost mystical sense of loyalty and union. The maintenance of the nation and of national identity depends on the reproduction of the paternal family unit to such an extent in *Citizen 13660* that the story of the instability of national identification is repeatedly comprehended as the forced breakup of the Japanese American family. In this regard, Okubo's memoir threatens to expose the precarious nature of demo-cratic national identity, which is symbolized here as less an enduring right than a material good, as just as vulnerable to dissolution and de-cay as the imperiled Japanese American body politic. But the text and illustrations never quite realize this potential. In the end, the memory of internment is suspended between at once celebrating and mourn-ing the loss of patriarchy, family, and nation, as Okubo indicates on the last page: "Here I was, alone with no family responsibilities, and yet fear chained me to the camp. . . . There was only the desert now. My

Fig. 2 Mine Okubo's illustration of women at Tanforan Assembly Center
(*Citizen 13660*).

thoughts shifted from the past to the future" (209). *Citizen 13660* finally expresses a disquieting ambivalence regarding the loss of the
family—the ultimate sanctioned social body, and one so critical to co-
hering history as narrative—as a vital structuring mechanism for citizenship; the narrative turns to a vague "future" offering the possibility
of alternatives for articulating the complexity of Japanese Americans'
wartime ordeal, especially for a woman "with no family responsibilities." The notion that the telling of her life story, a metonym for the
remembering of internment, might be effectively reimagined outside
the matrix of family and nation only momentarily appears as an attractive or feasible option.

In contrast, Carl Mydans tries in his article for *Life* to find a solution
to the burden of internment by attempting to revive the concept of a
Japanese American citizenship rooted in kinship forms. His report focuses much of its attention on tempering the disturbing effects of the
effort to remember internment by stressing the survival, despite the
odds against it, of the heteronormative family so obviously mourned in
Okubo's narrative. After the first section of the article, which includes

the opening photograph, a brief explanation of the camp's location at the "bottom of a drained lake," and a discussion of the waste of human and natural resources that define life at Tule Lake, the second section consists of several pages of photographs depicting various types of industry or community at the camp. The photographs, arranged in long panels running across the page, are accompanied for the most part by terse, descriptive captions; they are a clear attempt to document another, irreconcilable side of camp life. This series of portraits primarily contrasts with the reputation of the Tule Lake camp as dominated by "pressure boys" and "trouble makers." The images are distinguished by their attention to domestic scenes with women and children rather than threatening young male resisters. In this section, the American promise rejected by the "pressure boys"—who are blamed for provoking the riots at Tule Lake and for leaving to rot the rich fields cultivated by internees recruited as farmworkers—is assiduously recouped in the cramped spaces of family life, in the careless leisure of children, and in the camp stores that model the universalizing tenets of middle-class industry and domestic consumerism. This photographic section of a bustling community poised in hopeful preparation for the future contrasts sharply with the brooding desolation of Okubo's memoir.

The very first photograph in the section also indicates the sudden shift in focus and tone in Mydans's coverage of the Tule Lake camp. It depicts the Manji family of seven children, aged nine to twenty-two, enjoying the quiet pursuits of a family evening at home. The older daughters sit laughing at a small table, casually engaged in their various hobbies or projects, while their mother sits reading a magazine in the corner and their father sits patiently at the very edge of the frame. Two younger boys read comic books while sprawled on the floor, like any other young American boy. Within this scene of an otherwise idealized domestic arrangement, the noticeably narrow living quarters are not mentioned in the caption, although Mydans recognizes the obvious irony of this captive Japanese American family's demonstration of family freedoms at Tule Lake. "The Manji family," Mydans begins, "in their Tule Lake apartment, are all classified as disloyal" (28). The dissonance between the idyllic scene of middle-class American family life lovingly maintained in a camp of "trouble makers" is made even more apparent by Mydans's strategic observation that "the children are all U.S. citizens by birth" and that "on the bookshelf stand photographs of two more sons, both in the U.S. army" (28).

The levels of competing representation proliferate in this photograph, as they did in the opening image of the "trouble makers" roll call, but in this case in order to make a point Mydans clearly *wants* to highlight the opposition between the initial photograph of Japanese America's rebellious "Japs" and these law-abiding "citizens." Here, where *Life's* photographs of the Manji's photographs increase the levels of doubt, Mydans's framing of the scene and his carefully worded text cannot avoid the complicated levels of national recognition and strangeness made possible by the visibility of a quaint, idealized American family "all classified as disloyal." In a manner that seems to echo the corresponding promise and illusion of American freedom in the closing lines of Okada's *No-No Boy*, Mydans implies that in this "apartment," in a quadrant of one of ten internment camps, resides the kernel of redemption for Japanese Americans: the wholehearted pursuit of middle-class domestic ideals impossible to achieve in the camps. As an obvious developmentalist narrative, this section of the article presents the ascension to middle-class domesticity as the hope for a future for Japanese Americans, because through such domesticity they agree to transcend the rigid, ethnic past seemingly so tragically maintained by the "pressure boys."

The Manji family scene also serves to introduce or frame the stream of images that follow in the section, each of which attempts to emphasize further that the face of the "loyal" private Japanese American stands in direct opposition to the publicized resistance of the camp "trouble makers." The subsequent photographs include scenes of a nondescript elementary school classroom, which, except for the Japanese faces of the children, might exist anywhere in the nation, as well as a picture of the camp nursery where "a Japanese baby with silky black hair is held by a Japanese nurse" (29). Yet, despite the concentration on depicting the daily routines of a thoroughly American community, the general impression is repeatedly one of *both* recognition and strangeness, as these alien bodies and faces enact American life. Strains of the article's initial and uneasy presentation of the "pressure boys" as a domestic *and* an alien threat, one that is simultaneously fixed and yet remains elusive, are meant to be countered by the familiarity of these subsequent scenes. But the strangeness is inescapably captured in Mydans's description of "a Japanese baby with silky black hair" held "by a Japanese nurse." The article's celebration of Japanese American "loyalty" to the principles of middle-class domesticity fails to completely "annex" the conditions of internment as participant in the wider affluence and opportunity that will define postwar America. *Life*'s portrait of camp domesticity inevitably reflects the dubious terms of representation of, in the words of Shoshanna Felman, "the historical event that cannot be approached but must be distanced even in the very act of bearing witness to it."[29]

The description of the camp's setting in a later section of Mydans's essay merely reinforces the inconsistencies and contradictions that plagued attempts to represent the internment in the postwar years as "only a detour on the road of American citizenship," as Ansel Adams characterized it in *Born Free and Equal*, his collection of photographs from the Manzanar relocation center—an internment camp in the desert outside Los Angeles, California.[30] Published the same year that the *Life* article appeared, Adams's photographs of the landscape and people incarcerated at Manzanar echo Mydans's articulation of the internment as an anomaly in American history. "The spirit of Manzanar," according to Adams's account, "is fleeting and impermanent" (32) a living testament to the fortitude of Japanese Americans rather than an obstacle to their inclusion. The Japanese Americans' experience in the camp, turning arid land into "pleasure parks" (20) and erecting "a city built of shacks and patience" (26), is recast as a rich opportunity to prove their "loyalty" and suitability for the rewards of American life. The concept of the camps as a revival of the mythological pioneer spirit of America was common to most of the early postwar attempts to reinterpret the severity of the rugged living conditions of camps located in isolated and uninhabited areas.

Although it was typical in this period to depict the camps as "model communities" where Japanese Americans were being trained to be better citizens, the strikes and the lost harvest at Tule Lake the year of Mydans's visit made it impossible to cast the camp in this mold. Instead, the narrative summary of the latest troubles at Tule Lake emphasizes the tragedy of Japanese Americans' resistance in the face of so much potential plenty as a "waste" of camp "resources" and "opportunities." Reporting that Tule Lake is "some of the world's richest farmland," on which "the Japanese diked the land, dug irrigation ditches and produced a rich crop" (26), Mydans also observes that in the previous year their industry resulted in a near disaster just before harvest time. When a workman was killed in a truck crash on the way to the fields, a strike was quickly called by "the Japs" in order "to get more control of the camps" (26). Although workers from other camps, namely Manzanar, were transported to Tule Lake to complete the harvest, administrators decided to cut back on their plans to turn the camp into a model agricultural project. The tone of this description of the strikes implicitly indicts the strikers for their impudence, while neglecting the unavoidable suggestion of forced labor in the administration's use of a population held against its will. Mydans, who was there under the permission and guidance of the administration, clearly rehearses the military's view of the extravagance of the internees' demands, and thus includes no mention of the reports of brutality and harassment of individuals at Tule Lake that are now well known and that in fact helped to provoke this and other strikes.[31]

And yet, even allowing for the predictably biased nature of this account of internees' decisions to abandon their efforts on the verge of harvest, "They would do no work. They would not farm the fields" (26), the question remains why these otherwise hard-working Americans, those who had "diked the land" and formerly "produced a rich crop out of the drained lake area" (26), would reject the moment of their reward. Tule Lake cannot help but emerge as a metaphor for the dream of American success, historically enshrined as the noble industry of the storied American farmer, now lying fallow and unrealized. By pointing out that the land of Tule Lake itself is "not good for cultivation," while all around its barbed-wire borders is land "capable of grossing $1,000 an acre a year, and last month sold for $350 an acre" (26), Mydans unwittingly draws attention to the disparity between the barrenness of camp conditions and the plenty just out of reach. He ends by concluding simply that order has been restored in the decision "to take no chances" and farm only four hundred acres of the available surrounding lands in the coming year. But the troubling impression of the internees' dissatisfaction and their rejection of the importance of the "fertile adjoining acres" of America just beyond the camp's environs also signals the hollowness, and perhaps as a result even the declining appeal, of the "rich harvest" (26) of American democracy.

Citizen 13660 presses the point even further, positing the camps as an inversion of the narrative of pioneer existence, wherein the settler inevitably moves from fear and vulnerability in the new environment to an increasing sense of belonging and self-sufficiency.[32] Although authorities instruct Okubo's community to "be prepared" for "pioneer life" in the camps, she describes Topaz, "the jewel of the desert," as a hopeless experience. Internees tried to cultivate areas of vegetation and to spend their time in productive ways, but the vast periods of idleness were inevitable "as the result of the demoralizing effect of center life" (96). Buffeted by windstorms in the summer and the brackish mud of the alkaline soil after winter snows, Okubo comes to feel that despite their efforts "nothing was successful; the elements won out" (184). The pioneer theme of the conquest of a forbidding environment is never realized; instead many of the internees at Topaz grow increasingly dependent on their incarceration and fearful of the hostility and uncertainty that potentially await them in the outside world.

As a reminder of their entrapment at the mercy of the rude conditions, the stench from the sewer that was constantly under repair symbolizes the unavoidable and overwhelming nature of the physical obstacles that confronted Japanese Americans at every turn. In Okubo's memoir, the cruelty of the physical environment seems to materialize the racial obstacles confronting Japanese Americans. These obstacles, like the Japanese American body whose manifest history of trauma is constantly effaced but remains as a "faint" presence anyway, finally overwhelm the possibility of narrative closure, which, in turn, inverts the liberal assumption of historical developmentalism on which American exceptionalism turns. Judged by the wartime experience of Japanese Americans, the ideals of the American nation on the eve of V-E Day are arguably characterized by defeat and exhaustion rather than triumph and achievement.

Mydans's article, far from being merely a liberal celebration of the patriotic Japanese Americans (although it is that as well), openly acknowledges the "pressure boys'" unsettling challenge to the concept of pluralistic America and their questioning of the fullness of its democratic promise of liberty. Mydans depoliticizes the discursive instability of the memory of Japanese American internment, its resistance to the demands of national representation, and its stubborn denial of the historical progression of the American nation by subtly recasting its troubling of American ideals as a shared American anxiety about the postwar world. Although the first two-thirds of Mydans's photographic essay on Tule Lake is devoted to the attempt to distinguish between the "loyal" and "disloyal" internee, in the last few pages Mydans comes to a rather sudden recognition of the futility of this enterprise. In response, he attempts to quell the disturbance of the memory of internment by enveloping it within a larger story of the alienation of war and, in contrast to the early sections of the essay, by inviting rather than warding off the collapse of national boundaries and by embracing the death of national innocence. This movement comes in Mydans's photographic representation of a young resister he unwittingly but meaningfully describes as "killing time" in the camps, an apt description of the suspension of historical progress and the questioning of democratic promises that characterized the Japanese American experience of the war. "Killing time" also suggests the ironic utility of counterhistorical narratives, as Mydans subsumes and metamorphizes its opposition to history's "deceptive continuity" within a global, postwar atmosphere of anxiety that renders meaningless the critique of national history or domestic racism. Mydans's strategy of avoidance by "annexation" finally seems to manifest Foucault's observation that "oppositional histories resurface within the very unitary discourses they opposed."[33] The *Life* magazine article represents a critical gesture in the initial struggle to remember the internment against the demands of producing a postwar national history.

Midway through the third section of Mydans's article, in which he attempts to distinguish between the rejection of American ideals embodied in the "pressure boys" and the patriotic optimism of so-called loyal internees such as the Manjis, he includes a full-page photograph of one young "pressure boy" seated in his small cubicle in the stockade, against a wall lined with magazine cut-outs of glamorous white women. Clearly morose, the boy strums his guitar. Sporting a rich, dark pompadour, which recalls the rebellious youthfulness so evident in the opening photograph of the "trouble makers," he clearly stresses the troubling refusal of the Japanese American subject to be completely contained within Mydans's liberal framework. The caption reads:

> What it feels like to be a prisoner is shown in the expression of this young Japanese "pressure boy" in the stockade. He was singing *Home on the Range* when Mydans entered the stockade barracks. Reports Mydans: "He sang it like an American. There was no Japanese accent. He looked at me the same way I guess I looked at a Japanese official when he came to check on me at Camp Santo Tomas in Manila. At the back of my mind was the thought, 'Come on, get it over and get out. Leave me alone.' *This boy felt the same way. He was just waiting, killing time.*" (emphasis added) (31)

Although this photograph and its inscription come roughly halfway through the second section, they mark how Mydans's movement from his initial attempts to represent the threat of Japanese American resistance, through his attempts to distinguish and advocate for a distinctly different "loyal" Japanese American subject, exposes the impossibility of the terms of "loyal" and "disloyal" to contain the perceived threat of Japanese American difference. More overtly than the first photographs of "pressure boys," this image depicts a young "pressure boy" who straddles the presumed divide in the camps between the rejection of and identification with the familiar Western concepts of rugged individualism and unfettered freedom so ironically hailed in his sullen-faced singing of "Home on the Range." Here Japanese American resistance indeed threatens to invert the initial relationship between American loyalty and camp resistance by casting the prescriptions for proving national loyalty as the antithesis of this "pressure boy's" act of individual resistance, an American gesture that his song suggests is imperiled by the undeniable, unpardonable fact of internment.

The indelible impression left by this image of a "pressure boy" "killing time" in the camps, waiting for the song's vision of an unbridled American freedom to arrive, is carried over to the final section of this "first look" at the condition of interned Japanese Americans (fig. 3). At the end of the panels of photographs *Life's* editors pen a brief essay, tellingly titled "They Have Everything Except Liberty." "They are prisoners," the essay begins, "even though the War Relocation Authority tries to soften this fact by using the euphemistic name 'Segregees'" (34). Furthermore, the editors add, "because the problems which have arisen to plague the camp stem fundamentally from their loss of liberty, those problems can never really be resolved. Their life cannot be made pleasant. It can only be made endurable" (34). Although they stop short of condemning the existence of the camps, seeming to agree that those deemed disloyal "must, of necessity, be put in a place where they cannot hurt the U.S." (34), the editors are pressed to acknowledge the contradictions implicit in the preceding photoessay by Mydans by questioning, however mildly, the benefits of internment for either Japanese Americans or the nation as a whole. "It is too easy," they remind the reader, "to say that they are all disloyal and treat them all accordingly. Some 70% of them are American citizens" (34). Most remarkable, however, are the editors' expressed doubts about the system of relocation then underway for internees willing to pass an FBI check and take a public oath of allegiance. "This method of release sometimes does not work," they point out, given Japanese Americans' fear of vio-

Fig. 3 "Killing time" in the stockade at Tule Lake (*Life*, March 20, 1944).

lence and rumors of "irate anti-Japanese mobs" (34). The cumulative effect of this closing essay, as its title indicates, is to disturb further rather than to settle the reader's confidence in the process and outcome of the internment. And in rendering the meaning of the event uncertain, the article ultimately touches on the core power of the memory of Japanese American internment: it threatens to unravel the imaginary links between the body of the American citizen and the body of the nation by revealing the arbitrary nature of such constructions.

When Carl Mydans is finally permitted to speak in the last part of the essay, he tries once more to "annex" the contradictions of internment by containing the potentially explosive recognition of the experience of "disloyal" Japanese Americans in the camps within the terms of war expressed by his own ordeal as a POW in a Japanese camp during the war. The editors introduce his story as "an inevitable comparison," presumably because the mere fact of incarceration was bound to lead Mydans to consider his own time as a POW. But Mydans's comments go beyond simply expressing sympathy for life under such conditions. Building on his identification with the "pressure boy" in the stockade singing "Home on the Range," Mydans suggests a parallel between U.S. and Japanese experience of war that subtly denies the unique experience of Japanese Americans. According to Mydans, "Americans interned under the Japanese have a certain ease of mind in knowing that as Americans they are considered enemies and nothing will be done for them" (34). The fleeting recognition that the Japanese Americans he observes at Tule Lake seem to exist in a far more ambiguous and troubling no-man's land as neither enemy nor citizen gives way quickly to Mydans's suggestion that the legal and economic devastation of internment is only important as part of a much larger nexus of national conflict: "Over here we have the problem of American citizens being interned as aliens. There are political and sociological conflicts" (34). The poignant and unsettling loneliness of the patriotic "pressure boy," tagged as an enemy alien but enacting anyway the anthem of national identification, is called to mind. Like Mydans's narrative, it both hints at and tries to avoid the trauma of internment; for instance, he goes on to concede that Japanese American internees "are made physically comfortable out of all comparison to the comforts given us [American POWs]," only to remark that the U.S. camps are "dirty and empty" and "by American standards it is an ugly, dreary way of life" (34).

As an "ugly, dreary way of life," the internment camp as national phenomenon emerges in Life's article as an ominous foreboding of the potential decay of the American promise, which from the stockade in Tule Lake seems barely distinguishable from the Japanese prisons housing American POWs. The notion of American exceptionalism is fundamentally imperiled by the powerful suggestion that life in the United States has somehow failed to keep its vow and is, as a result, in danger of being indistinguishable in some respects from its most alien enemy, Japan. Magnifying the ugliness and the dreariness of the war for Japanese Americans in its scrutiny of camp life, the article on Tule Lake seems dangerously poised to render the entire nation, as emblematized by the "loyal" and the "disloyal" depicted among its ranks, little more than the "rockless bottom land" (26) on which the camp is constructed.

Fittingly, the photographs that conclude the essay focus not on the "pressure boys" of Tule Lake that began the piece, but on two groups of young women. The first is a "high-stepping" parade of drum majorettes practicing their moves along the dusty "fire-break" that separates the rows of dormitories that substitutes for the high school football field they might have occupied on any other Friday night. The facing page, in contrast, is a full-length photograph of "the same girls" performing a Japanese dance. The caption emphasizes that even in these seemingly innocent figures "there is a conflict between Americanism and Nipponism" (35) generated from the source of Japanese American memory and merely rendered in relief by the internment. The "high-stepping" drum majorettes and the "pressure boys" loom as inseparable, gendered elements of a remembered experience of America as stated by Okada's "faint and elusive insinuation" of promise.

"Why do you want to leave this country," Carl Mydans asks one Nisei who expresses his desire to be allowed to leave the United States. "I don't think they ever want us to come back," he reasons, "the feeling will be too much against us." When Mydans presses him on his future plans, he answers: "We want to go where there are new frontiers" (34). The rhetoric of the frontier once more swells, and with it the romanticization of the hardships of Japanese Americans as simply another cycle of pioneer life. But the power of the metaphor for imagining the terms of a renewed postwar nation and economy, one where all citizens are free to pursue new opportunities, ultimately rings hollow in the camps. "I think we'll find them [the new frontiers] in Australia," the young man decides, while in a parenthetical statement the editors simply observe: "Australia admits no Oriental immigrants" (34). To adopt the viewpoint and the counter-historical perspective of those interned, "to wait" for the promise of democracy while "killing time" was to be, like the "pressure boys" and the drum majorettes alike, a people without a country. It is this ambivalence in the wartime memories of

Japanese Americans that would continually thwart popular attempts to redeem them as a citizenry in a variety of public discourses. Remembering the internment was a vital prerequisite, as we will see, for constituting a postwar culture in the face of liberal crises, cold war politics, and racial restructuring.

TWO

The Internment of Anthropology:

Wartime Studies of Japanese Culture

On the one hand we dogmatically insist that anthropology rests on ethno-graphic research involving personal, prolonged interaction with the Other. But then we pronounce upon the knowledge gained from such research a discourse which construes the Other in terms of distance, spatial and temporal. The Oth-er's empirical presence turns into his theoretical absence, a conjuring trick . . . to keep the Other outside the Time of anthropology.—Johannes Fabian, *Time and the Other*

In *War Without Mercy*, historian John Dower's 1986 book on the racial discourses that informed the war between Japan and the United States, there is a fleeting but vitally important point about the terms of the national perception of Japanese Americans.[1] "The treatment of Japanese Americans," Dower begins, "is a natural starting point for any study of the racial aspects of the war, for it reveals not merely the clear-cut racial stigmatization of the Japanese, but also the official endorsement this received" (79). He then concludes that the key to understanding the terms of their treatment rests in the official program of "community analysis" or ethnographic study that the War Relocation Authority (WRA) "established in the ten camps in which Japanese-Americans were incarcerated" (79). Although Dower does not elaborate on the possible implications of community analysis, the ambitions of community analysts were well documented at the time, and they revolved around using interviews with the internees in an effort to develop theo-ries of Japanese behavior that would be useful after the war when the United States occupied Japan. Thus, anthropology's central role in the "treatment" of Japanese American internees begins to suggest something of the truth of Johannes Fabian's argument quoted in the epigraph to this chapter—that anthropology makes its Other (in this case, Japanese Americans) by using information gathered from "personal, prolonged interaction" in an effort to set the Other beyond the spatial and temporal realm of the examiner (in occupied Japan) and, thus, "keep the Other outside the Time of anthropology."[2] The work of the mostly liberal, white camp anthropologists or "community analysts," as they were officially known, was beset with problems peculiar to the national and institutional politics of the war, a fact that complicates the ways in which Japanese Americans were ultimately constructed as racial Others. American anthropological studies of internment became not just another example of the American propensity for seeing Japanese Americans as Japanese aliens, but more important, the studies became a clearinghouse for certain transitions in the deployment and power of anthropological theories about Asian Americans that were to have serious, long-term effects on the self-concept and political status of Japanese Americans. Beneath the circuits of influence and layers of obfuscation, community analysis programs allowed liberal, white anthropologists unparalleled power to reconstruct the Nisei in particular.

Government records indicate that during the early years of World War II the WRA, which was initially established to administer internment or relocation camps housing more than one hundred thousand West Coast Japanese Americans, created the community analysis program to assist in the administration of the internment camps. Termed the "community analysis section," it began at Poston camp in Arizona and eventually involved the assignment of social scientists as government agents in each of the ten internment camps.[3] Most of the social scientists involved were anthropologists whose chief qualification was their knowledge of and interest in Japanese cultural and behavioral patterns, although only a handful had ever actually visited Japan.[4] As community analysts they were primarily responsible for ensuring the smooth operation of camp life. But while stationed in the camps they were also explicitly encouraged to utilize Japanese American internees as informants on Japanese culture in the hope that the data collected might prove useful not only to the ongoing war effort against Japan but also to the postwar effort as well. The government hoped for insights useful for the control of both international and domestic Japanese communities: the reformation of Japan in the postwar period as well as the resettlement of Japanese Americans after the war.[5] Or, as Dower puts it, "observations based on work with these persecuted and uprooted Americans were superimposed upon the growing collective portrait of the Japanese enemy, and several social scientists who worked in the camps went on to participate directly in psychological-warfare planning pertaining to Japan."[6]

In truth, however, the relationship between the data drawn from community analysis and theories of Japanese character was even more complicated. Once the project was underway, some anthropologists began to recognize that the recruitment of dispossessed Japanese Americans as informants on Japanese culture occurred under such unique domestic conditions of suspicion and uncertainty that the uses of community analysis in postwar Japan must, at the very least, be compromised. The anthropologists' reservations about simply transferring methods of regulating camp life to the occupation of Japan were often explicit, especially as they begin to see their job as that of correcting misconceptions about Japanese Americans by highlighting their difficult ordeal during the war and promoting their chances for successful reintegration after the war. Ultimately, the relationship between Japanese Americans and Japanese cultural studies departed significantly from its founding intentions. Rather than simply using the internees as a resource for information on Japan, the anthropologists very quickly became invested in drawing conclusions about Japanese behavior that could be applied to a program of readjustment for Japanese Americans. Community analysts paradoxically found themselves willing to concede that the population was an "alien" culture in order to develop an acceptable argument for their assimilability. Thus, despite the obvious dilemmas posed by this loose exchange and substitution of data, the anthropologists continued to pursue the assumption that theories of Japanese behavior and policies for reforming Japan after the war might be confirmed and tested through "prolonged" analyses and observations of imprisoned Japanese Americans. The immediate, historical reasons for the liberal anthropologists' willingness to view the terms "Japanese" and "Japanese American" as interchangeable also followed in the tradition of early national sociological studies of "the oriental problem," which represented the peculiar American foundations of managing national anxieties about the "oriental" Other by reconstructing this "inscrutable" presence as an American in the making.

Scholars have only just recently begun to piece together the elaborate politics of internment anthropology that I synopsize here. Despite

the fact that the cultural anthropologists' participation in the administration of the Japanese American internment was public knowledge
during the war years, it is only in the past decade that this fraught part
of the history of American anthropology has been deemed a watershed
in the conceptualization of the Japanese American subject.[7] Peter Suzuki's work in the early and mid-1980s was groundbreaking in this regard, because he was the first to catalog the ethical and scientific problems suggested by the WRA's administration of the camps. In a series of
essays on the role of internment politics in the development of wartime
anthropology, Suzuki argues, among other things, that "anthropology
in the WRA camp was misapplied because it was largely used to control
and manipulate the inmates."[8] Suzuki's work was followed by Orin
Starn's 1986 essay, "Engineering Internment: Anthropologists and
the War Relocation Authority," a thoughtful and comprehensive over-
view of the motivations, processes, and results of the anthropologists'
misguided attempts to help Japanese American internees. Although
Starn acknowledges that the analysts were stationed in the camps in
order to gather data against Japan and to identify potential problems,
he also focuses on the paradoxical means by which the anthropologists
tried to use their positions to speak on behalf of the incarcerated. He
concludes that despite "their good intentions of improving camp conditions and defusing anti-Japanese public opinion," (700), WRA anthropologists ultimately produced work and followed policies that "unintentionally" promoted racial stereotypes about the Japanese and, by
implication, the Japanese Americans as well. Starn's impressive analysis remains indispensable for its synthesis of the evolution of the anthropologists' work in the internment camps. In his essay he also reiterates Suzuki's contention that the scholarly neglect of the meaning of
camp analysis has deprived American anthropologists of the opportunity for important insights into the development of postwar theories of
culture and behavior:

> It continually struck me how little the basic views of WRA ethnographers
> about their role in relocation have altered over the years. Historical
> changes have not inspired the kind of public self-examination found, for
> example, in the discussions of British anthropologists about their rela-
> tion to colonialism. . . . Continued convictions of having contributed to
> Japanese-American well-being in troubled times and to the war effort
> more generally would have to be the starting points for such an analysis.
> (717)

Echoes of Dower resound in Starn's description of the anthropologists' treatment of Japanese Americans as "starting points" for the understanding of American attitudes about the Japanese. Starn seems to suggest that Americans must come to grips with the extent of the anthropologists' participation in projecting Japanese Americans as an "alien" ethnic group in need of reformation, an enterprise that evokes an earlier, Western colonial paternalism.

Around the same time that Starn's work was published, Yuji Ichioka organized a two-day conference on the internment titled "Views From Within: The Japanese American Wartime Internment Experience," held at the University of California at Berkeley, the center for the original Japanese Evacuation and Resettlement Study (JERS). The book that came out of the conference gathered a wide-ranging series of essays on the politics of camp anthropology, essays that testify to the fact that the impact of community analysis is still being felt, although it is not by any means fully accounted for.[9] Like Dower, Suzuki, and Starn, Ichioka and the conference participants found themselves focused on the anthropological studies conducted in the camps as "the basis of a rich social history of concentration camp life" (22), but they also revealed the difficulty of categorizing the effects of community analysis. "It goes without saying," Ichioka concludes, with his characteristic cynicism, "that JERS was not a research project in the service of a political cause on behalf of Japanese-Americans. To say that it should have been is to engage in wishful thinking; to criticize it for not having been is to be naïve" (23). Although the disastrous effects of the tendency to view Japanese American culture as Japanese have been widely noted and have enriched numerous histories and memoirs of the period of Japanese American internment, postwar and Asian American critics have clearly just started to address the impact of anthropology's study of Japanese Americans' internment and resettlement.[10]

Still, as noted earlier by Dower, the underlying implications of the fact that theories of Japanese behavior were explicitly confirmed or tested by the administration of Japanese American internees remain unspoken. It is time to explain how the liberal anthropologists' conflation of Japanese American and Japanese culture allowed them not just to use an imprisoned population as a scientific resource but also to show how their reports from the camps reiterated earlier notions about Asians as "oriental Others" in America in an effort to revitalize the belief in an assimilable Japanese Other. More specifically, scrutiny of the work of the camp anthropologists suggests parallels between the earlier focus on Asian Americans as "marginal men" and the wartime obsession with the split character of the Japanese American Nisei. Despite their stress on presentism and their suspicion of historicism, cultural anthropologists recast the concept of the Asian American as the "marginal man" as one of Japanese "duality." According to Robert Park, who coined his definition in 1928, the "marginal man" was the result of global movement and cross-cultural contact, which created the conditions for the emergence of the alienated immigrant individual caught between two distinct cultures.[11] This concept metamorphosed into the wartime anthropologists' concerns with Japanese "duality," [the peculiar presence of warring impulses in an individual,] as they tried to show how the dualistic Japanese American might be pushed further toward the American pole. Community analysts argued that the presence of a tense generational struggle between Issei and Nisei internees was caused by the vestiges of a lingering, archaic Japanese character typified by the Issei, which the Nisei had to turn away from in order to progress toward full assimilation. As a result, the anthropologists determined to utilize the ancient filial piety of Japanese culture as a means of spatially and temporally fixing the problem of Japanese Americans, a problem that, thus parsed, inevitably necessitated their forced movement toward another more modern and thus American existence. Not coincidentally, this process of othering a group in space and time in order to create the imperative of colonial reformation was similarly deployed in occupied Japan, where the aim was to break the old, patriarchal Japanese traditions and replace them with a model of American democratic capitalism. In the end, however, the community analysis project was ultimately responsible for extending the "problem" of Japanese American difference by affirming the resilience of Japanese culture and, thus, maintaining the constructed alienation of the Nisei.

"Experience in Such Colonies":
Establishing the Camp Analysis Project

Mass hysteria in the wake of Pearl Harbor provoked widespread suspicion of Japanese Americans. Historian Michi Weglyn reveals that in February 1942, President Roosevelt signed Executive Order 9066, thereby acting against the findings of the prewar Munson Report, which had determined that "there is no Japanese problem on the Coast." This order designated much of the West Coast a "military area," and hence extended to the military carte blanche the power to remove any and all individuals of "a potentially dangerous" nature. Even though the order did not specify Japanese Americans for special scrutiny, they emerged as the order's intended target and remain the only ethnic group evacuated en masse under suspicion of disloyalty.[12] Ronald Takaki concludes that in signing Executive Order 9066 Roosevelt had in effect "signed a blank check, giving full authority to General DeWitt to evacuate the Japanese and place them in assembly centers and eventually in internment camps."[13] Despite the fact that almost two-thirds of the evacuees were U.S. citizens—Nisei who had been born and, in many cases, reared on the West Coast—a number of high-ranking government officials urged Roosevelt forward in the belief that, as Secretary of War Harry Stimson put it, "their racial characteristics are such that we cannot understand or trust even the citizen Japanese."[14] Within a year, virtually every West Coast Japanese American was sent to one of several remote relocation centers where he or she was officially quarantined and questioned to determine if imprisonment in even more isolated internment camps, reserved for those deemed disloyal and a threat to national security, was warranted. Ten relocation centers, often called "camps" even though they were supposed to be merely holding centers, were eventually established.

A central part of the task of assessing and containing Japanese American internees fell to the group of government social scientists who became part of the WRA's administration of the camps. As community analysts and as part of the Camp Analysts Section, or CAS, their explicit duties in the camps were to assess levels of residual "Japanese attitudes," including and especially the evacuated population's varying levels of loyalty to the United States; to recommend and direct government administration of the camps, including future plans for permanently relocating evacuees away from their lifelong homes in the West; and, later, to study the viability of training and using Japanese Americans as go-betweens in occupied areas of the Pacific.[15] Archival evidence reveals that the decision to place analysts in the camps was rationalized not only as a domestic necessity for the purposes of discovering how to deal with the unique problems represented by Japanese Americans, but also as a means of studying and confirming theories of Japanese behavioral patterns.

In an early memorandum from John Embree, the anthropologist who ran the CAS from Washington, D.C., to General J. L. DeWitt, Embree writes: "It is believed that various evacuees in the Japanese relocation centers possess information regarding Japanese social, political, economic and labor conditions which can be of great value in the prosecution of the war."[16] Although Embree clearly refers to Kibei, those Japanese Americans who had been born in the United States but educated in Japan, camp analysts regularly dealt with and depended on others in the camps as well. By 1944, Embree had broadened the initial focus on the Kibei to state simply that the evacuees were used as resources for camp analysts from "the time the administration was first set up." He also became more specific about the general uses of the data collected in the camps, saying, "the section was expected not only to be informed on social conditions in relocation centers but also on the social organization of the West Coast Japanese before the war, and on that abstruse phenomenon called 'Japanese psychology'" (278).

Here, the emphasis on historical context, on the specific social conditions affecting Japanese Americans, is in large measure the enduring legacy of Franz Boas, who established the terms for cross-cultural analysis as early as 1887 when, in response to Otis Mason's Social Darwinist view of the evolution of all cultures as governed by natural or biological laws, Boas argued for the necessity of historical specificity in assessing the culture of any people.[17] It is interesting to note that even Boas was not immune to such views. He entertained the validity of the physiological basis for comparison of cultures in his early theories of race and culture, even once acknowledging that some races were, at least in the then present day, "inherently" inferior to others. At the close of his career, however, he would adamantly insist that cultural differences were "dependent upon historical causes, regardless of race."[18] Although Boas and those who studied with him accepted that historical and social forces were the ultimate source of cultural differences, the debate did not entirely eliminate the resort to racial stereotyping in some cases. Embree's and perhaps others' willingness to consider that Japanese Americans might represent both a unique culture and yet remain direct symbols of a distant Japanese culture was indirectly influenced by this tendency in American social scientists' work on race and culture. John Embree saw no conflict between his Boasnian adherence to the historical foundations of culture and his casual assertion that with Japanese Americans "recommendations on labor relations, mess operations, etc., to be accepted, usually had to be made in terms of Japanese psychology rather than of prosaic labor-management relations."[19] The implementation of Japanese Americans as a resource for the study of Japan continued to develop under the auspices of Embree and anthropologist Alexander Leighton, the very first analyst installed at one of the camps. When unrest broke out in the Poston, Arizona, camp in 1942, it was decided that cultural anthropologists might be useful in resolving the differences between camp administrators and camp residents.[20] Thus, Embree's approach to the so-called problem of Japanese American status was shaped by his unselfconscious application of Boas's earlier arguments about racial differences.

Yet Embree, and Alexander Leighton in particular, were also compelled by the work of those social scientists who followed in Boas's wake to develop new theories that further explained the social and cultural origins of interracial contact and also suggested how solutions to the problem might be achieved. Chief among these problems was the question of the future role of Asian immigrants in American society. In a recent work, historian Henry Yu points out that "the 'oriental problem' in the 1920s created a set of ideas that structured the way that Asians were understood and the way they were given a meaningful place in American society."[21] Robert Park was the most influential proponent of "the oriental problem," which he perceived as a problem of assimilation because "the 'oriental' in America was still an exotic oddity, foreign and seemingly unassimilated."[22] According to Yu, Park theorized that such "an enormous cultural distance separated Western culture from 'Oriental' culture" that the universal cycle of contact, competition, conflict, accommodation, and assimilation was not allowed to develop.[23] Thus, the greatest task facing the social scientist was to determine how to move the "oriental" Other further along in the cycle so that he or she might achieve full assimilation.

More than any other single camp analyst, Alexander Leighton was vital to enunciating a set of strategies for dealing with the perceived "assimilation problem" of the Japanese American subject. He spent fifteen months, from June 1942 to September 1943, at Poston, a camp in Arizona in the Colorado River Valley, which was the first to use social scientists to observe Japanese American camp behavior. Not surprisingly, Leighton was also among the first to suggest publicly that analysts' experiences in the camps should play a major role in the nation's administration of the postwar reconstruction of Asia. John Embree, as

head of the WRA, viewed Leighton's anthropological project at Poston
as the model for the installation of community analysts in every one of
the camps housing evacuated Japanese Americans.[24] Because community analysis in the camps hinged on the presumption of the direct usefulness of Japanese Americans as informants on Japanese culture, Embree and Leighton were often compelled to focus on the similarities
between internment and the expected postwar dislocation of Japanese citizens. Any conclusions they might draw about the cultural differences that Park had theorized as preventing Asian Americans' assimilation in America had to be applicable to the occupation effort in
postwar Japan. Although camp analysts did not in practice mistake Japanese Americans for Japanese, in theory they did rely from the start on
viewing the government's administration of Japanese American displacement as a direct analogue for the military's later occupation of Japan. As a result of this reliance, the anthropologists' observations and
opinions regarding the administration of internment were later quite
influential in developing and confirming theories of the best way to
manage Japanese differences and, as a "natural" extension, the best
means of restructuring Japanese American subjectivity to achieve
Park's final stage of assimilation.

    In hindsight, the disastrous effects of such a fundamental oversight
seem glaring, and it is important to recall that these ramifications were
barely considered in the first public description of the camp analysis
project and its aims. Although the project may now appear a rather obvious instance of social engineering, one that seems stamped with the
imperialism of an earlier age, Leighton—perhaps also reflecting imperialist rationalizations—believed his work would ultimately achieve
the liberation of his subjects. In July 1942, Leighton published an essay
titled "Training Social Scientists for Post-War Conditions," just as he
was assuming his position at Poston. In this work, he outlines an optimistic plan for the use of social scientists during and after the war, in
which he cites the invaluable benefits of the "practical application" of
their results.[25] After providing a synopsis of his experiences in "an Es-
kimo village in Alaska" as an example of how the social scientist could
be "both an observer and a social doctor to a community" and utilize
the information gathered toward "the development of better living and
better relations," he suggests that "there are many similar opportunities in the United States under the widespread administration of the
Office of Indian Affairs" (27–29). His statement refers to the Poston

camp, which, because it had been established on Indian land, was the only camp to come under the administration of the Office of Indian Affairs. He concludes his essay by rendering a sketchy portrait of the nature and meaning of the camp analysis project: "Colonies of American Japanese have been formed," he offers, with the belief that "experience in such colonies can *naturally* lead to positions in reorganizing the Pacific areas when the war is over" (emphasis added) (29). Leighton only briefly questions the applicability of "experience in such colonies" when he cautions against compromising social science by placing the scientist "under pressure to deliver goods of immediate value or cease to exist" (25). The significance of this early wartime piece rests in its prescience: it anticipates the profound influence government social scientists would have on postwar foreign policy in Japan; it predicts that the camp analysis project will play a vital part in realizing that future; and it projects the latter two ambitions at the expense of considering the ethical and procedural obstacles inherent in the use of "colonies of American Japanese." Yet despite the early optimism over the cross-cultural uses of community analysis, in a very short period of time Leighton's faith in the postwar benefits of wartime social science would be tempered by his growing knowledge of the unique situation of Japanese Americans and the problems inherent in collecting and assessing data in the uncertain environment of the camps, and by an implied recognition of the manipulation of time and space that would prove to be an integral part of social science's approach to the "oriental" unassimilability of Japanese Americans.

"Groping in the Dark":
Patterns of Erasing Japanese American Culture

Although Leighton had originally expressed tremendous confidence in the potential of the Poston project, by 1943, less than a year later, his commitment to the cas would increasingly be shadowed by an awareness of the difficulties in identifying evacuees' attitudes in the camps as universal to all dislocated Japanese. In "Assessing Public Opinion in a Dislocated Community," Leighton peppers with caveats and disclaimers his argument for seeing the administration of the camps as an analogy for postwar occupation of Japan.[26] The essay looms now as an illustration of the contradictions and generalities that beset early attempts to use the internment as a corollary for occupation as well as the means by which the anthropologists eventually rationalized their efforts in the face of mounting doubts about their mission.

"Applied social science has no magic formula with which to provide infallible answers," Leighton begins, "no matter what is done, there will be groping in the dark." Although he retains hopes "to reduce both the groping and the darkness" (653), Leighton remains ambivalent throughout the essay about the advisability of using for international purposes information gathered under extraordinary domestic circumstances. In his report on the community analysis project, WRA chief John Embree confirms that "because of special local problems in establishing rapport with the Poston community there was a reluctance on the part of the research unit to communicate its findings directly to the Washington office of the WRA."[27] Yet Leighton ironically finds a way to resolve his dilemma by highlighting rather than obscuring in his essay the "special local problems" encountered by analysts; that is, by emphasizing rather than by ignoring the purely functional aspects of the specific conditions shaping internment resistance. Focusing on the most extraordinary events in camp history—the strikes and protests that occurred in several camps early in the internment—Leighton recasts their particularity as emblematic not of distinctive historical and political contexts unique to U.S. domestic culture but of the universal problems of dislocation. He suggests that the general benefits of community analysis lay in the lessons learned at these critical times of crisis, and he specifically argues that the methods employed by community analysts to quell Japanese American dissent could be used just as effectively by occupation leaders in postwar Japan dealing with similar episodes of resistance by a "hostile" people of Japanese descent.

The outbreak of "special local problems" chronicled by Leighton resulted from the daily psychological pressures of incarceration on Japanese Americans, two-thirds of whom were citizens under constant involuntary surveillance, as well as from the heterogeneity of the evacuated population, a fact that often made it difficult for camp analysts to pinpoint the essence of Japanese American much less Japanese difference. Leighton early concludes that the evacuees at Poston "varied greatly in background" and that there was a prevalence of "much conflict of opinion and a breakdown of the previous forms of social control" (654). At times, "different pressure groups sought power," he reports, "each trying to convince the government that it alone represented the feelings of the people" (654). Despite the fact that the

Japanese American Citizens League (JACL) was officially acknowledged by the administrators as the voice of Japanese Americans, "the transmission of information and point of view in both directions was a problem of first magnitude" (655), because the administration was equally at sea in their treatment of evacuees. Although some "looked upon the people being governed as enemies to be punished and never trusted, others emphasized the official policy of rehabilitation. The net result was a marked inconsistency of action with consequent confusion" (654–55). The evacuees in turn responded with "a community attitude of hostility toward any form of investigation or inquiry" (656). Those few who did participate with the analysts in the collection of information, mostly younger JACL members or their sympathizers and not necessarily Kibei, were under the stigma of being doubly marked as "informants" because they were viewed by a substantial number of Japanese Americans who refused to cooperate with what they considered their illegal incarceration, as having "reported names to make money, to settle grudges, or to ingratiate themselves with the law enforcement agencies" (656–57).

Leighton's published account of the problems at the Poston camp suggests that the community analysts' assignments to collect and interpret the responses of Japanese American evacuees were plagued from the very beginning by overt administrative hostility, the evacuees' resulting apprehension of government agents, and reliance on a pool of informants distrusted by most in the camp. Leighton's description of the early camp period as a tense and even volatile environment is born out by the written record of subsequent events in other camps as well. Position alone witnessed a major strike by evacuees over food and living conditions and the later indictment of 101 young Nisei men for refusing to volunteer for military service.[28] Resistance was also encountered at, notably, the Manzanar and Tule Lake camps in California, where the rigors of incarceration, interrogation, and, in isolated cases, violence, precipitated major episodes of protest later reconstructed in the memoirs of Japanese Americans held there.

Remarkably, what Leighton proposes in his article is that the organized resistance encountered in the camps at these times, although specific to the domestic conditions of internment, is most instructive as an example of the tensions inherent "in a variety of administrative problems in countries where human life has been severely dislocated and where the people are very different from the average American in racial descent, traditional values, and predominant attitudes."[29] Notwithstanding liberal anthropology's arguments against biological determinism, the chief point of comparison between wartime internment and postwar occupation is the shared racial origins of the two populations. In the case of Japanese Americans, Leighton tries to complicate this fact by suggesting that the resistance often resulted from the mutually perceived racial and cultural differences between those of Japanese descent and "average Americans," differences that made communication difficult. "The greater the ethnic difference between the governing and the governed," Leighton asserts, "the greater becomes this difficulty" (652). Here Leighton recalls the conclusions of the United States Immigration or Dillingham Commission, which was established in 1907 to explore the impact of and suggest solutions to the perceived problems of immigration. In its introduction the commission focused on "an inquiry into the assimilation of the immigrants with the American people as far as the form of the body is concerned." Drawing on Franz Boas's work for the commission article, "Changes in Bodily Form of Descendants of Immigrants," which argued that over time the immigrant's body was transformed by American life,[30] the commission found that the "oriental" would probably find it impossible to adapt to American life because their extreme racial and physiological difference from white or "native" Americans would render such transformation impossible.[31] The Social Darwinist influence is undeniable here.

Although Leighton warns against "transferring too literally the lessons learned in one to the other," particularly in situations such as internment "where social relations are largely artificial and everything has an air of being temporary," he simultaneously suggests that the cultural motivations of the strikes and the specific techniques used to circumvent the strike at Poston in November 1942 should logically carry over to occupation policy with other Japanese.[32] Believing that "the community attitude of hostility toward any form of investigation or inquiry," "one of the toughest problems" faced by camp analysts, was a "universal" quality that "went far back in Japanese culture," Leighton concludes that internees' hostility "was a parallel of *what must be met* in occupied areas" (emphasis added) (656–57). Leighton's suspicion of historicism resulted in the neglect of the political and material conditions motivating Japanese Americans' "hostility" in favor of a functionalist approach that ends up reinforcing the very racism that Boas and his liberal successors decried. The problem of using the dislocation of Japanese Americans to provide theories about Japanese behavior meant that Leighton and others working with him subtly reinforced the belief in racial difference as a means of collecting and organizing knowledge. Leighton's argument effectively reconfigures the internees as dislocated Others who are removed both spatially and temporally from the national situation; in effect, they became indistinguishable from the Japanese peoples whom military administrators would later encounter in Japan. This gesture is, as Johannes Fabian points out, a feature of "modern anthropology" that "constructs its Other in terms of topoi implying distance, difference, and opposition" in the interest of constructing "ordered Space and Time—a cosmos— for Western society to inhabit, rather than "understanding among cultures."[33]

Yet at the same time Leighton makes a strong argument for the efficacy of peaceful negotiation in dealing with any dislocated Japanese populace. The decision of the administration to handle the Poston strike by initiating a negotiation with the strikers and allowing for the venting of limited grievances is offered as an illustration of what might be done in Japan in the event of a similar phase of resistance. "Even in the occupation of enemy territory, the chief aim of the agents of a democracy will not be to out-Fascist the Fascists, but, after the necessary housecleaning, to rehabilitate the country," according to Leighton, who offers Poston as an illustration of the benefits of negotiation over force with enemy peoples.[34] The community analysts at Poston had rightly predicted that "if the [Poston] Administration negotiated carefully, it would come out of the situation with much better influence in the community than it had previously wielded" (663). Furthermore, the use of peaceful methods by the administration at Poston compared favorably with the use of military force at Manzanar in the face of a similar internee strike, a strike that subsequently resulted in two deaths, months of turmoil, and "a marked increase in operating expenses" (663). The aversion to the use of force in administering "hostile" groups is "nothing but the consistent application of common sense," Leighton confesses, and he acknowledges that its use "is far from new" (667). Here Leighton more explicitly traces the Poston administration's reliance on negotiation with the Other to the late-nineteenth-century colonial structures developed by sympathetic colonialists such as T. E. Lawrence, whose words close the article and, at least for Leighton, encapsulate the methods of control developed in the camps: "They would follow us, if we endured with them, and played the game according to their rules. The pity was, that we often began to do so, broke down with exasperation and threw them over, blaming them for what was a fault in ourselves" (667).

Although the "exasperation" plaguing the camp analysts resulted from a very specific set of domestic and institutional struggles, the existing literature on Japanese or "oriental" behavior clearly influenced their interpretations of the meaning of their conflicts and negotiations with internees. Henry Yu points out that Robert Park's concept of the "marginal man" was one that came to exert a powerful influence on not only white, liberal social scientists but also on Asian American intellectuals who drew on their theories as a concept of their positive function in American society.[35] Park's description of the "marginal man" as "the stranger in the community" who "learns to look upon the world in which he was born and bred with something of the detachment of the stranger" appealed to social scientists because it explained the modern condition of "cosmopolitan" alienation.[36] It appealed to Asian American writers and intellectuals because, according to Yu, Park had "celebrated this new social type, the 'marginal man,' as being freer and more creative, released from the bonds of custom and tradition . . . a cosmopolitan ability to move among and understand different cultures."[37] Yet the celebration of this concept as one that helped to redeem the perception of Asian Americans in general was premature, as David Palumbo-Liu notes, because the Asian American as "marginal man" is relegated to a different, although progressive, plane of consciousness, an act that effectively maintains the distancing of the Japanese American as Other: "Sometimes racial others are read as synonymous with the general exotica of modern forms; at other times, they are markers of a 'racial frontier' that cannot be crossed without cost."[38]

In addition, because the "marginal man" was described as lacking national identity, a person "without direction and control," he would also find it virtually impossible to complete the process of assimilation as Parks described it. Although Park points out that "the chief obstacle to the cultural assimilation of races is not their different mental, but rather their divergent physical traits" that prevent them from being fully accepted by the dominant white society, elsewhere he promotes the importance of "mental" activities in achieving assimilation.[39] In

Old World Traits Transplanted, published in 1921, Park lays out the "psychology of assimilation" as one in which "a certain identity of experiences and memories between immigrants and Americans is of main importance."[40] The "marginal man" by virtue of his characteristic "detachment" is naturally unable to give himself over completely to a common stock of cultural memories; he must, on some level, remain apart. To embrace uncritically the concept of the Asian American as a "marginal man" is, then, to prolong rather than resolve the alienation of Asians in America.

The psychic or sentimental remove of the "oriental" as "marginal man" was also projected in spatial terms. Anthropologist Conrad Arensberg, a friend and fellow analyst of Leighton's who was stationed with him at Poston, advocated for the rights of Japanese Americans even as he expressed a belief in their immutable and inherent difference from white Americans. In an essay on conditions at Poston, he argued that, as Japanese by origin, the Japanese Americans were naturally accustomed to different treatment and that the administration was wrong to treat them as aliens.[41] Most interesting is Arensberg's visualization of an entirely different relationship to space and thus social relations. He conjectures that although "for a Caucasian group much of this might perhaps be extraordinary . . . the Japanese, both rural and urban, have a long history of living in crowded conditions and subjecting one another to strong conventional controls" (8). Sympathetic to the futile efforts of Japanese Americans "to bust the shackles" of their incarceration, Arensberg nonetheless chooses to view their daily reactions and immediate impulses as falling under the umbrella of Japanese conventions described in John Embree's late 1930s study of life in a small Japanese village, *Suye Mura*. Arensberg's recognition of the unique psychological hardships of internment follows a dead end that leads one back to the unavoidable difference of Japanese Americans parsed as "the paramount importance of the local group" (8). He was typical of many wra camp analysts in that he consistently vacillated between both obscuring and acknowledging the racism that created the camps as the situation demanded. In the end, as Arensberg readily admits, he was obligated to view the internment "from the vantage point of Mr. Burge's office [as camp director]" with the purpose of separating "cooperative evacuees from those who were not" (8).

In addition to the work of Park and Boas, Conrad Arensberg, like most other wra anthropologists including Alexander Leighton, had been deeply influenced by a 1930s structural-functionalist approach. According to Orin Starn, this view occasionally moved him to regard the camps as "a complete functional system" threatened by the internees' resistance, and thus "in all seriousness [he] termed the camps 'communities' in need of stabilization."[42] In later decades, Leighton referenced British anthropologists' theories of the "functional variability of social institutions" and systems as concepts that framed his own approach to internment camp life, which he concluded merely "laid bare the existence of these systems" for anthropologists.[43] Expressions of liberal sympathy on the part of camp analysts, who wanted to transcend the racialist views of a U.S. government suspicious of Japanese American difference, eventually came to embrace the universality of functionalism. Functionalism, in turn, realized the needs of bureaucratic efficiency. Unlike British anthropologists of the early twentieth century, such as Bronislaw Malinowski and especially A. R. Radcliffe-Brown, who likened cultures to naturally functioning organisms that followed their own laws and allowed little room for individual agency, Leighton and his colleagues in the camps wanted to learn how to alter and redirect the internment camp societies and subjects they studied.[44] They sought to learn how to make the camps—and by extension occupied postwar Japanese culture—work as normal communities that might nurture the residents rather than punish them.

Like Leighton, Arensberg encouraged administrators to adopt a program of outward sympathy for Japanese Americans' complaints on the grounds that the best way to control "emotional outbursts" is "to let such emotion play itself out harmlessly and to deflect the released energies to other things, after emotion has been discharged."[45] This argument for a policy of tolerance of cultural difference became common in the reports of camp analysts who hoped to sustain a progressive vision while also carrying out their duties as government agents committed to controlling the internees in their charge. Yet pleas for tolerance of Japanese American resistance eventually played into the designs of the government, because reports from camp analysts became less a means of acknowledging the unique dilemma of the internees than an argument for understanding internees' problems as natural manifestations of Japanese behavior coming into conflict with the norms of (white) American society. The implied purpose of social scientific work with the "oriental Other" remained the task of discovering the hidden means by which to affect the Americanization of the Other. And although this task was certainly shaped by earlier theories in American social science, it was equally, at least, affected by the changing wartime status of anthropology as an American institution.

Virginia Yans-McLaughlin's comment on Margaret Mead's wartime "compromises with scientific objectivity" might also apply to the camp anthropologists' reasons for downplaying the cultural uniqueness of Japanese Americans: "A nation at war could not be a nation divided. In a nation of immigrants, the immigrants were now given short shrift."[46] In the face of the seemingly greater threat posed by Hitler's Third Reich, anthropologists who were hired to help in the war effort were forced to suspend any vigorous critique of ethnic Americans' experiences. More often than not, under pressure to deliver goods useful in the war effort against Japan, community analysts resigned themselves to making their arguments, as John Embree initially described it, in terms of "that abstruse phenomenon, called Japanese psychology."[47] Johannes Fabian offers a similar assessment of American anthropology in the first half of the twentieth century as a "conflict between evolutionary-genetic (time-centered) and structural (timeless) theories of explanation."[48] Rejecting the eugenics-based research of early social science, wartime social scientists opted for a cultural relativist approach that might do away with ethnocentric conclusions. Yet, as Fabian observes, if the influence of structuralism-functionalism meant that social scientists "showed disregard for Time (i.e., for Time as past) this does not mean that anthropology ceased to serve as a time machine. . . . The denial of coevalness becomes intensified as time-distancing turns from an explicit concern into an implicit theoretical assumption" (39). Social science, in other words, continued to view the Other in terms of a premodern or "primitive" time, often by focusing on the Other's existence in a completely separate temporal and spatial sphere, so that "whatever happens behind the walls [of relativism] occurs in a Time other than his" (52). The cultural relativism that defined the work of community analysts followed this pattern. More specifically, their insistence on avoiding the historicism they associated with Social Darwinism guaranteed that they would favor universalizing cultural models for explaining the confusion that marked Japanese American experience in the camps. Increasingly, this model became grounded in the perception of an unpredictable and even erratic Japanese behavioral pattern, a behavior deeply ingrained by early childhood and later reinforced by cultural practices peculiar to those of Japanese descent.

The chief proponent of this theory of Japanese character was the

British anthropologist Geoffrey Gorer, who worked for the Office of War Information (OWI) during the war as well as for the British government, and whose theories were widely influential for anthropologists attempting to develop theories of Japanese behavior in the absence of direct access to Japanese culture. In early 1941, Gorer presented his findings in a talk at Yale University in which he proposed that a series of antagonistic preoccupations and responses constituted what he then called "Japanese character structure."[49] As a proponent of the culture and personality school of anthropology, which believed in deploying the tools of psychoanalysis on nations or cultures in order to map national character types, Geoffrey Gorer provided a scientifically based model by which Westerners might explain Japanese behavior. Adopting a childhood deterministic approach common in psychoanalysis, Gorer eventually expanded on his 1941 talk to pen an analysis of Japanese child-rearing practices for the OWI titled "Themes in Japanese Culture."[50] The report became immensely influential, finding that the observed preoccupation with order and ritual in Japanese life could be traced to the supposedly harsh and repressive toilet training and the withholding of maternal affection characteristic of Japanese culture. The result of these childhood influences was "a deeply hidden, unconscious and extremely strong desire to be aggressive" (285) that was constrained only by equally severe social prohibitions against such desires. The illustrative effect was observed in an individual who is caught between controlling these extreme desires and an unresolved infantile resentment against them.

Perhaps the most remarkable aspect of Gorer's study of Japanese character is that he, like the camp anthropologists, tested at least some of his theories and conclusions about Japanese character through interviews with Nisei informants. He furthermore admits to having discarded any information given by Nisei that contradicted "practices not reported by others" on "the theoretical ground that the individuals observed were probably aberrant" (275). Although we can draw many conclusions from Gorer's study, seen strictly within the framework of wartime work on Japanese character this famous essay reveals that a circular logic linking Japanese American and Japanese behavior existed even before the camp analysis project was begun. And, like the camp analysts, Gorer sought to refine knowledge of the conflicted or "dual nature" of Japanese character structure as part of a progressive historical thrust, long recognized in cultural anthropology. Again, like his liberal American colleagues, Gorer's work was part of ongoing efforts within anthropology to replace racist views of cultural differences as fixed and physiological with a more humane understanding of the fluid, culture-based origin of those same differences. Beginning with Franz Boas's efforts to counter the racial eugenics of the late nineteenth century and extending to the generation of anthropologists that included Americans educated in that tradition—such as Robert Park, Margaret Mead, Ruth Benedict, Conrad Arensberg, and even Geoffrey Gorer (who, although he was an Englishman, was deeply influenced by American culture and personality techniques)—cultural anthropologists of the 1940s followed in the liberal tradition set forth by Boas, which meant maintaining, however subtly, the Othering of racialized peoples. It is not hard to see, for instance, how Gorer's concept of Japanese "duality" takes up and recirculates the notion of the "oriental" as a "marginal man" caught between two realms.[51]

The influence of Gorer's conclusions on other anthropologists' developing theories of Japanese character is undeniable. Ruth Benedict cites his study as pivotal to her own conceptions of Japanese behavior in *The Chrysanthemum and the Sword*.[52] And, although he could not have anticipated it, Gorer's famous essay also provided a means for community analysts to explain Japanese Americans' behavior as the unresolved vestiges of childhood without ever needing to factor in the complicated politics of camp administration. The popularity of Gorer's concept of Japanese "duality" was a move vital to American anthropology's continuing practice of Othering the mostly native-born Asian American population.[53] Suggestive of colonialism's view of Others as premodern races, the widespread acceptance of Japanese "duality" as a sign of a lack of development is casually reiterated in Leighton's article on dislocated communities, where he describes the "confusion" of internees as "emotional complexes similar to those of the child who has unpredictable parents and who never knows whether he will receive approval or a slap."[54]

Within the camps, the resort to Gorer's prototype of Japanese character, together with the turn toward a universalizing functionalist view of dislocation and resistance, sometimes resulted in the repeated pathologizing of evacuees' behavior and, more particularly, of Japanese American culture. Extreme in this respect was the work of anthropologist Weston LaBarre, who while stationed at the Topaz camp in Utah appeared to ignore altogether the hardship of incarceration for Japanese Americans as he gathered data for his confirmation of "character structure in the Orient."[55] LaBarre never doubted that his forty-four-day period of observation of confused behavior in many evacuees was proof of the inherent "duality" in Japanese character structure that Gorer had previously described. In addition, he felt no reservations about uniting his studies of camp behavior with his later interviews with Japanese prisoners of war; both sets of interviews were treated as pieces of the same Japanese puzzle. In Japanese American evacuees La-Barre cataloged behavior that to him underscored the compulsive, neurotic core traits of the Japanese character structure: "Secretiveness, hiding of emotions and attitudes; preservation and persistence; conscientiousness; self-righteousness; a tendency to project attitudes; fanaticism; arrogance; 'touchiness'; precision and perfectionism; neatness and ritualistic cleanliness; ceremoniousness; conformity to rule; sadomasochistic behavior; hypochondriasis; suspiciousness; jealousy and enviousness" (322). Years later LaBarre continued to defend his methods and conclusions in the study, arguing in another essay that "anthropologists and sociologists, plainly upset by its analytic clinical approach, have long found it a convenient target as a presumably 'early impressionist' culture and personality study, without any method beyond hunch-ethnography. It was not" (23). He maintains that contemporary critics "failed to discern the method," to comprehend the careful "listing of all the traits which clinical work indicates are characteristic of the compulsive personality" and the careful attempt "to ascertain whether there was a deductive matching between the clinical and the ethnographic" (24). "There was," LaBarre concludes the Japanese Americans he observed at Topaz; "QED, I thought . . . the Japanese are surprisingly compulsive."[56] Faced with the complex tensions and levels of distrust that pervaded the camp, LaBarre deployed Gorer's thesis of a duality in Japanese character structure to make sense of Japanese Americans' behavior. In so doing, he helped to secure the further applicability of Gorer's thesis to a functionalist camp analysis in cases that tended to ignore the environmental and cultural roots of internees' behavior. In this way, Japanese "duality" was implemented in the camps as an essential behavior possessed by all persons of Japanese descent.

The expressed reliance of the community analysts on functionalism, along with its more obscured roots in Park's work on "orientals," conditioned the analysts to be confident that Gorer's thesis of Japanese duality would once more deploy scientific explanations of the "Japanese character" of internees to forego the discussion of domestic racism and the politics of social science, just as the concept of the "marginal man" had done earlier in the century. The tendency to ignore how the pressures of internment might have affected their own views of the camps, to say nothing of how such pressures affected the views of Japanese Americans held there, obviously undercuts the camp anthropologists' attempts to advocate for cultural tolerance on behalf of the interned community. According to Orin Starn, "the culture and personality approach tended to lead to 'scientific' restatement of conventional stereotypes" that "helped produce extraordinarily ahistorical analyses of camp society" as "a timeless manifestation of Japanese character and culture."[57] The anthropologists assumed that the reproduction of Japanese American trauma as an emblem of Japanese duality that transcended historical and social arguments ultimately prepared the way for acceptance of the possibility for assimilation of Japanese Americans, but by nationally and historically dislocating the Japanese American subject the community analysts ultimately sealed the Japanese Americans' continuing fate as "oriental" Others. If they could not share space and time with modern Americans, then they could not share in the cultural memories and nationalist sentiments so critical to assimilation. The temporal and spatial processes of Othering Japanese Americans were most visible in arguments about the generational conflict between Issei and Nisei. In the effort to make way for a new generation of Americanized Japanese, the community analysts would designate the Nisei as the future of Japanese America, with the Issei doomed to symbolize the archaic reservoir of Japanese memories and experiences that must be amended. In much the same way, finessing the role of powerful patriarchal figures in Japan would prove critical to the success of the American occupation.

Turning It to Good Account: Saving the "California Japanese"

Writing in late 1942, after less than three months at Poston, Conrad Arensberg stated: "I believe it is well not to exaggerate the importance of the Issei-Nisei conflict" given that "there is not an immigrant group, and very few regional and class groups either, in the United States that does not face intergenerational conflict."[58] Arensberg's cautionary words did not, however, keep him from concluding that "the whole

WRA will have to learn to live with that conflict among the Japanese and to turn it to good account" (9). In large measure, the WRA anthropologists' attempts to help the Japanese Americans by preparing them to be integrated into the postwar world derived from their attempts to do just as Arensberg suggests, to turn the Issei-Nisei conflict "to good account."

Most published community analysis reports were particularly concerned with the role of the relationship between Issei and Nisei males in affecting camp attitudes toward the administration. Despite the fact that the authority of Issei fathers had been clearly damaged by their initial exclusion from participation in camp councils, an act that also tended to destabilize relations within the family as a whole, within a relatively short period of time the camp analysts witnessed a "reemergence of patriarchal control." In spring 1946, Edward Spicer's closing report on the history of community analysis states that "the decision of the older people" was consistently responsible for "the response that the younger people felt impelled to make" in regard to the infamous loyalty oaths required of all Japanese Americans in 1943.[59] Although a few "resisted parental pressure for some time," in the end most assented, according to Spicer and his staff, because of "the feeling of loyalty to the old people" (22–23). By "the old people" Spicer clearly means to indicate Issei men, noting that "the women will follow their lead" (26). Influence in the interned family, and especially over the decisions of the majority of the Nisei men who were often merely spokespersons for their fathers, "was the last as well as the strongest refuge of this older generation, the only spot where the word and advice of the [male] elders still carried weight and authority" (23). Like Arensberg four years before him, Spicer warns that "the price of neglecting this fundamental social fact is evacuee resistance to administration" (26).

What the WRA anthropologists proposed was not a rejection of the power of traditional patriarchal figures, but an acceptance of its limited future in America without the hybridizing influence of the Nisei. According to Arensberg, they believed that the Nisei's inevitable transcendence would mark the transition to a new kind of Japanese American and that it would "reflect itself in political development, where it has already made its appearance at Poston."[60] The primary shortcoming of community analysis is that "nothing has been done to enlist the skills of the older people and the forms of authority and expertness that are theirs" (11). Although this report appeared quite soon after the estab-

lishment of the community analysis sections, and well before the anthropologists had worked out the official means of enlisting "the forms
of authority" held by Issei fathers, Arensberg nevertheless conjectures
that the solution might be to utilize father figures and their spokespersons, the Nisei men, in "roles very like those of the 'white man's Indian' among the Indians." "The administration must ask itself," he
continues, "if that is not one of the prices it will have to pay, if the Japanese Americans are to be taught the forms of American municipal government" (11). Despite its obvious colonialist perspective, this description of the necessity of the merging or sharing of responsibilities and
duties between distinctly different individuals owes more to Robert
Park's belief that assimilation of American cultural memories did not
mean the denial of previous cultural memories for immigrants.[61] "Any
fine fund of feeling is valuable," Park concludes, "in identifying the
present with the past" (286) because "the values and attitudes he
brings with him from his old life, is the material from which he must
build his Americanism" (280).

According to Edward Spicer, in an attempt in summer 1943 to cut
down on rising levels of "insecurity in the centers" and to procure the
internees' good faith in the administration's plans to relocate and resettle Japanese Americans in the Midwest away from historical Japanese
American communities, the WRA anthropologists suggested "embodying approaches to the evacuees through Issei leaders and through family discussion."[62] Their proposal for relying on the power of loyalty to
paternal authority to influence camp sentiments immediately became
a part of the official program of the WRA.

Once again, complex circuits of influence linked anthropological
concepts of Japanese American and Japanese culture. The WRA's view
of paternal authority and its emphasis on understanding the significance of paternal control was immediately derived from Geoffrey Gorer's previous prewar theories regarding the layers of paternal authority
constituting Japanese society. In Japanese culture, attitudes toward authority were almost exclusively framed as relations between males, according to Gorer, as "from the Emperor (with his divine ancestors as
his superiors) to the newborn infant (with the outcasts as his inferiors)
every male has his exact place in this male world that gives orders and
expects obedience."[63] The thought of breaching this system of male obligation and filial obedience was unimaginable, and "no Japanese can
feel safe and secure unless the whole environment is understood and

as far as possible controlled" (289). In particular, Gorer argues, "the Japanese can never feel safe unless, as some of their more bombastic military leaders have proposed, the Mikado rules the whole earth" (290). Any social hierarchy attempting to encompass Japanese subjects therefore must necessarily include some version of this order of paternal authority, because without it the anthropologists predicted that the Japanese individual would be at sea and all administrative designs rendered moot. Gorer would reiterate this belief in the power of the emperor in the final months of the war, when he, along with other anthropologists, advocated retaining the emperor rather than destroying his position in Japanese culture. They relied primarily on Gorer's findings that the father figure was indispensable to the functioning of any Japanese society. But their belief in the wisdom of this approach also gained support from Park's earlier injunctions that the "attitudes and values" from "the old life" are "the material" of Americanization for both Japanese postwar subjects, and as their domesticated screens, Japanese Americans.[64]

The strategy of utilizing a stabilizing paternal symbol to limit resistance in any dislocated community was also concurrent with a program to relocate selected Nisei away from Japanese American enclaves, to produce in effect a geographical and spatial mapping of the theoretical Othering of Japanese Americans. The divisive cultural effects of the Issei fathers' influence on the younger internees' suspicions of relocation were evident at Poston from the beginning, when Arensberg reported that "fears among the Japanese of the 'breakdown' of family life and family authority" often led to resistance and even delinquency on the part of younger internees, who represented the majority of the camp population.[65] The Issei men's resistance to their geographic relocation disrupted the discourse of Othering practiced by the community analysts by denying its realization both spatially and temporally. Spicer would later conclude that the occasional crises precipitated by food shortages or the infamous loyalty oaths only reinforced the need of Japanese Americans to cling to traditional forms of authority and "increased their hesitation to re-establish themselves elsewhere" and thus to develop a full sense of their place in American life.[66] Heart Mountain, Wyoming, anthropologist Asael Hansen concurred with Spicer when he reported that "in crises . . . differences between Issei and Nisei tended to fade. The community as a whole assumed an anti-administrative stance" that presented problems for the community analysts.[67]

The anthropologists quickly recognized the usefulness of paternal authority to camp administrators. Spicer maintained that "through their leadership and their parental relationships they [Issei fathers] can council their children in favor of relocation,"[68] while Hansen observed that "during 1945, when some Issei informants of long standing began to relocate," their decisions "helped a great deal" in establishing meaningful contacts and authority for the anthropologists.[69] In light of Alexander Leighton's related argument for the success of negotiation over forceful measures as a means of controlling internees in the camps and Japanese citizens in occupied Japan, the WRA anthropologists began to experiment with manipulating Issei authority to influence Japanese American culture from within. At both Heart Mountain and Poston, the staff actively sought to rely on paternal authority to convince the camp as a whole to go along with the administration's plans for them by agreeing to their literal reinscription in the landscape and history of the American nation.

This line of reasoning about the administrative benefits of paternal symbols in ruling Japanese American subjects would be mirrored in arguments for retaining the emperor during the occupation. "As the father of his people," the emperor offered a way to control the nation's actions in a time of crisis and transition. "It seemed to us," asserted Alexander Leighton and Morris Opler in a 1946 essay taken from a previous report titled "Applied Anthropology in Psychological Warfare Against Japan," that "resistance both in battle and on the home front could be lowered by a clear and repeated statement declaring that the fate of the Emperor" would be left to the Japanese.[70] Drawing on their work in the camps during times of crises, they predicted that "attacks on the Emperor would remind the people of their allegiance and tighten their grip on their belief at a time when other aspects of morale might be giving away" (258). Although this recommendation gave the appearance of respecting Japanese traditions, in truth its aim was to deploy the emperor as a kind of puppet figure, one who might subtly ventriloquize U.S. goals for the reformation of Japan. Policy makers in Japan would benefit from recognizing that "the Emperor can serve the welfare of men, self-government and good international relations" (260). Or, as Leighton would reiterate in his 1984 essay on applied anthropology, "the problem was to facilitate this [change] by appealing to those value elements within Japanese culture that would encourage the transition from hold out to surrender."[71] Believing along with Leighton and Opler that the emperor "can fulfill the needs of very different sorts of persons," Ruth Benedict would argue even more explicitly for relying on the emperor as a titular monarch or "secular chief" existing alongside MacArthur to effect MacArthur's rapid preeminence as the new "blue-eyed American Mikado."[72] Benedict would cite the Japanese army and navy's historical use of "his name to force through their measures" (91) as a precedent for U.S. policy in this regard. Whether in the United States or in Japan, the posture of reasoned concern for maintaining cultural differences, although vital to postwar liberal anthropologists' successful promotion of their particular brand of cultural tolerance as simply the most judicious means of maintaining the peace while encouraging the evolution of relations, more often than not veiled an agenda of cultural assimilation that, in the case of Japanese Americans, exposed American anthropology's Othering of the nations' immigrant "orientals."

The advocacy of cultural tolerance resulted in efforts to deny the historical and legal restrictions that maintained the Japanese Americans' racial difference, because it was vital to the future of American exceptionalism and the promise of postwar renewal. Although it is also true that most camp analysts sympathized with and tried to assist the evacuees in getting hearings for their political objections to the ordeal of internment, the efforts of the analysts often merely effaced Japanese Americans' claims to rights and justice by simultaneously embracing them within and then distancing them from the national agenda. The problem of Japanese American internment was thus effectively turned away from questions of camp conditions and, beyond that, of civil rights, to proving that Japanese Americans could somehow merge their Japanese behaviors with American traditions and thereby foster the flowering of a new generation or type of Japanese American. But this vision depended on Japanese Americans' submission to the paternalism of the state and its institutions in a manner that banished them from full participation in the political discourse vital to their agency as citizens.

Alexander Leighton, while continuing to project the problem of Japanese American identity as a problem of Japanese reformation, also encouraged authorities to remember the unique wartime position of all the evacuees "that their relocation was a forced one which they interpreted as discrimination and rejection."[73] Yet Leighton's earnest articulation of the need to rectify the injustices directed against Japanese Americans resided with a reluctance to critique those tenets of American social science that promoted the scientist as the best arbiter of the lot of subjected peoples. He held on to the hope that liberal social science might yet be the answer to the hostilities of society by instructing Japanese Americans how to operate in a mainstream, European-based U.S. culture. In a very real sense, then, in their suggestion that the Nisei take on new American mentors in the postwar period the WRA anthropologists indirectly substituted their leadership for that of Issei patriarchs. By defending Japanese Americans as "good Americans" in "The Japanese Family in America," one of his final wartime reports, Leighton makes a last revealing plea for filial obligation in achieving the reformation of Japanese Americans.[74] In his report Leighton announces that "after spending months in the centers, about 10,000 [Japanese Americans] were resettling in the Middle Western states, hoping to become reabsorbed in the life of the Nation" (15). In pursuit of their successful reconversion, he offers a sympathetic portrait of Japanese Americans' wartime trials, attempting to explain "the special adjustment problem of the Japanese" by contrasting their feelings of postwar uncertainty "with the war worker or soldier, who is rewarded for his discomforts and sacrifices by a feeling of fuller participation and acceptance in the national life and an increase in prestige, if not in income" (151). The problem, as Leighton understood it, was the marginalized "status" of Japanese Americans in the United States, a position that he argues derives from the belief "that racial heredity is more important than the factor of culture" (152) in determining the Americanness of immigrant groups. In the tradition of liberal anthropology, Leighton holds up social science as a field of thought opposed to such racist arguments by asserting that "it is a basic postulate of social science that no inherent differences in biological stocks of the human species exist that make it impossible for individuals of one stock to assimilate the culture practiced by another" (151). And because there is no racial or biological reason why Japanese Americans may not assimilate into the "melting pot" of U.S. cultures that Park had forecasted as an inevitable process, there is thus little to be gained by "walling it off in society" (152–53). Because many anthropologists actually viewed the camps as "a new stage in the modernization of Japanese Americans" (153), as "ideal cities" wherein the prewar pathology of Japaneseness residual in Japanese Americans might be reformed, Leighton's perspective was influenced by the idea that the camps, while objectionable, might also provide an opportunity to affect Japanese Americans' inclusion as Americans.

As an anthropologist committed to applying the results of data on living communities, Leighton sought to light the path to acculturation into mainstream European culture, which was never considered as less than a move toward progress and enlightenment. Never did Leighton or any of the other anthropologists who favored this renewed acculturationist strategy of bringing Japanese Americans into line with the dictates of mainstream Anglo culture stop to consider the costs of "inclusion" to the community.[75] Indeed, before we can fully account for the effects of community analysis, we must recognize that they found confirmation and sanction for this policy of acculturation from among leaders in the internee population, whose views of themselves bore the legacy of Park's theories about the "oriental problem," as Henry Yu notes.[76] Given Park's sympathies with the "orientals" he wrote about, and his clear intention to privilege their "marginal" status as a benefit, Asian Americans hoping to claim their place in America embraced his theories. Yu's description of the effects of Park's theory on the Asian American anthropology students who worked for him may also describe the situation of wartime Nisei: "For them, the marginal man theory was like a release from bondage, naming them as the future and giving them the most important role in race and cultural relations. Accordingly, the concept had a profound impact on their self-identity" (199). The ramifications of Yu's argument are profound, for he suggests that the Asian Americans' views of themselves may be more affected by the ethnocentrism of white, liberal social science than has been previously recognized.[77] In addition to this historical phenomenon in ethnic self-conception, the inordinate power of community analysts to set policy for dealing with Japanese Americans ensured that the internees would be especially vulnerable to accepting their conclusions.

For years the JACL had been active in trying "to better the status of their own minority in the U.S."[78] They had early on in the internment process recommended a "route of superpatriotism" for Japanese American evacuees, advising that they "obediently allow themselves to be relocated in order to better prove their allegiance to the U.S.," and, in addition, that they "vehemently disavow all things Japanese" (255). Not surprisingly, JACL members worked most closely with camp administrators such as Leighton to weed out disloyal elements, a practice that earned them the label inu, or dog, the camp name for a collaborator. Years later, Wayne Collins, the San Francisco attorney who argued

the cases of many Japanese American resistors against the Justice Department, continued to condemn the JACL in no less vivid terms as the
group "that pretended to be the spokesman for all Japanese Americans
but . . . wouldn't stand up for their people. . . . They led their people like
a bunch of goddamn doves to the concentration camps" (255). Although the JACL promised the internees that their patriotism and per-
severance would be rewarded after the war, the Japanese Americans
who returned to their communities found that their homes and businesses had been confiscated and sold by the government, and, in many
cases, that they were excluded from renting property and holding jobs
out of a persistent view that somehow they were still more like Japanese
enemies than American "superpatriots."

Following the JACL's lead in many respects, in a plan that would prolong financial ruin and social alienation for many Japanese Americans
in the early postwar years, Alexander Leighton strongly advised against
the maintenance of "Japanese customs," citing the "natural and often
unconscious attempts [of Issei] to pass on their culture to their children" as helping to create "definite barriers to assimilation."[79] Rejecting historical fears of and restrictions against miscegenation, fears
that would be widely maintained by many white Americans well beyond the 1940s as later struggles to integrate southern society and
northern schools would testify, Leighton promoted limited interracial
relations, specifically the social mixing of Nisei with white peers, as integral to any program of successful acculturation for Japanese Americans. He argued that "it was largely from such white friends—who
were in a sense patrons—that the Japanese children acquired their
goals and ideals in American life, as well as manners and language"
(153). In the process of acculturation, contact with whites worked to
break up "a kind of family that is protective, reactionary, and atavistic"
while maintaining "filial duty" as "a trait of Japanese family life" that
may be "a potent force for the creation of good citizens" (156). The implied new head of this reformed "California Japanese" family would be
the so-called white patrons, a term derived in fact from the Latin "pa-
ter," or father. These new white patrons inherited the responsibilities
previously assumed by Issei fathers, who were now deemed an obstacle
to postwar acceptance.

Leighton's argument suggests that, paradoxically, it is difference itself that must be eradicated in order to realize a world of respect for
cultural difference. But because Japanese difference is seen as cultur-

ally and not biologically encoded, one need only reconfigure and redirect the strains of a culture and not do away with the actual bodies of persons. This strategy of retaining certain habits of ethnic cultural or familial life as a means of recasting political manipulation and submission as cultural encounter and negotiation finds a correlate in developing postwar arguments for the retention of the emperor.

In September 1946, occupation policies were beginning to turn to "steering a middle course" in dealing with the former imperial power. By the end of 1946, even the Pentagon submitted that now Japan was deemed a partner with the United States rather than an exenemy. Ruth Benedict's work served to bolster these attitudes by reassuring Americans that it was not too late for a benevolent relationship with Japan, that the United States "has not impeded that course by insisting on using techniques of humiliation."[80] Although political observers argued about whether the occupation was too "hard" or too "soft," Benedict addressed the debate by insisting that "the real issue was not between hard and soft [peace terms]" (299). The real task was to "break up old and dangerous patterns of aggressiveness and set new goals. . . . The means to be chosen depend upon the character of the people and upon the traditional social order of the nation in question" (300). General Douglas MacArthur and others in charge of occupation policy consistently viewed Japan as a country of naughty children in need of a new, better father figure, so that the job of occupation was "the job of rearing seventy million problem children" (302). Reflecting prewar and wartime anthropology's emphasis on the childhood origins of Japanese character structure, MacArthur testified before a senate subcommittee, "they [the Japanese] would be like a boy of 12 as compared with our development of 45 years."[81] Certainly descriptions of the erratic nature of Japanese character structure suited this view of Japanese culture as one of puerile adolescents in need of adjustment and guidance. MacArthur's stated approach to reforming Japan indirectly echoes Leighton's arguments on behalf of Japanese American acculturation, as well as Leighton's adherence to colonial logic, the Lawrencian belief that "they would follow us, if we endured them," if we "played the game according to their rules."[82]

Alexander Leighton's project is representative of the means by which liberal anthropology's desire to critique American ethnocentricity, and the white racism that often fueled it, ultimately resecured the Asian Americans as "oriental" Others. The rejection of ethnocentric biases was the explicit goal of every liberal anthropologist in the postwar period. "One of the handicaps of the twentieth century," writes Benedict, "is that we still have the vaguest notion and most biased notions, not only of what makes Japan a nation of Japanese, but of what makes the United States a nation of Americans."[83] She reminds her readers that "a course of action is not necessarily vicious because it is not the one we know" (13). U.S. citizens must recognize that in Japan "western arrangements will not be trusted tools with which to fashion a better world, as they are in the United States" (303). By following an approach designed to contain and manipulate identifiable Japanese differences, Leighton is caught between two irreconcilable desires: the need to speak for the right of the Japanese to rebuild their country after their own concerns and purposes and the resurfacing tendency to find that inherently Japanese social pressures, "no matter how voluntarily embraced, ask too much of the individual," that "they have to repress too much for their own good."[84] Thus, despite Park's injunction against the loss of the values of "the old life," Japanese Americans must finally concede to be remade in the image of white American ideals, what cultural critic Christopher Shannon rightly arraigns as a portrait of the Other "equally endowed with the capacity to value western ideals of individual freedom."[85]

In terms of Japanese American identity after World War II, the work of the WRA anthropologists seems to suggest that future examinations must take account of the presence, however dubious or obscured, of Japanese American internment politics in the development of postwar theories about the Japanese. As much of the historical record reveals, the anthropological approach to redeeming Japanese differences was tested, at least in part, within a program ultimately designed to assimilate Japanese Americans. In addition, because anthropologists advising on occupation policies in postwar Japan honed their plans while attempting to administer an internment process most of them felt was unjust, U.S. postwar policy toward Japan inevitably reflected a brand of anxious liberal paternalism that derived from the anthropologists' misguided efforts to improve the lot of disenfranchised Japanese Americans by managing them as the distant and familiar "oriental" Other.

THREE

How Rose Becomes Red: The Case of Tokyo Rose
and the Postwar Beginnings of Cold War Culture

The violence of the body reaches the written page only through absence, through the intermediary of documents that the historian has been able to see on the sands from which a presence has been washed away, and through a murmur that lets us hear—but from afar—the unknown immensity that seduces and menaces our knowledge.—Michel de Certeau, *The Writing of History*

For a narrative's authority always relies on a referent outside the narrative, the part that always remains different from the narrative itself, the part that is not the same as the language that refers to it.—Alan Nadel, *Containment Culture*

Perhaps no single media event in the immediate postwar years was as potentially damaging to the recovery and readjustment of Japanese Americans as the 1949 trial and conviction of Iva Toguri d'Aquino, a Nisei and a graduate of UCLA who was identified as the legendary Japanese radio propagandist Tokyo Rose. Just how a young American came to be Tokyo Rose is a story almost as fantastic as the origin of the Tokyo Rose legend itself, which was always acknowledged to be a myth, a fabrication of homesick soldiers adrift in the Pacific in the final days of the war. Although it is true that during the war the Overseas Bureau of the NHK, or Japanese Broadcasting Corporation, regularly aired propaganda broadcasts in an attempt to demoralize Allied troops fighting in the Pacific, most of the programs were highly unpopular and certainly ineffective as propaganda. The only real success NHK could claim came from a series of English-speaking female disc jockeys who hosted popular music broadcasts ostensibly designed to play on GIs' homesickness and fears. Immensely popular with lonely GIs, who generally considered the broadcasts more amusing than threatening, the collective of female disc jockeys soon became known by the single moniker Tokyo Rose. Despite the fact that in 1945 the Office of War Information had determined that "there is no Tokyo Rose; the name is strictly a GI invention," and notwithstanding the relative failure of the so-called Tokyo Rose broadcasts to damage Allied spirits, when the United States began its occupation of Japan in September 1945, the rush was on to find the living symbol of Tokyo Rose. Thus the orientalized figment of GI fantasies quickly became embodied in an unlikely and unsuspecting real person, Iva Toguri d'Aquino, by an almost incredulous series of accidents and miscommunications.

Some two weeks before the occupation of Japan officially began, a *New York Times* reporter attempting to unmask the elusive figure who had captivated GIs during the war asked his readers: "Tokyo Rose is a figment of the fertile brains of the propaganda office. Or is she?"[1] He went on to suggest that Tokyo Rose might be anywhere in Japan, and he even went so far as to question the identity of his female guide in Japan, a Nisei woman from California whom he reported "smiled slyly" when she mentioned Tokyo Rose and seemed to know more than she would say. "Come on now guide," he cajoled, "weren't you Tokyo Rose?" By the time General MacArthur landed in Japan, he was followed by a flock of other reporters eager to break the story of life in the American occupied country. In addition to coverage of the trial of General Tojo and other Japanese war leaders, another major news story was the identity of Tokyo Rose.

According to Masayo Duus, who wrote the first book-length account of d'Aquino's ordeal, two men ultimately became responsible for the "discovery" of Tokyo Rose.[2] Journalist Clark Lee landed in Tokyo with orders from his boss at International News Service, the Hearst-controlled media conglomerate, to find Tokyo Rose. He soon teamed up with *Cosmopolitan* reporter Harry Brundidge, who had the financial resources to buy an interview with Tokyo Rose, and they set about flushing out a likely candidate. Through a series of contacts at NHK, Lee finally pushed Kenkichi Oki, another Nisei living in Japan during the war, to identify Iva Toguri d'Aquino as one of the five or six female broadcasters on the "Zero Hour" music programs who might be one of the voices GIs knew as Tokyo Rose. Born Iva Toguri in the United States, she was in Japan taking care of a sick aunt when the war started, and like most other Japanese Americans there at the same time, she was not allowed to reenter the United States after the attack on Pearl Harbor. Unable to find a steady job by which to support herself because she refused to denounce her American citizenship, and with the war shortages making food more scarce, she finally took a job as a typist at NHK. When Japanese officials at NHK realized she could speak English, they coerced her into making broadcasts for the Japanese that had been written by POWs under threat of death. Along with the POWs and other Nisei women, Iva Toguri d'Aquino had unwillingly become a part of the Japanese propaganda machine in the final years of the war. It was also at NHK that she met a young biracial Japanese-Portuguese immigrant, Filipe d'Aquino, whose father was a Portuguese citizen in Japan who had married a Japanese woman. D'Aquino helped Iva to survive the difficulties of life as an enemy alien in wartime Japan, and in early 1945, she married him while both were still in Japan. Her marriage to a Portuguese national, who had been educated in Catholic mission schools in Yokohama and who was strongly pro-American in his views about the war, would later play a part in her attempts to escape U.S. prosecution as a citizen guilty of treason. At one point, when it became clear that the Justice Department wanted to deport her for trial on charges of treason, d'Aquino desperately tried to claim Portuguese citizenship. Given her earlier claims to U.S. loyalty and citizenship, her efforts not only failed but also further complicated her status as a "loyal" American. Iva Toguri d'Aquino's naïveté about the repercussions of such gestures would aid her pursuers in making the case against her.

When Lee contacted d'Aquino in September 1945, she was anxious to raise the money to return to the United States. He and Brundidge promised her $2,000 for an exclusive interview in which she admitted she was Tokyo Rose. Through Leslie Nakashima, a Hawaiian-born Nisei and prewar friend of his, Lee encouraged d'Aquino by telling her that by granting the interview she was not only procuring the money to return home, but she was also helping to stem rumors about Tokyo Rose by setting the record straight. D'Aquino agreed, even signing a contract in which she stated that she was "the one and original Tokyo Rose," although both she and Lee knew her claim was a false one. The biggest story of the occupation of Japan amounted to nothing more than a publicity stunt in the end, but the stunt would soon turn tragic for d'Aquino.

When Harry Brundidge's editor at *Cosmopolitan* refused to pay for the story, Brundidge feared d'Aquino might sue. In order to head off her claims and protect his reputation, he contacted the Counter-Intelligence Corps (CIC) in Japan and suggested that they detain d'Aquino for questioning. Despite the fact that the story ran in the *Los Angeles Examiner* under Lee's name and the title "Traitor's Pay—Tokyo Rose Got $100 a Month—$660," d'Aquino was never paid by either reporter.[3] To make matters worse, the breaking story provoked the CIC to question d'Aquino's assertion in the article that "circumstances had forced her into broadcasting" and that "she believed Americans would enjoy her music and laugh at her propaganda" (41). Although d'Aquino's admission that she was Tokyo Rose initially had been received with great fascination and even amusement by Americans in Japan, in time officials felt mounting pressure to investigate her. She was interrogated and placed under arrest at Sugamo Prison in Yokoyama, a prison reserved for the incarceration of Japan's worst war criminals. A full year later, after a failure to substantiate charges of treason, the CIC finally released d'Aquino on the grounds of insufficient evidence. As journalist Mark Gayn asserted, "broadcasting prepared propaganda is not regarded as a war crime. If it were hundreds of broadcasters in Tokyo would have to stand trial."[4]

But the nightmare was only just beginning for d'Aquino. When she tried to return to San Francisco she was again detained, and subsequently she was charged with eight counts of treason. On October 6, 1949, some four years after d'Aquino's naïve attempt to placate what she perceived as an amused American public and raise money for her return to the United States in the process, she was convicted of one count of treason and jailed. She served six years, was fined $10,000, and was stripped of her citizenship for thirty years for being Tokyo Rose, even though all reliable sources conceded that "there was no Tokyo Rose." How, then, did the American public come to support the belief that "the one and original" Tokyo Rose had been discovered in the person of Iva Toguri d'Aquino? The complicated answer to the question of how an American of Japanese ancestry came to be seen as the embodiment of a mythic Japanese war criminal resurrects an important and little examined watershed event in the postwar history of Japanese Americans, one that metonymically implicates Japanese Americans in the establishment of a cold war culture that was characterized by narrative containment of the collapsing categories of Western subjectivity, namely east and west and native and foreign and the larger cultural binary shaping them, the "natural" distinction between man and woman.

The case of Tokyo Rose is linked to the changes in the period both in U.S.-Japan relations, which has historically been rationalized by heteronormative gender relations, and in the status of Japanese Americans in the United States, who were then in the process of a tremendous transformation from wartime internees to peacetime citizens. In many ways, the extraordinary treatment of d'Aquino's case allows us to reflect on the passage from postwar to cold war ideology and the impact of this transition on a woman who came to represent, all at once, the threat of both Japanese and therefore Japanese American subjectivity, the unsettling persistence of the woman who exceeds social concepts of woman, and, as a radio announcer, a timely example of the paradoxical function of popular culture and entertainment in spreading the McCarthyist doctrine. The anxious shifts in U.S. perceptions of domestic and foreign politics during the middle to late 1940s included the final bitter battles in the Pacific theater and the residual resentment of Japan, the exhilaration and then uncertainty of the first years of the postwar, and the emerging strains of a distinctly different cold war mood— one that would eventually lead to McCarthyism and the involvement of the United States in the Korean conflict with Communist Chinese forces in the early 1950s. The early 1950s would give rise to an amazing reversal of postwar sentiment about Japan, as Americans embraced the conviction that Japan was now a partner to the U.S. endeavor in Asia rather than a threat. The late 1940s reveal no more than the vague beginnings of this transformation, however, as the nation moved uncertainly from the war-weary anticipation of Americans on the eve of a complete Allied victory to a growing fear of rampant internal security threats and unseen but clever subversive elements in the very body politic of America. It is important to the understanding of what happened to Iva Toguri d'Aquino to distinguish the period during which she was pursued, tried, and convicted as one in which changes were occurring that would pave the way for a cold war with China and Russia and for the McCarthy hearings, as well as for the later reversal of opinion about Japan. This network of related changes in global and domestic politics determined the need for and the fate of the pursuit of Tokyo Rose. It also made her story a site for the making of what Alan Nadel describes as a cold war culture of containment in which "the rampant performance of narratives" in a variety of sites created "the illusion that national narratives were knowable and unquestionable realities."[5]

The late war years, which saw the bloody Pacific battles between the Allied and Japanese forces, were the theater for the various NHK female announcers who were forced by Japanese officials to act the part of the beguiling and dangerous oriental siren as part of a propaganda effort in the last months of the war. Set down in the midst of a strange environment in the South Pacific in 1944, thousands of Allied GIs had endured an interminable sentence only occasionally broken by the lively NHK "Zero Hour" music programs that were hosted by female voices who intoned: "Greetings everybody. How are my victims this evening?" or "Hello you fighting orphans in the Pacific. How's tricks?"[6] The GIs' active imaginations, as the OWI termed it, inevitably supplied the rest, shaping the collective of disc jockeys into Tokyo Rose, a catchphrase for the oriental seductress so familiar to them from Western lore and clearly invoked by the broadcasters themselves. The myth of Tokyo Rose might easily have remained a faint mythic emblem of the war, except for the problem of the U.S. occupation of Japan. When the war was won, and the difficult, daily Allied restructuring of Japan had begun along with the trials of Japanese war criminals, the desire to project the jumble of female voices reading prepared texts into a single, self-motivated individual—the mysterious seductress whom GIs imagined pursued them during the war—quickly overwhelmed the fact that there was no one at NHK who had ever used the name "Tokyo Rose" and that there were several similar women announcers who were broadcasting at the same time. The story of a single, living Tokyo Rose who could be identified, revealed, and punished became almost inevitable in the atmosphere of the Tokyo war trials, which offered a narrative means of containing and making "knowable," to quote Nadel, the peculiar conditions of d'Aquino's wartime history.

From early 1946 until 1948, once-revered military leaders, including no less than General Tojo, were publicly tried, convicted, and later executed for their wartime acts against the Allied forces in an exercise deemed by many observers as a thinly veiled form of U.S. propaganda, an event that primarily served to punish Japan and to purge the nation of its faith in its wartime government in preparation for its total acceptance of U.S.-enforced democracy.[7] The line between fact and fiction became irrelevant in the pursuit of this aim, in anticipation of what would come to be a common feature of cold war anticommunism, which often obscured political and cultural complexities by interpreting them as variants of a narrow range of existing narrative forms. From as early as 1947, according to cold war cultural critic Andrew

Ross, newspaper reports about atomic espionage began to take on a "sensationalist" edge derived from spy fiction as political discourse increasingly became a "mass-mediated" event.[8] The trial of Tokyo Rose and the predicament of its Nisei protagonist were indirectly implicated in the early manifestation of this lurid paranoia about the effects of popular culture on the political fortunes and security of the nation.

Of course, the fascination with discovering and later convicting a Nisei as "the" Tokyo Rose might also be said to represent simply a revival of the fear of a "home-grown" Japanese menace of the war years. Yet it seems more likely that the desire to pursue d'Aquino was motivated less by a residual fear of Japanese Americans, who by this time had been utterly demoralized and dispersed by the internment and resettlement processes, and more by the need to punish Japan's most legendary and elusive female figure. This is not to suggest, however, that the threat of Japanese American internment was irrelevant, for it remained a nagging problem throughout the postwar period. U.S. Justice Department officials had to avoid the disturbing facts of Japanese American displacement during the war, a displacement that had forced d'Aquino to be caught in Japan against her wishes at the same time that it attempted to identify her as an American in order to deport her and try her for treason. The Justice Department, in other words, had to force d'Aquino's story to fit the needs of a rising cultural discourse of treachery avenged that had little to do with unearthing the "real" facts of her wartime status and activities. Instead, the trial and conviction of d'Aquino was an attempt to contain her story within the larger cultural investment in the mythic narrative of a beguiling Japanese nationalist vixen and her pre-cold-war chastisement. In significant ways, the submerging of Iva Toguri d'Aquino's story under the myth of Tokyo Rose is, according to Nadel, an early U.S. containment narrative, "the name of a privileged American narrative during the cold war" that sought to impose itself on all stories in order to reproduce the Manichean world of good versus evil, of democracy versus communism, that made U.S. supremacy and its structuring trope, the heteronormative order, necessary.[9] Thus, "containment equated containment of communism with containment of atomic secrets, of sexual license, of gender roles, of nuclear energy, and of artistic expression" (5). As a harbinger of this cold war culture of containment, the situation of d'Aquino reveals the often neglected functions that Japan and, by association, Japanese American subjectivity were to play in the cultural and gender anxieties underlying so much of the postwar buildup to the McCarthy period of the 1950s.

The need to embody d'Aquino as Tokyo Rose during the early postwar years altered the initial wartime allure of Tokyo Rose as the sexualized female figuration of the Japanese threat. Although the obsession with identifying domestic traitors to the American cause—not all of whom were actual communists—was only just solidifying by the time d'Aquino was convicted in late 1949, Winston Churchill had already delivered his ominous "iron curtain" speech in 1946, in which he predicted the coming darkness of a communist "iron curtain" descending between Eastern and Western Europe. In response to these early fears of communist influence across the globe, and in a reversal of the initial antagonism and apprehension of occupation forces in Japan, Japan would ultimately emerge as a necessary partner to the United States in the ideological struggle with the Soviet Union over control of Asia. But this was later. The corridor of time during which "Tokyo Rose" was tried and convicted, roughly early 1946 until late 1949, represented instead a period of transition between the wartime antagonism toward Japan and all things Japanese and the later cold war mood of a marriage or partnership with Japan as a safeguard against the influence of communism.

In key ways, then, d'Aquino's conviction captures a historical and cultural moment when the generally restricted status of Japanese Americans—before, during, and, to some extent, after the war—provided fuel for and was in turn reinvigorated by the growing tide of suspicion of communism and of subversive agents within the national body. In short, it marked a moment when Japanese Americans' displacement, postwar occupation history, and cold war anticommunism converged, although there has been little to no analysis of the terms and implications of these buried lines of connection. Although there are two exhaustive book-length accounts of Tokyo Rose, Masayo Duus's *Tokyo Rose: Orphan of the Pacific* (1979) and Russell Warren Howe's *The Hunt for Tokyo Rose* (1990), both are journalistic histories of the discovery and trial of d'Aquino rather than close, critical analyses of the function of her ordeal within the related frameworks of Japanese American internment and later cold war politics.[10] More specifically, no one has yet explored how d'Aquino's transformation from a rather plain Nisei schoolgirl to the bodacious Tokyo Rose, an enemy and alien female figure whom everyone admitted did not exist, indirectly invoked the public's anxiety over the meaning and boundaries of not just Japanese and Japanese American identity in the 1940s and 1950s but over national gender roles as well. The story of Iva Toguri d'Aquino is critical, then, not just because it provides the literal link between the initial postwar uncertainty and the later, well-known history of the excesses of McCarthyism but also because it allows us to approach the recollection of this link within the terms of the comparatively obscured story of Japanese American counter-history during the same period, thereby revealing how the ambivalence of Japanese American identity became implicated in a trial that was a harbinger of the cold war to come.

"It Should Have Been Ava Gardner": Drawing the Boundaries

Even though, in the words of Masayo Duus, the trial of the woman presumed to be Tokyo Rose "had nothing to do with the Communist menace" so familiar from the early 1950s, still, in the late 1940s, "the label of 'traitor' touched a deep and sensitive nerve in the popular psyche."[11] According to Ellen Schrecker, as early as the late 1940s "previously innocuous activities came to seem increasingly ominous."[12] In 1947, the House Committee on Un-American Activities (HUAC) opened hearings on the communist presence in Hollywood, setting off an unprecedented government campaign to purge radical left political figures from almost every area of culture, under the assumption that such figures represented a serious threat to the security of the nation. Although the most legendary victims of the committee's right-wing ire were well-known intellectuals and writers who were arguably in a position to influence the masses, the anticommunist crusade was ultimately more effective in inventing the enemy as an ordinary citizen than it was flushing him or her out of high places. Consider that the most infamous of all of McCarthyism's victims, Ethel and Julius Rosenberg, were described by Blanche Wiesen Cook as "two ordinary Jewish New Yorkers who believed in a non-fascist future" or even more broadly, by David Suchoff, as a couple "associated with a Jewish past that most New York [Jewish] intellectuals thought they had left far behind," and it becomes clearer just how McCarthyism worked to discredit whole segments of the population in its selection of only apparently isolated victims.[13] In the case of the Rosenbergs, according to Suchoff, government prosecutors hoped to "use subversive Jewishness as a means of containment" by exacerbating "American Jewish fears of the charge of double loyalty" (162). Although the guilt or innocence of the Rosenbergs is still debated nearly fifty years after their execution in 1953, they nonetheless remain representative of the most vicious tactics and effects of McCarthyism: the need to personify imagined dangers, wherever they might hide. And this need would be met despite the fact that the Rosenbergs "were convicted on rather meager evidence by a judge who colluded with the prosecution" (162).

If the hysteria of the period demanded an enemy, then none could be more threatening or more unexpected than the enemy among us. According to Victor Navasky, "the success of the hunters depended on their ability to link the menace without to the menace within," thereby making the domestic, private lives of citizens the imperiled site of betrayal and corruption from without.[14] The stated objective of Red hunters was to purge and purify this inner circle by eradicating the ideological otherness that communism typified. Often, the communist or traitorous Other was figured as a social deviant, as one who defied the presumed natural order of human relationships and hierarchies. The Red purges sweeping the nation in the late 1940s and early 1950s had the particular effect of punishing individuals whose actions or lives challenged gender roles or expanded the rigid bounds of middle-class heterosexuality. The domestic space became a primary forum for the control and perpetuation of normative heterosexuality in the nation and, as such, a focus of anticommunists. Although feminist scholars consistently point out that the notion of a protected and private sphere of national life is largely a social construction emanating from the need to naturalize the boundaries limiting the cultural involvement of women and ethnic minorities, policing the home front as the perceived realm of women's influence and affective intimacies became seen as a means of controlling the fear of women's autonomy and gender and sexual deviancy in general.[15] In the era of McCarthyism, the concept of the domestic scene soon became doubly feminized as both the site of women's lives and of familial sexuality rendered weaker still by the influence of foreign ideologies.

Citing previous studies of postwar culture, Wendy Kozol concludes that "anti-Communist iconography elevated patriarchal emblems of masculinity into weapons necessary for the fight against Communism, whereas stereotypes of dangerous women and effeminate men signified the threat of subversion."[16] Focusing on the apparent feminization of national character ironically enabled the success of McCarthyism, because "depicting the enemy as male, and the United States as female, intensifies Cold War dangers not only by conceding power to the enemy but by emasculating the signifier of the nation" (111). The most effective antidote to a degenerating female nation is, of course, "a revitalized masculinity," which was expressed in HUAC's aggressive pursuit and punishment of suspected spies and traitors such as the Rosenbergs.

When Ethel Rosenberg was arrested in the summer of 1950, prosecutors vigorously pursued her interrogation, hoping to use her as leverage against her husband. According to a study by Ronald Radosh and Joyce Milton, the prosecutors presumed she would break under the pressure of such intense questioning, as well as out of concern for her children, and admit to the crime of espionage in order to lighten her sentence.[17] But what they discovered was a strong-willed woman who refused to be manipulated into admitting guilt, who repeatedly referred to her rights amid intense legal pressure, and who almost certainly upset their expectations of a woman's and a mother's weaker constitution. In fact, to many observers, like Joyce Antler, Ethel Rosenberg gave the impression of a "cold, well-composed woman lacking 'normal' feminine characteristics" (205). The jury foreman later stated that she seemed to him to be a "steely, stony, tight-lipped woman. She was the mastermind. Julius would have spoken if she would have permitted him. He was more human. She was more disciplined" (206). Antler adds that the final FBI report further determined that all pleas for leniency and for a commutation of execution in the interest of protecting a mother and wife were negated by the sense that "in this instance, it is the woman who is the strong and recalcitrant character and the man who is the weak one."[18] In the end, the greater fault for the Rosenbergs' conviction and execution was laid at Ethel's feet, because she dared to overturn the public's expectations of the role to be played by a wife and the mother of two boys. The execution of the Rosenbergs was, whatever one thinks now of their guilt or innocence, effective in repudiating their marriage as gender pathology and in openly condemning Ethel's seemingly *unnatural* femininity. Ethel Rosenberg became the living model of the obstinate postwar woman so feared in an era that encouraged social and political conformity as a national characteristic. As the woman who refuses to submit, who does not shrink from public censure and exposure, Ethel Rosenberg embodied the unconventional femininity that Red hunters unconsciously targeted. Her execution remains the ultimate tragic act of purging the nation of radical, political, and cultural otherness.

As the dual personification of insubordinate woman and radical Jew, Ethel Rosenberg dared to mix motherhood with an open expression of sexual desire. Much has been made of Ethel and Julius Rosenbergs' passionate letters and gestures to each other in the face of execution. Carol Hurd Green reports that guards at Sing-Sing prison were so shocked by the Rosenbergs' "hungry embrace" at their first meeting after their separate arrests that they never again allowed them to touch, finding that "their open sexuality was intolerable."[19] Awash in condemnation for the Rosenbergs, Louis Nizer's account of their prosecution in the film *The Unquiet Death of Julius and Ethel Rosenberg* reflects the biases of many other observers in its descriptions of Ethel Rosenberg as chiefly responsible for the "intolerable" nature of the Rosenbergs' sexuality.[20] According to Nizer, when on a regular visit to Sing-Sing Ethel Rosenberg's lawyer pointed out her depressed appearance— "Look at you—no lipstick, hair all over the place"—Ethel shot back, "Wait till Julius gets here. I'll doll up to kill." Whether in fact these were Ethel Rosenberg's words, the impression of her in Nizer's words as a "plump, deceptively gentle-looking Lower East Side housewife" who openly affirmed her sexual desire, made motherhood and sexuality synonymous in perhaps the most inexcusable challenge to cold war Americans' anxieties about the state of middle-class American femininity. The terms of containment culture, as Nadel defines it, ensured that the punishment of Ethel Rosenberg's unnatural expression of female sexuality became one with the punishment of her left-wing, communist beliefs.

The free-floating national anxiety about the subversive power of women over men was also at the heart of the appeal for the prosecution of Iva Toguri d'Aquino (although her case preceded the Rosenbergs' trial by almost five years), and ultimately it owed its life to the particular play of postwar gender politics with d'Aquino's status as a Japanese American woman. According to Elaine Tyler May, in the early postwar years the nation was still obsessed with the terms of the return to peace, and a great part of the burden for the success of the nation in peace was the willingness of women who had "manned" the factories that supplied the war effort to return dutifully to their culturally sanctioned roles as homemakers.[21] Add to this widely expressed anxiety about women's potential power in postwar culture the antagonism toward all things Japanese, and one perceives the complicated national concerns that began to form around Iva Toguri d'Aquino's willingness to claim that she was Tokyo Rose. Tokyo Rose, as myth, blended two more general Asian female stereotypes: the "dragon lady," the monstrous reptilian, orientalized female, and that of the exotic, sensual oriental doll. But because the broadcasts of Tokyo Rose were reported to have taunted GIs with news from the home front, she very soon became an exclusive emblem of the dangers of the oriental femme fatale, luring white men to their destruction by exploiting their sexual vulnerability as could be done only by an oriental enchantress: half dragon lady, half geisha doll. When, for instance, Jay Walz in the *New York Times* reported in August 1948 the announcement that d'Aquino had been arrested and would be tried as Tokyo Rose, it set the tone for popular perceptions of her alleged crimes by emphasizing the destructive power of women's sexual power and men's unwitting vulnerability: "In sweet-toned chit-chat the various Tokyo Roses talked to their American listeners as 'forgotten men,' and made frequent mention of wayward wives and sweethearts back home. It is in connection with such broadcasts that Mrs. d'Aquino, a native of Los Angeles who once attended the University of California, will be prosecuted."[22]

Although Walz made it clear that d'Aquino was "only one of a half dozen women who took part in Tokyo broadcasts," his article simultaneously cast doubts on d'Aquino's innocence by calling hers "the Tokyo Rose case" and by repeatedly prefacing her denials with phrases such as "according to her story," and "she once told reporters." Although Mark Gayn and a handful of other reporters had earlier cautioned Americans to be careful to review the facts of the case and to consider whether d'Aquino had not been "a victim of circumstances," most journalists were not so ethical. They opted to play up the story of Tokyo Rose.[23] Before a grand jury had even been convened to hear the case, the press was already feasting on the intrigue and subterfuge that shrouded d'Aquino's statements as the suspected Tokyo Rose.

Iva Toguri d'Aquino's life as Tokyo Rose had an undeniable appeal for a Western audience raised to believe in Asian women's natural predisposition toward sexual duplicity. Thus in one sense it was not hard to cast d'Aquino, as a young woman of Japanese descent, as the living essence of the exotic feminine fantasy dreamed up by thousands of American men who listened to the wartime broadcasts she was reported to have made. She provoked even more public censure because she simultaneously emblematized the woman who unapologetically controlled men, rather than was controlled by them. And, in keeping with containment culture, the nation's global interests in asserting its power over the former enemy nation of Japan were ultimately synonymous with the need to embody and then punish d'Aquino's sexual power as well. Thus her initial appearance as possessing a youthful naïveté and a willingness to please, in time yielded itself to the influence of a larger cultural narrative that combined the collective Western fears of feminine power and Asian influence that have historically plagued the nation's perception of all Asian women.

Yet even in the face of such powerful cultural cues, framing d'Aquino as the sultry and sinister Tokyo Rose was not without its problems. Although d'Aquino was twenty-nine when she was first identified as Tokyo Rose, her appearance and demeanor were consistently described as that of a much younger and less sophisticated "girl." Masayo Duus describes the initial meeting with Clark Lee and Harry Brundidge as disappointing to them, not the least because of d'Aquino's unimpressive appearance:

> Lee and Brundidge were a bit put off by Iva's appearance when they first saw her in Lee's hotel room. Tokyo Rose, the GI's idol, wartime woman of legend, should have been gorgeous and alluring. Instead there stood Iva, slightly tense, and looking like a schoolgirl. To Lee and Brundidge she seemed about twenty years old, although in fact she was twenty-nine. "It should have been Ava Gardner," Iva later recalled, "but instead it was me." Iva stood just a bit over five feet tall, her hair in pigtails . . . but even by the farthest stretch of imagination, she was not sexy, not even very feminine.[24]

Amazingly, in an example of the coming cold war propensity for concocting something ominous in even the most innocuous figure, d'Aquino's slightly homely "schoolgirl" demeanor ultimately did not impede the public's willingness to accept her in the role of Tokyo Rose. She was, quite literally, cast in the role of the oriental vixen, the alien woman who needed harnessing if the nation were to reaffirm its power and if the last vestiges of imperial Japanese arrogance were to be eradicated. The story of Tokyo Rose served not only the needs of the U.S. occupation of Japan but also proved to be a cultural narrative tailor-made to succor rankling fears about postwar gender reconversion, which hinged on the willingness of women to return to the home, to be restrained. The public interest in Tokyo Rose would turn d'Aquino's claim that she "should have been Ava Gardner" into a historical certainty by filtering her story through broader narratives that obscured the unique circumstances of her presence and actions while in wartime Japan. Like the spy stories that shaped the public fascination with a communist conspiracy, popular culture would also become the means of bringing d'Aquino-as-Tokyo Rose to justice by refiguring her as the oriental "Ava Gardner" the moment needed. Just as radio had been the conduit for the commission of her alleged original acts of propaganda against the Allied forces, after the war the combined media of film, radio broadcasts, and newspaper features would be critical to her conviction.

When news broke in occupied Japan of the discovery of Tokyo Rose, the army commissioned d'Aquino to make a news film for GIs in which she demonstrated her activities as Tokyo Rose. Unwilling or unable to see the potential for self-incrimination in playing along, she agreed. According to Masayo Duus, d'Aquino found that "the atmosphere was fun, and it all seemed to be a big joke."[25] The film begins with d'Aquino being interviewed, during the course of which she describes her activities at NHK. As the film progresses, however, scenes of d'Aquino's descriptions begin to be dramatized by actors, including brief scenes of GIs huddled around the lone radio listening to Tokyo Rose, a.k.a. d'Aquino, from a hillside hut in the South Pacific (33). In addition to the army's news film, the navy also attempted to make a film about Tokyo Rose, casting d'Aquino as the Japanese propagandist. According to Russell Warren Howe, as Ensign Vaughn Paul later explained to the FBI agents building a case against d'Aquino, he coaxed her into appearing in the navy's version of her story by telling her that his main objective was not to judge Tokyo Rose but merely "to give a face and a body to the legend they [the GIs] had heard on shipboard radios."[26] Although the navy's film was never used because of its poor production quality, Paul, as the director, followed the army's approach of dramatizing d'Aquino's alleged wartime activities as Tokyo Rose by alternating a series of interviews and flashback vignettes with hired actors playing the key parts. Although in both the army and navy films d'Aquino appeared in these vignettes playing herself, the role of Tokyo Rose was more often played by an alluring actress. The ultimate effect of both of these early official attempts to frame the story of Tokyo Rose for a military audience was to replace d'Aquino, the "slightly tense schoolgirl," with an actress who more appropriately embodied the exotic "Ava Gardner" mystique presumed to be Tokyo Rose's signature effect. These now destroyed films were the first, crucial steps in the construction of Tokyo Rose the myth over and against the contradictions posed by Iva Toguri d'Aquino's body, her repeated insistence that her broadcasts were harmless, and her expectation that the American public would embrace her as a heroine of sorts.

The elusive power of visual and popular media is a theme running throughout the story of the pursuit of Tokyo Rose. The modified terms of America's attention to popular culture was, for instance, primarily responsible for the overturning of the occupying army's initial fascination at d'Aquino's announcement that she was Tokyo Rose. Andrew Ross's point about the mediazation of politics during the cold war period is especially relevant to the early years of the postwar when "the domestic Cold War climate was also shaped by intellectuals' contradictory responses to the domestic development of mass-produced popular culture."[27] "Surely nothing could seem more at home in the new 'prosperity state' of postwar consumer capitalism than the domestic forms of the popular industries," Ross observes, "and yet, these were the same cultural forms which bore all the 'foreign' traces, for Cold War liberals, of an achievement in Stalinized taste" (16). Thus, in the words of Victor Navasky, the early HUAC hearings on Hollywood and other "attempts to cleanse the cultural apparatus can be understood only within the larger framework of the efforts to cleanse the political apparatus."[28] The belief in the potential of popular cultural forms to carry hidden or subversive messages resulted in their paradoxical position in postwar and cold war culture. Popular cultural narratives like the atom-spy thriller, for instance, provided a critical narrative form for promoting the worst fears voiced by anti-communist forces, who, in turn, rejected the power of mass culture to influence the public and were often contemptuous of popular culture.

Following closely on the heels of the military's attempts to stage d'Aquino's story for GI audiences, the 1947 campaign to make d'Aquino answer for Tokyo Rose's crimes quickly built up support among the often wolfish watchdogs of anti-Americanism who were not averse to manipulating popular culture despite underlying fears about its insidious effects on the dull American masses. D'Aquino, the pigtailed UCLA coed, was gradually being transmuted into the sultry siren of the Pacific. Although the CIC in Japan had exonerated d'Aquino of all treason allegations in 1946 with J. Edgar Hoover himself finding no substantial evidence for trial, conservative political factions in the United States were not yet convinced. While awaiting a Justice Department decision on her request to return to the United States and be reunited with her family, d'Aquino became the object of a sustained campaign started by the American Legion and later taken up by the sensationalist reporter Walter Winchell, who did more to whip up public outrage than perhaps any other single figure and who relied on precisely the tactics of spy fiction and treasonous intrigue that would be the staples of McCarthyism, however much its liberal or intellectual abettors also decried the influence of these mass-cultural narratives.

On October 28, 1947, James F. O'Neill of the American Legion, which had vigorously condemned Japanese Americans during the early months of the war and supported their internment in the camps, began to put pressure on the State Department to pursue the prosecution of d'Aquino despite the initial findings of the CIC and the FBI. The American Legion induced its members to bombard the Justice Department with protest letters throughout early 1948, an auspicious moment, perhaps, because the HUAC hearings on anticommunism in Hollywood were set to begin later that same year and had attracted enormous public attention. High treason was the watchword for the times, it seemed. The American Legion was quickly joined by the Native Sons of the Golden West, an anti-Asian organization active in California since the turn of the century. As reported by Masayo Duus, together the two powerful organizations exerted so much pressure that on December 8, the Los Angeles City Council passed a blanket resolution barring d'Aquino's return by declaring "this council does herewith vigorously oppose the return to this county of this person or any other person treasonably connected with the 'Tokyo Rose' wartime propaganda broadcasts."[29] Although she was not specifically named in the resolution—which, in the fashion of the military's news films, substituted the idea of Tokyo Rose for d'Aquino herself—it was clear in the context of the flurry of hostility surrounding d'Aquino's case that the act was designed to condemn her as a traitor in the public's mind by appealing to its growing appetite for salacious stories of betrayal.

But it was undeniably Walter Winchell's Sunday night radio broadcasts against d'Aquino that finally sealed her fate. Like Clark Lee, Winchell was "an archetypal Hearst man, whose job was not to win Pulitzer Prizes but to 'raise hell and sell newspapers' in any way possible" (111).

With a national audience estimated at seven million, Winchell signed on after receiving a letter from the irate mother of a soldier killed in the Pacific campaign in which she protested d'Aquino's exoneration and return as a miscarriage of justice and an insult to her son's memory. Rather than question the letter's use of d'Aquino as a target for a parent's understandable grief and anger at the tragic loss of a son, Winchell instead reacted in his typical knee-jerk fashion and channeled the mother's ire into his regular exhortations that the Justice Department and Truman in particular prove to the American people that they were not "soft" on traitors; he demanded no less than the indictment and conviction of d'Aquino. The irony of Winchell's radio broadcasts is that they trafficked in precisely the sort of relentless manipulation of public sentiment that attempted with a barrage of accusations and insinuations to wear down the listener that he despised d'Aquino for. The fact that the Justice Department had doggedly looked for evidence against d'Aquino while holding her in prison for a year without trial did nothing to silence Winchell's campaign. As a former Hollywood reporter who still maintained his connections there, and as a rabid anticommunist who agreed that the culture needed purging, Winchell personified the contradictions of a media at once embraced and despised that beset popular culture in the period.

When the attorney for the United States, James M. Carter, tried weakly to placate what he perceived as Winchell's dangerous suggestion that d'Aquino had not been thoroughly investigated, he underestimated the subtle appeal behind both the mother's and Winchell's combined attacks on d'Aquino. For, in addition to the sensationalism that was Winchell's hallmark, his attack on d'Aquino provided a timely outlet for Americans' varying degrees of frustration and doubt about the end of the war and the uncertain domestic peace ahead. Winchell cared little for the facts or the figures involved. His business was fantasy, and he clearly relished the notion of ensnaring the living Tokyo Rose, not primarily as a manifestation of the combined Western fantasies of the Asian menace and the bad woman—in contrast to the suffering mother figure—but especially as a figure against whom both he and his audience might vent tensions held in check during the war. These domestic tensions were evident, in fact, on the very eve of the postwar period, on V-J day, August 15, 1945, when the nation was visited not only with jubilant victory celebrations in major cities, but also by the worst labor strikes and layoffs in years. The victory parties competed in the headlines with the news of striking automotive, steel, and rubber plant workers, with expectations of more layoffs and troubles ahead once the GIS returned to reclaim their jobs. Add to these economic fears the more abstract worries about the reconversion of GIS and the occupation of Japan, and the future of the national victory begins to be shrouded in doubt. If nothing else, Winchell correctly gauged the mood of the country and the fact that nothing less than a kind of exorcism would do to stem the growing sense that the nation was perhaps ill-equipped to rebuild Europe and Japan. If it could be proven that the real problem was treason in high places, then the possibility for a complete redemption from these fears was, at least symbolically, much greater.

The unconscious urge to embody and enact this national purging gradually overwhelmed coverage of d'Aquino's story throughout the rest of 1948 and until her formal arrest for treason in August 1949. It was no longer d'Aquino who interested the reporters but the icon of war for which she was merely the most immediate medium. The body of her story and the body that merely "should have been Ava Gardner's" were replaced by the drama, the shadowy outlines of which were first enacted in the army and navy films. The theatricality of the Tokyo Rose story, such as it was constructed, was not missed by Winchell's Hollywood peers. Earl Carroll, the Broadway impresario and Hollywood musical producer known for his ostentatious stagings, was intrigued by d'Aquino's predicament and seized on the public furor over her freedom. He arranged to meet d'Aquino in the interest of discussing a film version of her life as Tokyo Rose, with Japanese actress Yoshiko Yamaguchi in the title role. He also agreed to deliver a letter to Winchell in which d'Aquino defended her actions in exchange for d'Aquino's cooperation in making yet another film of her life, although he promised that his drama would be sympathetic to her version of events. When his plane crashed on the way from California to New York to discuss a compromise with Winchell, d'Aquino's hope to use popular media once again, but this time to change the tide of public disdain, was lost.

Although there may be little reason to believe that Carroll's film would have followed through on his earnest promise to tell the "real" story of her involvement at NHK—especially given his demonstrated penchant for elaborate and glamorous productions—his involvement culminates the struggle to reconcile the plain-spoken d'Aquino to the

mysterious secrets that even casual observers assumed were hidden behind her bland exterior. Against the backdrop of increasing stories of
communist spy rings operating out of otherwise unlikely places, the
growing popular cultural myth of Tokyo Rose overtook the rather
dreary person and story of Iva Toguri d'Aquino. By the time of her trial,
most American readers knew her face simply as Tokyo Rose. The *San
Francisco Chronicle* wished d'Aquino, who was born on the fourth of
July, "No Happy Birthday!" as she went to trial in that city on July 5,
1949.[30] It referred to her in its announcement of the upcoming trial as
either "Tokyo Rose" or "the American born Japanese girl" and promised readers "day-to-day" coverage of an event that was "as exciting as
a spy thriller, as informing as history." The packaging of Iva Toguri
d'Aquino as Tokyo Rose is an early representative of the cold war substitution of "spy thriller" for "history," an example of the ways in
which preexisting cultural narratives confirm and fix the ambivalence
of the nation's future.

But the production of the necessary myth of the traitorous oriental
seductress out of d'Aquino's demonstrated naïveté was not easy. The
question of who *was* Iva Toguri d'Aquino was never comfortably settled
by the trial nor by attempts to typecast d'Aquino as the evasive, alien
propagandist. The confused attempts of prosecutors to match the bodies of "Tokyo Rose" and d'Aquino during the court trial were not resolved by the dramatization of military films or Winchell's bombastic
broadcasts, because none of these narratives could prevent the inevitable encounter with the precarious and discomfiting fact of d'Aquino's
identity as an American unwillingly exiled from her nation. Even
though the "hunt" for Tokyo Rose was arguably successful because it
led to the prosecution of d'Aquino, there was always the shifting questions of her status as a Japanese American living in Japan, her cooperation with POWs in making the broadcasts, and her marriage to a Portuguese nationalist to contend with. In yet another level of contradiction,
the unresolved meaning of her national affiliation or cultural identity,
and thus the meaning or intent of her broadcasts, fueled as well as
dampened the need to prove that there was something amiss about
d'Aquino's person, something excessive about her life and her identi-
fications that prevented easy categorization. In hindsight, the conflicting facts of Iva Toguri d'Aquino's status and her wartime story both
aided and frustrated the government's attempts to characterize her as
a traitor. How much did the public really want to know about d'Aquino,

about the vicissitudes of Japanese Americans' wartime lives, or about the nature of propaganda, including the nature or meaning of the propaganda that ensnared her?

Despite the success of the campaign against d'Aquino, doubts about her treasonous activities lingered, even through the final stages of a jury trial that seemed from the beginning to have been designed to ensure her conviction. The attorney general with the Justice Department who reopened the case after Winchell began his radio campaign was Tom Clark. Clark was familiar to Japanese American organizations as a civilian coordinator for the relocation authority that had organized their internment. In addition, according to Masayo Duus, he was remembered for taking "a hard line toward certain elements in the Japanese American community," including those who resisted the government's plans or doubted the strength of their allegiance to a government that would violate their civil rights.[31] In addition to the Justice Department's now widely acknowledged practice of suborning testimony from witnesses in the d'Aquino trial under threat of prosecution, the trial was presided over by Judge Michael Roche, the same judge who had during the war denied a writ of habeas corpus to Mitsuye Endo, a Nisei who had tried to argue that her internment on the basis of ethnicity alone was unconstitutional and violated her rights as a citizen.[32] Not surprisingly, then, Roche's management of the proceedings was weighted to favor the case against yet another Japanese American. The judge repeatedly overruled the objections of d'Aquino's lawyer Wayne Collins, the famous defender of many other Japanese American defendants, and often limited the scope of his direct examinations of key defense witnesses. Russell Warren Howe points out that when Collins put Toshikatsu Kodaira, an AP reporter during the war, on the stand to testify about how Harry Brundidge had tried to bribe with gifts his testimony against d'Aquino, Judge Roche sustained every one of the prosecution's objections. The result was that 103 of 131 of Kodaira's replies were stricken from consideration.[33] Similarly, Masayo Duus observes that Judge Roche's later decision to deny evidence that Brundidge had tampered with witnesses was "shocking" to many court observers because it clearly called into question the legality of the case against d'Aquino.[34] Roche's final instructions to the jury dealt the coup de grace, all but destroying the defense's most effective and lasting contention: that d'Aquino had only broadcast out of fear for her life and for the lives of the Allied POWs who were forced to write the broadcasts. As reported by Howe, Roche determined that in d'Aquino's case, "excuse from a criminal act on the ground of coercion" did not cover "fear of injury to one's property or remote bodily harm," nor was it enough "that the defendant thought she might be sent to a concentration or internment camp" or "that such threats were made to other persons and that she knew of such threats."[35]

Sent to deliberate with these instructions, the jury nevertheless stalled at ten to two for acquittal on all counts. When after a full day of deliberations they reported back to Roche saying that they were hopelessly deadlocked, he pressured them to return and deliver a decision, reminding them of the expense of the trial. Aware of the expense to the taxpayer, and affected by the pressure to punish d'Aquino, they finally found her guilty of one lesser count of treason, and acquitted her on the five more serious counts. According to jury foreman John Mann, the jury opted for the lesser charge because they believed that d'Aquino, who had already spent two years in jail awaiting trial, would not serve any additional jail time. When Judge Roche summarily sentenced her to ten years and a $10,000 fine, Mann "was unable to sleep for days." Years later, when interviewed by reporters, he maintained his shame over the jury's verdict, saying he still felt "I should have had a little more guts and stuck with my acquittal vote" (293). Just why Mann and his peers did not "stick with" their acquittal votes is perhaps difficult to assess in retrospect, although their actions, like the courts' violations of d'Aquino's rights, were almost certainly affected by the residual suspicion of Japanese Americans that persisted beyond the bounds of wartime hysteria and became inextricably linked with the occupation politics that had initially launched the pursuit of Tokyo Rose.

D'Aquino's situation as an American living in Japan during the war obviously confused the terms of her identification as a loyal citizen, but her wartime experience also reflects a fragment of Japanese American history only nominally explored by historians. Iva Toguri d'Aquino was one of approximately ten thousand Japanese Americans, some of them Nisei, caught in Japan when the war began. The Nisei especially quickly found themselves in difficult straits resulting from actions beyond their control that impinged on the terms of their national allegiance. Before the war it had not been uncommon for the Issei to have their children's births listed in the family register in Japan, an act that legally claimed Japanese citizenship for the Nisei along with their status as

American citizens by virtue of birth. D'Aquino was one of these Nisei holding dual citizenship at one point, although, according to Duus, after the Japanese invaded Manchuria in 1932, her father, following the route of many other Issei in the years leading up to World War II, had her name stricken from the register in an effort to clarify her national allegiance, as well as his own.[36] The Issei's actions, which at worst can be said to express the ambivalent national field they negotiated as aliens legally forbidden to become U.S. citizens, left an indelible mark of indecision on the record of the Nisei caught in Japan during World War II. The United States was reluctant to agree to their return, and the Japanese security police tried to pressure many Nisei into signing the family register once more thereby reclaiming their Japanese citizenship and making themselves available for war service. D'Aquino was also approached by Japanese officials as she waited for permission to return to the United States, but she repeatedly refused to give up her American citizenship and even demanded to be interned as a foreigner in Japan.

The pressures on d'Aquino and her fellow Nisei were immense, and included difficulty getting rations and jobs. In the face of these hostilities many Nisei eventually relented and entered their names on the family register, and even more followed when they heard about their families' internment in the United States, an action that signaled to them the United States' complete rejection of their communities. D'Aquino was one of the few who refused and who, according to her acquaintances, "was the most outspoken" in her desire to return to the United States (55–56). When the State Department refused to certify her citizenship in 1942 and allow her to go back to the United States, d'Aquino had no choice but to settle into some sort of existence in Japan. Ironically, she was remembered by her Japanese neighbors as the object of much scorn and suspicion as a spy for the Americans and was frequently interrogated by the Japanese security police for her resistance. A spy in America and Japan, and a citizen of neither, d'Aquino's life in the 1940s and 1950s encompassed the frustration experienced by Japanese Americans who tried in vain to prove their allegiance to a nation that both required and refused it. In fact, one might argue that the government's view of the chief instrumentality of Japanese Americans was in their usefulness as leverage with Japan, and thus it had an investment in maintaining the indeterminacy of Japanese Americans' status, although the state would also be increasingly committed, if only for rhetorical purposes, to the job of eradicating the conditions of post-war racism as part of its "war on communism."

In a manner akin to the way in which d'Aquino's body was quite literally caught between Japan and the United States, Japanese Americans interned at home were considered an official part of the wartime exchange of bodies between the two nations, the beginnings perhaps of the tendency of the United States to utilize the so-called problem of Japanese American identity to reinforce national boundaries and to consolidate national security interests. Convinced of the potential of the Japanese American community to harbor treasonous elements when the war began, Secretary of the Navy Knox, among others, opined that "the most effective Fifth Column work of the war" had been committed by West Coast and Hawaiian Japanese Americans working in concert.[37] Although the mounting hostility against Japanese Americans was primarily succored by the relocation and internment of the entire West Coast population, other proposed measures included plans for a "repatriation program" in which Japanese American bodies were to be traded for those of American citizens not of Japanese ancestry who were detained in Japan. In fact, in a letter to Cordell Hull, Secretary of War Harry Stimson even recommended the "threat of reprisals against many Japanese nationals now enjoying negligible restrictions in the United States" to force better treatment of American citizens and POWs in Japan.[38] In the U.S. government's view, Japanese Americans in the United States during the war were hostages as well as aliens, valuable instruments of battle or leverage in the fight to gain an upper hand in the war in the Pacific. In a manner reminiscent of the pressures exerted by the Japanese security police on the Nisei, American officials also tried to coerce Japanese Americans into renouncing their American citizenship so that it might procure willing volunteers for a massive repatriation program that some hoped would cast out the Japanese American presence for good.

As late as summer 1944, the desire to rid the country of the Japanese Americans was still strong enough to motivate the passage of Public Law 405, which allowed in time of war for the renunciation of citizenship and repatriation of individuals who formerly had been deemed citizens. According to Michi Weglyn, the law "was primarily intended for the easy postwar disposal of the Kibei (Japan-educated Japanese Americans)," who were concentrated at Tule Lake, the camp for those deemed "disloyal" or "bad apples" and presumably in need of deportation.[39]

But for most Japanese Americans, particularly for the Nisei, the law's passage was a depressing sign that the public's animosity toward Japanese Americans was unabated. It cast further doubt on their perceptions of the possibilities for a postwar life in America for any person of Japanese descent. The Nisei's predicament was one of suspended displacement, caught between returning to Japan, a country that the Munson Report had determined "is afraid of and [does] not trust the Nisei," and a U.S. government that often seemed to jump at any opportunity to divest itself of what it perceived as the problem of Japanese American communities. Added to this national mood were the pressures coming from within the Japanese American population itself. At Tule Lake, for instance, it was not uncommon for "neutral Nisei and Kibei" to be subjected to intense peer pressure to denounce citizenship in a country that so obviously resented their presence as citizens: "For those consumed by fear, indecision, and hopelessness, the argument was persuasive. Why risk the chance of falling victim to Caucasian atrocities or the possibility of not finding work and starving to death on the outside? By simply declaring loyalty to the Emperor and tossing off what amounted to a mere 'scrap of paper,' they could cancel out forced resettlement, rule out the draft, and extend protective custody for the entire family until such time as they could depart for safer shores" (236). Even within the population there were rumors that failure to renounce American citizenship would mean that the Japanese government might take action against relatives in Japan. It seemed, regardless of where one looked, that the weight of the war with Japan and the combined fate of both nations rested heavily on the actions and claims of the Nisei, most of whom were still in their twenties at the time.

Getting out of the war merely unharmed and with their citizenship intact seemed the best promise of a future to many Japanese Americans, who tried hard to forget the internment period and to rebuild their lives when the war ended. For the government, the need to forget the internment period was linked to the broader desire in the late 1940s to ignore the threats posed by the frustrated lives of its many disenfranchised citizens, including African Americans, Mexican Americans, and the working poor. According to Sucheng Chan, this effacement of national inequities was particularly critical as an ideological weapon in the growing war against communism where, "perceiving itself as the leader of the 'Free World,' the United States competed with the Communist bloc of countries for power and influence in the

rest of the world."[40] Thus, the containment of subversion or questioning of the preconceived success of democratic capitalism, whether
expressed through the trial of d'Aquino or in the hunt for anticommunists in Hollywood, was always shaped by the war to contain communism abroad. On the surface, at least, as Robert Lee notes, "the political
logic of the Cold War and the logic of liberal universalism required an
adherence to a doctrine of racial equality" that obviated the erasure of
the memory of internment, as well as the reformation of Japanese
Americans along either side of a line between "loyalty" and "disloyalty" that threatened to replay the injustices of the war.[41]

One key to ensuring d'Aquino's conviction while also maintaining
the illusion of democratic equality was the complicity of Japanese
American leaders such as those in the Japanese American Citizens
League (JACL) who turned away from her defense. Although the JACL
had been active in trying to help the Nisei in Japan to cancel their parents' registration of their names as Japanese citizens, in the postwar
period the organization adopted a consistent policy of steering clear of
controversy and promoting only unquestionable examples of the patriotism of Japanese Americans. When they were asked by d'Aquino's father to raise funds for her defense, they refused. In addition to their
long-standing struggles with d'Aquino's lawyer Wayne Collins, who
had been critical of the JACL's accommodationist tactics during the
war, the JACL had proven itself to be a mostly conservative force within
the community, cautioning subordination and patience in the face of
discrimination. Thus representatives of the Japanese American community separated themselves from d'Aquino, despite the fact that her
case might have offered them an opportunity to clarify their ambivalent status by articulating finally and publicly the specific conditions of
their existence as citizens caught in between two warring nations while
adamantly trying to claim one. Although the JACL's attempts to control
and moderate the voice identified as Japanese American, to lend it ideological coherence and, thus, national recognizability, were understandable, their silence could also serve to prolong the community's precarious position. In the case of d'Aquino, for instance, it allowed the
government's concocted case against a citizen of Japanese ancestry to
go largely unchallenged.

Parts of the Japanese American community went even further to
condemn d'Aquino and, in so doing, perhaps disassociate themselves
from the specter of disloyalty that seemed to follow her despite the facts

of her case. In 1956, some seven years after the trial, when d'Aquino was being released from prison, *Newsweek* printed a letter from Lincoln Yamamoto in which he deemed d'Aquino's conviction a "miscarriage of justice," and stated "we nisei are proud of Mrs. d'Aquino, and we're going to give her a heroine's welcome."[42] Other Nisei readers, however, balked at his reasoning. Yamamoto adopted the resistant pro-Japan stance of those who were so outraged by the government's treatment of their communities that they, in turn, rejected the government. "It's our custom to consider ourselves citizens of Japan, regardless of where we were born," Yamamoto declared, "and our first allegiance is to Japan" (227). The national director of the JACL in San Francisco, among a number of others, wrote in to clarify the official position of the community by declaring with equal force: "Our first and only loyalty is the United States of America" (228). This exchange throws into relief the issues at stake for a population that was still struggling to establish its basis for national inclusion by allaying lingering fears of Japanese American subversion. What was lost in the process, however, was the critique of the unequal terms of national identity embedded in Yamamoto's provocative assertion that, as a Nisei, even so distant a cultural context as Japan represented a far more substantial basis for selfhood than the presumed preeminence of American citizenship, the full entitlements of which had been historically denied to Japanese Americans anyway. But rather than recognize and incorporate the underlying power of Yamamoto's refusal of America, the JACL chose to embrace the only alternative it felt was left to Japanese Americans: to accept the restricted terms of American inclusion in the postwar period in exchange for denying its most progressive political voices or, in d'Aquino's situation, by refusing to confront one of the most challenging postwar cases of injustice against its members.[43]

The terrors of the McCarthy period, following in the wake of the trauma of internment, were nothing if not extremely effective in suppressing the potential for resistance among so many marginalized communities. The charge of "double loyalty" that had been so effective against Jews, beginning during the HUAC hearings and culminating with the execution of the Rosenbergs, seemed to have worked equally well against Japanese Americans in this earlier period. No one dared to touch d'Aquino's case for fear of the repercussions. Yet the government also took a risk that involved invoking the memory of internment, which tended to indict the United States in an era in which it was clearly critical to avoid revelations about racial discrimination and civil rights violations. In the end, d'Aquino's conviction would depend on the containment not only of her narrative within the larger drama of subversion from within but also, as a necessary part of that process, the resituating of her body and its chief instrument of treason: the very pitch and tone of the so-called Tokyo Rose voice, emitted on so many waves of uncertainty in the middle of the vast Pacific.

Voices in the Dark

As yet another example of the complexities underlying d'Aquino's conviction, the postwar invisibility or silence of Japanese Americans did not just aid the public's willingness to believe that Iva Toguri d'Aquino's broadcast messages matched the voice and the intentions of the ultimate American traitor, but that same community silence was also extended through her conviction and the loss of her citizenship rights. In light of the nation's recent appetite for embodied fantasies of fifth-column Japanese American activity over and beyond the often complex realities of Japanese American histories, the jury's rejection of d'Aquino's defense, the rejection of her voice, of her narrative of meaning, is in some measure also the state's rejection of the voices of those Nisei members of the JACL who hoped to empower themselves by tacitly agreeing to the cold war logic that found her guilty by reason of narrative necessity. In effect, the JACL leaders unwittingly conspired to reinforce and indeed affirm the need for the alienated Asian subject as a continuing, "natural" element of American nationalism. But the JACL would perhaps have been better served as the historical "voice" of the Japanese American community by noting the slippage in the state's prosecutorial arguments, arguments that both inaugurated and ex- posed the coming McCarthyism. Although the government prosecu- tors repeatedly insisted that the voice of "Tokyo Rose" was d'Aquino's alone and that the message of that voice was undeniably treasonous, in reality the speaker and her message often avoided clear identification as either. Similarly, d'Aquino's status as a Japanese American en- trapped in a network of complicated wartime circumstances, and not the feared apotheosis of orientalist fantasies, was entirely misrecog- nized by prosecutors and the public alike. The story of a proclaimed "loyal Nisei" enduring the war in Japan was not even intelligible within the narrative conventions of a redeemed postwar Japanese American subjectivity, a narrative promoted by the JACL during the late 1940s and early 1950s that concentrated on the revival of the community around the figure of the patriotic Nisei who vehemently rejected all associations with Japan.

But the misrecognition of any body, literal or narrative, is also critical to enabling the metanarrative that obliterates it, as in the case of containment narratives as Alan Nadel points out. Drawing on Michel de Certeau's theory of the narrativity of history, Nadel describes this process as one in which the "mute body" is the "raw material that enables the production of discourse about it"; the body remains irretrievable, accordingly, because it exists "in a place not just physically but temporally different from the site that produces the discourse."[44] The body of d'Aquino's story, then, remains unsalvageable from the swamps of the trial and its coverage, where the story of a loyal Nisei is shielded, both geographically and historically, from discovery. In its absence, the story of Tokyo Rose blossoms, ensured by the oblivion to which Japanese American experience is consigned. But it was not a simple case of exploiting geopolitical displacement, because the trial transcripts bear the uneasy burden of maintaining the misrecognition of d'Aquino, whose counter-history indeed, in the words of de Certeau, "lets us hear" through a "murmur [the] immensity that seduces and menaces our knowledge."[45]

The problem of identifying Iva Toguri d'Aquino as Tokyo Rose hinged on finding clear-cut evidence matching her image and actions to those of the fabled Japanese propagandist, but from the outset there were considerable obstacles. First, of course, there was d'Aquino's rather plain and naïve demeanor. She had initially been a disappointment to reporters Lee and Brundidge who had hoped to find a more alluring figure to cast in the role of Tokyo Rose. Although the media was subsequently successful in its deft substitution of the public's fantasy of Tokyo Rose for the literal body of d'Aquino—a practice in which it was, at least initially, aided by d'Aquino herself—there remained a second and perhaps more troubling dilemma: d'Aquino's noticeably raspy and unappealing voice. According to Masayo Duus, Charles Cousens, the Australian POW who wrote d'Aquino's broadcasts, described her voice in court as "a gin fog voice" that was "rough, almost masculine, anything but a femininely seductive voice."[46] D'Aquino's voice seemed in obvious contrast to the GIs' reports of a "sweet-toned" feminine voice, enticing them into its seductive web of self-doubt and resignation. When d'Aquino was introduced to the public as Tokyo Rose on September 4, 1945, in a press conference in Yokohama, an Australian reporter remarked that her voice "was nothing like what he had heard in the South Pacific" (29). The director of the army news film concurred, asking d'Aquino during the filming if the voice she was using was in fact her own, because "it certainly does not sound like anything we heard in the South Pacific" (33). The dissonance between d'Aquino's "masculine" voice and the storied femininity of Tokyo Rose's voice would preoccupy prosecutors who tried hard to find GIS who could definitively identify both as the same.

On one level, the ensuing rush to fix d'Aquino's voice as that of To-kyo Rose was simply another means of controlling the cultural particu-lars of her story, particulars that threatened to indict the nation's treat-ment of a professed "loyal citizen." But the focus on her voice in this case, rather than on her physical appearance, is also related to a much broader trend in the popular cultural representation of women. In *The Acoustic Mirror: The Female Voice in Psychoanalysis and Cinema*, Kaja Silverman builds on cinematic criticism about the synchronization of sound and image in early-twentieth-century motion pictures to argue that women's voices in early films quickly became subordinated to their bodies in a manner that increasingly deprived them of an impor-tant measure of autonomy as speaking subjects.[47] This attempt to re-duce women's representation to the physical at the expense of verbal articulation was conditioned, according to Silverman, by the need to secure the primacy of the male spectator, for whom the female figure acts as "an acoustic mirror" that is "thick with body" when she speaks (61). In an analysis of this effect in Alfred Hitchcock's films from the 1950s, Robert Corber expands the terms of Silverman's argument by pointing out that "the conventions governing the representation of the female voice in classical Hollywood cinema can also be explained his-torically."[48] Corber links the subordination of female voices to early twentieth-century efforts to contain the threat of the New Woman and her disruption of "the gender-specific division of labor" (119). How-ever, what Corber does not address is how this initial, historically spe-cific need to contain the female as a speaking subject continues to be modified by subsequent changes in the social positioning and cultural perceptions of women, suggesting the need for greater critical atten-tion to the danger of theoretically (and falsely) fixing the terms of "gender-specificity."

In many ways during the late 1940s the gender anxieties rampant in U.S. culture seem relatively obvious and certainly familiar; women's wartime years working in traditionally male-defined jobs had provoked a fear, not unlike the fear of the New Woman, that traditional gender economies had been irreparably disturbed. Certainly this was true of the need to fix and thereby manage or control the voice of Iva Toguri d'Aquino. Furthermore, her silencing was at least equally motivated by the demands of asserting U.S. control of Japan, as the discussion has previously noted. But the need to establish patriarchal control over d'Aquino's voice as a substitute for that of Japan's was not yet fully conceived as a "marriage" or partnership, as it would be shortly. Instead, in early 1949 the U.S. presence in Japan was still committed to MacArthur's early proscription against fraternization between GIS and Japanese women because it considered the possibility of such relationships unseemly for conquerors. According to Yukiko Koshiro, "Americans were increasingly annoyed at Japanese willingness to fraternize with their troops. The Japanese were seen as presumptuous, like servants presuming friendship with their masters."[49] MacArthur went so far as to guarantee that divisions would be maintained because "the general aloofness of the American soldier, based upon his innate self-respect, is one of the most noticeable characteristics of the occupation."[50] But in time his assurances would give way to occupation policies that depended on physical segregation to try to prevent the growing incidence of fraternization between Japanese women and the less than aloof American soldier. By late 1948, U.S. occupying forces had been so embattled by criticism resulting from increases not only in fraternization but also in the number of GI marriages to Japanese women that the occupation army faced something of a crisis. How could it continue to assert its power over the Japanese nation by appealing to patriarchal forms without allowing the presumption of patriarchal, male privilege to become synonymous with interracial sexual relationships involving GIS? As the cold war with the Soviet Union heated up, the embarrassment of fraternization was viewed as an obstacle to the achievement of the nation's postwar objectives.[51] Thus, once again, d'Aquino's case was playing itself out within a moment of political and cultural uncertainty that involved the complex interworkings of gender, racial, and national anxieties about the postwar order.

When the State Department eventually issued a call for GIS who felt they could identify Tokyo Rose's voice to come forward, they indeed found men who adamantly believed that d'Aquino's voice was that of Tokyo Rose. Among the group was naval officer Marshall Hoot, who testified that he knew all along it was a Japanese American voice he was hearing. His testimony as an American soldier was devastating; it not only indicted d'Aquino as a Japanese propagandist but also delivered what seemed like critical evidence that she had consciously used her "American" status to make her broadcasts more damaging to Allied morale. "Nobody but someone raised in America could have picked out the records that appealed to the boys," Hoot stated, "I don't think a Jap from Japan could have done it. We had her pegged in as being American by her style. Intelligence also, they knew."[52] According to Masayo Duus, prosecutors were also inadvertently helped by testimony that Cousens had worked at NHK to train d'Aquino to speak differently, "to speak slowly and cheerfully," or "as though she were in the midst of a group of GIs kidding with them."[53] The testimony of former GIs was hard to dismiss or discount in 1949, and the added stipulation that Cousens had indeed seemed to manipulate d'Aquino's voice to suit his scripts explained the discrepancy between d'Aquino's "natural" voice and her radio persona, but the patriarchal control of her voice that his management indicated did virtually nothing to succor prosecutors' fears. Given the scandals besetting the occupation in Japan, the working relationship between Cousens and d'Aquino instead stirred up the then heightened resentment of Japanese presumptions of equality with Americans and the potentially subversive outcome of any friendly relations with the Japanese, especially one between an Allied soldier and a Japanese woman. Cousens's full testimony reveals that the reasons for changing d'Aquino's voice were more complicated than many understood, just as the issue of d'Aquino's sympathies and intentions as a Nisei working in wartime Japan were also more difficult to discern, given the international political stakes in Japan. But few were willing or able to grasp the nuances of their relationship or the complicated purposes of their recorded broadcasts.

Neither d'Aquino nor Cousens ever denied that they had complied with the Japanese military's demand that they make broadcasts, but they also testified that the message they had tried to send, and the means of that message, was meant to be subversive to the Japanese cause. According to Russell Warren Howe, special agent Charles Hettrick, a CIC investigator who had initially interviewed Cousens and a few other POWs who had worked with d'Aquino at NHK, testified that

Cousens and his comrades had actually selected d'Aquino for the job of a radio disc jockey "because her voice would sabotage the program."[54] When Cousens had endured charges of treason himself in July 1946, he was summarily exonerated and all charges dismissed when he explained the complicated machinations of the POWs to avoid helping the enemy. These Allied machinations clearly involved d'Aquino's full and active participation. According to reports: "Cousens suggested that Toguri [d'Aquino] should take part in broadcasts to U.S. troops in the Pacific, mainly because of her extraordinarily rough voice and blunt manner. Her voice came through the microphone as he hoped it would, and he knew that if he could get away with it he would have an opportunity of presenting a comical program."[55] In short, the efforts to manipulate d'Aquino's voice, and the impression Cousens tried to give while at NHK of encouraging d'Aquino to be more charming and feminine, were part of an elaborate ruse designed to placate Japanese officials *and* circumvent the effectiveness of the propaganda that Cousens was forced to write. According to Howe's study, rather than coaching d'Aquino to be more alluring Cousens was in fact trying to achieve "a voice that sounded like a woman army officer *ordering* her troops to be cheerful."[56] Far from working with the enemy, Cousens and d'Aquino were actively and consciously working to undermine the intentions of the Japanese officials, and to save their lives and the lives of other POWs in the process. Or, as Cousens himself is purported to have told d'Aquino: "All you've got to do is look upon yourself as a soldier under my orders. Do exactly what you're told. . . . You'll do nothing against your own people. I will guarantee that personally, because it's my script" (46).

The defense had badly misjudged the tensions of the day by believing that Cousens's testimony would be reassuring to the jury or to government prosecutors. All it did was exacerbate already sensitive cultural and political issues because it cast d'Aquino as an equal in the Allied war effort to defeat Japan, as simply another "soldier under my orders." In the face of this revelation, the fact that the broadcasts were, in fact, Cousens's words ("it's my script") was less convincing. His testimony only irritated discomfort with the way in which anticommunist campaigns in Hollywood seemed to be revealing the indeterminate and unstable nature of language and representation. The recognition that cultural images and voices were easily manipulated threatened to undo the security of not just male or physical bodies but, even more than this, of the discursive forms that helped to produce them.

It did not matter that Cousens's testimony was supported by a slew of other defense witnesses. According to Captain Wallace Ince, a POW who became acquainted with d'Aquino at NHK and to whom she often slipped extra rations, all those involved with the broadcasts understood that "it was quite easy to rephrase and condense the news in such a way that it told just the opposite story of the same broadcasts, or to set off by phrases the army communiqués, so that anyone listening in would know it was a fake from beginning to end" (170–71). In d'Aquino's case this often meant presenting an ironic parody of the Western image of a dragon lady weaving her web of propaganda. Following Cousens's suggestion, d'Aquino often addressed the GIs as "honorable bone-heads," but dropped the "r" in order to caricature the stereotyped accent of a Japanese announcer. "The tone," according to Masayo Duus, "was self-mockery."[57] Rex Gunn, an AP reporter who had heard Orphan Annie's broadcasts while on Saipan, described them in similar terms to another reporter: "She was the complete lampoon of the oriental seductress. . . . She would say, " 'Beware, this is vicious propaganda. I'm going to sneak up on you GIs with my nail file and murder a whole battalion.' "[58] The government's case against d'Aquino, however, ignored the function of sarcasm and parody in her broadcasts, preferring to write it as yet another familiar attempt at oriental obfuscation and pointing to her signed contract with Brundidge and Lee and her willingness to make the military news films as Tokyo Rose. The hint of disloyalty, particularly where an American of Japanese descent was concerned, was enough to overwhelm the corroborated, extenuating circumstances that had, in the case of Cousens, been enough to dismiss all charges. The prosecution's and the public's rejection of the defense's presentation of d'Aquino, however, ultimately reflected the early cold war attempts to limit discursive ambivalence by resorting to narratives of containment: the image of the treacherous and inscrutable oriental femme fatale was not merely familiar, it also necessitated the urgent exertion of U.S. paternal retribution to set right the upended order of things.

The prosecution's case blindly and successfully insisted that someone *must be* Tokyo Rose. Although the legal case against d'Aquino never cited her as Tokyo Rose, the trial of Iva Toguri d'Aquino continues to be called the trial of Tokyo Rose, as most newspaper accounts promoted it and as the Justice Department initially announced it. But in another shift in perception, among the many that obscure the d'Aquino story and conviction and, with it, the status of Japanese

American women in the postwar years, the Justice Department, which initially pursued her because she was Tokyo Rose, soon backed off its original belief that d'Aquino was Tokyo Rose when the facts of the case emerged as clear roadblocks to such a charge. In addition to the fact that Tokyo Rose was always acknowledged to be several women rather than one single voice, there were the conflicting reports and memories of many of the GI witnesses of the Tokyo Rose broadcasts. Thus, although both then and now *stories* remember it as "the trial of Tokyo Rose," in fact it was, at least legally, a case of treason by a woman who could not have been Tokyo Rose.

What is more, d'Aquino was almost certainly not one of the many anonymous voices heard and identified as parts of the myth of Tokyo Rose. Records indicate that she was probably one of the clearly sympathetic voices countless GIs remembered as enlivening their South Pacific nights. D'Aquino always identified herself first as Ann, short for "announcer," on NHK, and later, at Cousens's request, as Orphan Annie. The latter name was suggested as a clever moniker that picked up on d'Aquino's habit of opening her broadcasts with the greeting "Hello, you orphans of the Pacific!" It also subtly suggested a potential alliance between the speaker and her audience, a fact completely overlooked by *both* the defense and the prosecution during the trial. This implied alliance might account for the affection held by many GIs for the myriad of female voices they heard, believing that at least some of them were comical and sympathetic. In fact, it was the obvious and successful satire of d'Aquino's broadcasts that had initially interested the late Broadway producer Earl Carroll, who claimed at least to understand the rich theatrical possibilities of d'Aquino's and the POWs' subversive participation with the Japanese. Despite the fact that the Justice Department was aware of the inaccuracy, they never corrected the press's consistent references to the trial as "the trial of Tokyo Rose," perhaps preferring the simple term "spy thriller" to overtake completely the complexities of the case.

Iva Toguri d'Aquino was not a spy and was not guilty of treason, although the U.S. government punished her for both crimes even as they admitted these crimes had been committed by a phantom propagandist who never existed. In addition, d'Aquino's message as an American loyal to the Allied cause and her satire of oriental femininity using the persona of Orphan Annie were clearly detailed during the trial. Yet by grounding the myriad and "mysterious" radio voices heard by GIs in even so imaginary a figure as Tokyo Rose, and in turn finding this fantasy of oriental femininity convincingly embodied in d'Aquino's body and voice, the disturbing and untranslatable ordeal of a female Nisei "soldier" in the war was overwhelmed. In the words of Russell Warren Howe, the only coherent function for d'Aquino given "the widening circle of ignorance and hysteria surrounding the case" was for "the little typist to become a dragon lady."[59] Where no treacherous oriental influence was found, one was concocted in the most lurid terms available during the period, even in the face of conflicting testimony and the fact of d'Aquino's American sympathies and status. When chief prosecutor Tom De Wolfe delivered his closing remarks, his rhetoric demonstrated the cold war propensity for ignoring the documented and unique circumstances of d'Aquino's wartime life when he pronounced her "a female Nipponese turncoat and a female Benedict Arnold" (132). Yet, in Masayo Duus's view, d'Aquino's fate more accurately looms as a symbol of "the tragedy of being a Nisei" during and after the war against Japan.[60] D'Aquino's prosecution dramatized the trauma of subjectivity that beset many other Japanese Americans during the war who also found they had become, even if merely in psychological terms, stateless persons in a postwar saturated by bitter ironies and facing a government's blatant disregard for and ignorance of what had always been the geopolitical and gendered complexities of Japanese American women's experiences. Caught between her embodiment as, alternately, alien menace and opportunistic woman, d'Aquino's message, in effect her counter-history, continues to be relegated to historical obscurity.

The record shows that she was finally convicted of treason for allegedly broadcasting the following: "Orphans of the Pacific, you are really orphans now! How will you get home now that your ships are sunk?" (Duus 223). Today, this message, at once so ominous and yet, as the circumstances of the war prove, so innocuous, seems sadly to arraign the nation's rejection of an ethnic and immigrant community in distress, as well as its continuing failure to understand the critical and purposefully deployed ambivalence at the heart of Iva Toguri d'Aquino's broadcasts. In hindsight, d'Aquino's case may now speak to us through the dull static of national and political anxieties during the postwar years and the containment strategies that obscured her identity. Perhaps it tells us that the ambivalence in the cultural discourse on d'Aquino as Tokyo Rose reflected the lingering dilemma of Japanese

Americans' public perception in the cold war years, as they remained a haunting, if unidentifiable, threat to the notion of the United States as a democratic nation. In the years leading up to rampant anticommunism, forces were still devising the means of ferreting out this threat, and thus the object of inquiry often evaded historical recognition, caught in the intersections between fact and fiction, certainty and oblivion.

FOUR

"A Mutual Brokenness": The Hiroshima

Maidens Project, Japanese Americans, and

American Motherhood

There are many ways to frame the postwar memory of the internment, but few fictional accounts can rival the imagistic power of Joy Kogawa's 1982 novel *Obasan*.[1] In Kogawa's narrative the history of North American internment of Japanese immigrant communities is primarily revitalized by placing that seemingly limited domestic tragedy within the context of the atomic bombing of Japan, a move that asks the reader to imagine a plane of tragedy beyond the national, beyond the ideological. On the surface, of course, *Obasan* narrates the story of Naomi "Nomi" Nakane, a young Nisei girl whose family endures the relocation ordeal in British Columbia, Canada, only to discover that they are irrevocably broken and divided after the war ends. Nomi is molested by a trusted white neighbor, her father suffers from poor medical care and eventually dies, and her brother Stephen experiences a chronic leg injury, growing daily more bitter and withdrawn. After the war, Nomi becomes a teacher and Stephen an accomplished musician. He is written up in the local papers as "a young man with a future" (257), although in truth he has learned to hate and deny his Japanese heritage. Notwithstanding the profound grief that marks the Nakanes's lives after relocation, their shared tragedies are finally overshadowed by the enduring mystery at the heart of the novel: the unknown fate of Nomi's revered mother, a symbol of the family's prewar domestic bliss, who is caught visiting relatives in Japan when the war begins and is later presumed dead. The circumstances of the mother's death are shrouded in secrecy for years, until Nomi's obasan, or aunt, finally produces a letter from Japan that recounts the mother's ordeal at Nagasaki on August 9, 1945, a victim, along with Nomi's grandmother, of the U.S. bombing of that city. The revelation provides an obvious end to Nomi's search for the truth about her mother, and makes it possible for her to begin to recover from the pain of the war.

But the invocation of the atomic bombing of Japan in a story about Japanese Canadian relocation also suggests something much more compelling about Japanese Canadian and, by implication, Japanese American wartime history's function as a counter-history. The conclusion of Joy Kogawa's novel propels that history into new territory by exceeding the conventional boundaries of Canadian history, both geographically and ideologically, and by asking the reader to consider the connection between the horrific effects of the atomic bomb in a Japanese city and the less obvious damage of relocation for Japanese bodies in North America.

The horror of the victims of the atomic bombings becomes a corollary for the plight of Japanese Canadians, who were, after all, treated as if they were the enemy. When victory comes for the Allied forces, it is overwhelmed by a sense of defeat for all the Nakanes. They find themselves publicly shamed, stripped of their property, and forbidden even to return to their old neighborhood for years. Lamenting her mother's forced separation from her adopted country Canada, and indirectly encompassing the experience of the Japanese Canadian community, Nomi laments, "by the time this country opened its pale arms to you, it was too late. First, you could not, then chose not to come" (290). She wonders how often "did Grandma and Mother waken in those years with the unthinkable memories alive in their mind, the visible evidence of horror written on their skin, in their blood, carved in every mirror they passed, felt in every step they took?" (281). "That this world is brokenness" (287) seems to be the novel's resigned philosophical conclusion as well as the primary link between the two catastrophes of war. But *Obasan*'s final pages also resonate with the force of Nomi's identification with Japan's devastation after the bombing, as Joy Kogawa turns the stigma of Japanese identity into a potentially subversive transnational taxonomy of suffering.

As we look back through the lens of Kogawa's poignant reconstruction of Japanese Canadian relocation, what are we to make of the provocative suggestion of a relationship between the atomic bombing of Japan and the devastation of Japanese communities in North America? If the relationship were limited to Kogawa's novel then we might reasonably dismiss it as history reshaped through the distorting kaleidoscope of literary imagination. But the record of postwar America's attempts to come to terms with the destruction of the atomic bombings actually lends historical valence to Kogawa's fictional speculation that a mutual "brokenness" continued to link all those bodies marked as "Japanese," both over here *and* over there. This quality of "brokenness" was especially associated with Japanese women's bodies, as proven by the history of American efforts to correct the "brokenness" of those bodies.

As news of the horrific effects of the atomic bombings began to filter back through the American press, some liberals in the United States felt compelled to reach out to the victims of the bomb (often called Hibakusha, or "bomb-affected persons") in an attempt to assuage the widespread anxiety that the atomic bomb provoked in America. Thus was born the Hiroshima Maidens Project, which in 1955 raised enough funds to bring some twenty-five young Japanese women disfigured in the bombing to the United States for corrective plastic surgery in the hope that such an act would, quite literally, help to heal the wounds of the war. Under the auspices of Japanese peace activist Reverend Kiyoshi Tanimoto and the influential liberal editor of the *Saturday Review*, Norman Cousins, the Hiroshima Maidens Project ushered in a remarkable if brief period of postwar atonement and reconciliation between the United States and Japan, as ordinary American citizens donated money and volunteered to board and assist the young women as they recovered from their operations. These volunteers were often deemed "adoptive families," because the first appeals for donations in the *Saturday Review* were under the banner of the Moral Adoption Plan, which implied that as victors in the war Americans should adopt moral responsibility for those less fortunate. When the Reverend Tanimoto appeared on Ralph Edwards's *This Is Your Life* in 1955, Edwards appealed to Americans to be generous, "for this is the American way."[2] The media paid particular attention to the benevolence demonstrated by the older white American women who took in the unknown young Japanese women, as the Hiroshima Maidens Project blossomed into a concerted attempt to salvage the scarred femininity of the Japanese bomb victims. These American "mothers" became the conduits of feminine salvation for the Hiroshima Maidens, as indeed American domesticity in general became the site of their transformation from girls who were physically and psychologically damaged by the war into confident and attractive women. In the story of the Hiroshima Maidens Project, the white American mother and the idealized American home she produced were portrayed as the solutions both to the problem of damaged femininity and to the lingering ethical doubts about American democracy caused by the devastating effects of the atomic bombings.

But American motherhood and domesticity were not without their own problems in the 1950s. The end of the war in 1945 had revived the debate about the perils of the domineering mother and wife, as conservative forces tried to ensure that wartime women workers would return to their homes and relinquish their positions to white men. Statistics now show that women in general continued to work outside the home in large numbers, complicating the collective memory of the 1950s as a period when the single-paycheck nuclear family reigned.[3] The disjunction between the ideal of the fifties American family and the frequent pressures of family life extended and, in some cases, exacerbated the anxiety of the late 1940s concerning the nature of women's functions and domestic family life. The Hiroshima Maidens Project momentarily allayed these anxieties by casting the white American mother and her home as the site of regeneration for the worst catastrophe of the war, the atomic bomb. In addition, the project succeeded in affirming the idea of American dominance through the celebration of the white American homemaker, who represented a way of life that distinguished America as a land of privilege and progress, safe from the pressures and problems of the outside world.

However, there was one problem in this success story of redeeming American womanhood and domestic bliss that could not so easily be resolved. Although a majority of the so-called American mommies were white, two very influential figures in the project were Japanese American, and their presence as "American mothers" disturbed the promotion of American domesticity as the private world of self-fulfilled individuals, safe from public intrusion. Helen Yokoyama and Mary Kochiyama, both Nisei and born, raised, and educated in California, were by all accounts pivotal to the smooth operation and management of the Maidens Project, and Kochiyama continues to be a source of information for historians. Still, their presence in the project is repeatedly overlooked in contemporary accounts of the Hiroshima Maidens Project in favor of focusing on the interracial networks of white "mothers" and Japanese "daughters" that grew out of the project. The meaning and impact of these other Japanese American "mothers" have remained difficult to parse against the conventional portrait of postwar America as a nation of white suburban subjects and thriving middle-class nuclear families coming to bond with Japanese female victims. Yet Japanese Americans like Yokoyama and Kochiyama remain factors in the making of postwar history in America despite the penchant for ignoring the terms and the challenges of their participation as Americans whose private lives had been recently shattered by public and political pressures.

Perhaps what the atomic destruction of Hiroshima and Nagasaki and the internment of Japanese Americans share is that they both, in the words of Marita Sturken, "disrupt the compelling narrative of the United States as the triumphant country of World War II."[4] But although both the atomic bombing and the internment may have frequently threatened to disturb the image of the United States as an ideal democracy, the two events had very different functions and effects in the unfolding story of the Hiroshima Maidens in America. The story of disfigured young Japanese women willingly rehabilitated by white American families did much both to ameliorate Americans' guilt about the use of the bomb and to enshrine further the 1950s American home as a model of comfort and security available to all. In contrast, the history of Japanese American internment and its lingering postwar effects could serve no such purpose. It was not possible to address the abuse of Japanese Americans, as Americans had addressed the damage done by the bomb, without admitting, on some fundamental level, the abandonment of democratic processes during the war and, more important, the subsequent widespread destruction of the prewar American homes and families created by those in the camps. The enforced separation and division of family life for Japanese Americans, a condition that continued into the 1950s in some cases, contradicted the suburban bliss reportedly experienced by the young bomb victims recovering in East Coast homes.

If public discourse was able to turn the fallout from the atomic bomb to redeeming national service with the promotion of the Hiroshima Maidens Project, it was clearly not so successful with regard to the story of Japanese American recovery from the internment, which continued to challenge the image of an affluent and cohesive American domesticity. As a result, the story of the Japanese American involvement with the project was suppressed, and to a large degree Japanese American experience continues to be suppressed in postwar histories written today. However, renewed critical attention to the meaning of the presence of Japanese American "mothers" in the Hiroshima Maidens Project may finally begin to complicate our portrait of the cold war era and the furor over the atomic bomb that was so characteristic of that era. The American faith in its democracy as the site of international goodwill and postwar healing is contradicted by the domestic histories of Japanese Americans. Including the participation of Japanese Americans such as Helen Yokoyama and, especially, Mary Kochiyama in the narrative of the Hiroshima Maidens Project reveals much more than the mutual "brokenness" of Japanese bodies after the war. Japanese American postwar history highlights the inconsistencies of domestic ideology in the postwar period as well as the postwar dependence on maintaining the illusory boundary between the private and the public. This boundary had already given way for Japanese Americans, whose private lives had long ago been officially surrendered to national scrutiny and socioeconomic upheaval. During the height of the fifties domestic ideal, Japanese Americans' struggles to remake families and homes offered a radically different perspective on the promise of postwar democracy.

Selling the Story of the Hiroshima Maidens Project:
The Making of "a Personal Event"

In his book *The Hiroshima Maidens*, Rodney Barker provides the most comprehensive story of the 1955 project to bring young female victims of the bombing of Hiroshima to the United States for medical care.[5] Although his interest in the Hiroshima Maidens Project is personal— his Quaker family boarded two of the young Japanese women when he was nine years old—his book maintains a journalist's objective tone and narrative framework, offering a straightforward account of the project's inception, duration, and effects. Yet, like most other accounts of the project, Barker's story cannot avoid comprehending the Hiroshima Maidens Project as a story about love and compassion, a supreme example of the potential for sacrifice and generosity across cultural and racial lines. Barker's story begins with the selfless acts of

Reverend Kiyoshi Tanimoto, the Japanese clergyman from Hiroshima who was famous to Americans as one of the chief figures in John Hersey's best-selling book *Hiroshima*, the brave young Methodist minister who is depicted carrying victims on his back through the burning rubble and firestorms with no thought of his own safety. Tanimoto had devoted much of his life after 1945 to educating people about the bomb's effects, although he had escaped virtually unscathed. The plight of the victims "woke such a deep sorrow in him," according to Barker, because "he was ashamed that he had no such cross to bear, and he wanted to do all in his power to help" (56). Tanimoto's subsequent speaking tour of the United States attracted the attention of a number of charitable groups and church organizations dedicated to peace, and it gave him the idea of setting up the Hiroshima Peace Center Foundation to address the physical damage wrought by the bomb and to "explore the ways of peace" (56). Through Tanimoto's initiative, the transnational effort to assist the victims of the atomic bombings was founded as a philanthropic venture appealing to the purest motives of humankind: compassion and generosity.

Tanimoto was particularly interested in assisting "innocent victims of the bombing—the orphaned children, the widowed women" (57). In many ways, the eventual success of the project depended on Tanimoto's initial strategy of selecting only those sorts of victims who could arouse the sympathies of Americans in particular without posing an overt political or ideological threat. Young women of marrying age soon became the focal point of Tanimoto's efforts, and his choice was instrumental in securing the commitments of American intellectuals. Along with John Hersey and Pearl Buck, Norman Cousins was among the first Americans to offer substantial assistance by exhorting the readers of the *Saturday Review* to make donations to help Japan's "atomic orphans" and by assuming the chair of the board of directors of the Hiroshima Peace Center Foundation in 1949 (57–58). As it became clear that the medical facilities of Japan could not accommodate many of the victims' injuries, in 1953 Tanimoto began to enlist Cousins's help in organizing a medical mission to the United States for a selected group of young women who had been dubbed the "Atomic Bomb Maidens" in the Japanese press, "an image of horror defiling innocence" (60). Cousins was so impressed by his first encounter with the fifteen badly disfigured young girls, ranging in age from sixteen to twenty-one, "hands folded primly in their laps," that he eventually arranged for the group's "transportation, hospitalization, surgery and home care free of charge" (65). He also arranged for them to appear in a television tribute to Tanimoto on Ralph Edwards's *This Is Your Life* to set up his appeal for viewer donations to cover their other expenses. Throughout the months of fundraising, both Cousins and Tanimoto promoted the Hiroshima Maidens Project as a campaign to rehabilitate the innocent victims of war in return for having the girls "become symbols to the entire nation of Japan of American generosity and enduring friendship" (73). Calling it "The Moral Adoption Plan," Cousins encouraged his readers to see their participation as a selfless, missionary-like effort. Despite this humanitarian appeal, Cousins and the other organizers were not above reminding a skeptical State Department that "if his [Tanimoto's] group was not allowed to do something for these poor girls, the Russians might get to them first" (74).

The suggestion that "the Russians might get to them first" was an example of the not so subtle politicking that often lay behind descriptions of the project as purely an altruistic gesture that was lacking in political meaning and effects. In fact, the initial skepticism from the State Department, which wondered if the women's visit might be construed as an admission of national guilt or responsibility, may have increased Cousins's efforts "to keep the project a personal event" (98). Cousins and Tanimoto hoped to overcome these political fears by casting the young women as the innocent representatives of Japanese damage from the atomic bomb, and, even more important, by the repeated suggestion that the project's ultimate goal was to heal the scarring of their femininity by rendering the disfigured young women more marriageable. Cousins's aim was in some respects impossible: to depoliticize an event already rife with political overtones. In fact, the visit of the Hiroshima maidens was so laden with the potential for controversy —if the operations should fail, or if the girls should attempt to criticize their American hosts, for instance—that senior State Department officials unsuccessfully tried to ground the mission minutes before the plane bearing the maidens and their entourage took off from the American Air Force Base at Iwakuni, Japan, on May 5, 1955. Once the project was underway, however, every effort was made to promote the women's visit as the "personal event" Cousins envisioned by proclaiming the theme of damaged Japanese femininity in need of American aid and support.

In "The Maidens Are Coming," the first editorial that appeared in the *Saturday Review* after the women left Japan, Cousins describes the maidens as women who "had reached marrrying age" but who, because of their scars, "had withdrawn almost totally from community life."[6] Their singular form of escape was a weekly trip to the movies, where the young women "like to see the pretty American girls and imagine that we are they" (12). Before the Hiroshima Maidens had even touched down on American soil, their function as young Japanese women desirous of an American brand of femininity was already being established. Cousins's editorial reports on the maidens' progress repeatedly imagined their visit as an interlude of personal rehabilitation and emotional training, whereby they would be rendered better young women by becoming more like "the pretty American girls." The focus on the feminine recovery and domestic longing of the young women avoided at least one obvious contradiction in the organizers' appeals to Americans, namely the sense of guilt or responsibility that must have lay behind the appeal of "Moral Adoptions" in the first place. The attention to containing the story of the Hiroshima Maidens Project as "a personal event" about the healing power of American femininity also limited any consideration of the broader uneasiness about women's changing "nature."

As feminist historians of the period have long pointed out, despite the long-held view of the fifties as a time of domestic conformity and maternal productivity, widespread public anxieties about the security of both concepts repeatedly surfaced, with the mother figure often the focal point of cultural concerns. Although the practice of scapegoating mothers was not new, its increased popularity in the late 1940s and early 1950s America was clearly the result of then current ideological crises about the domestic stability of presumed traditional heterosexual gender roles.[7] Elaine Tyler May, for instance, points to the necessary reconversion of the returning soldier as a force that initially precipitated fears about the willingness of women, particularly white women, to return to the home in the late 1940s.[8] The subsequent recognition that, by and large, women were not returning to the home but continued to work only added to the fears.

The rising popularity of psychoanalytic interpretations of sexual identity and development in the late 1940s resulted in the reemergence of fears of "the dangerous mother" who ruined her children by trying to run their lives. Philip Wylie coined the term "momism" to describe this phenomenon in his 1942 book *A Generation of Vipers*, and he was also instrumental in drawing on the Freudian focus on the male child to designate "momism" a particular threat to sons and, by implication, to national masculinity.[9] After the war, Wylie's thesis experienced a rapid revival as it fed on apprehension about the process of the white male soldier's reconversion. It was soon followed and supported by the work of popular psychoanalysts such as Helene Deutsch, Edward Strecker, and Ferdinand Lundberg and Marynia Farnham, each of whom promoted the idea that the nation faced a potential disaster if women and the domestic spaces they were presumed to rule continued to be affected by a rapidly modernizing culture. The fear of the modern woman was, of course, not new, having first emerged in the early 1900s in response to the rise of the so-called New Woman or career woman. Writers such as Thorstein Veblen, Charlotte Perkins Gilman, Henry James, Theodore Dreiser, and Edith Wharton had confronted the issue in their works mainly as an effect of the consolidation of industrial and consumer capitalism, which were perceived as threatening the boundary between public and private and, along with it, gender roles.[10] And surely the advent of an industrial, capitalist economy irrevocably altered the relationship of women and men to their gender roles, as increasingly they came to rely on popular cultural ideals to construct their identities as gendered citizens. In the postwar era, the opening up of the nation to the rebuilding of Europe and Asia similarly altered concepts of gendered citizenship, as these concepts became linked to issues of international relations and national security. Thus, while the dread over the condition of the modern American woman seems to cast it as an exclusively national problem, suffusing the twentieth century and chiefly impacting women's private lives, in fact, the problem in the postwar period was neither exclusively national nor privately female in scope.

In many ways, normative heterosexual gender roles provided the central framework for comprehending international relations during the entire twentieth century, particularly, as several critics have pointed out, the relationship between east and west.[11] Thus, reemphasizing the naturalness of the heterosexual relationship between men and women, whether living in the nation or beyond, became an indispensable ideological tool for promoting the logic of U.S. masculinized domination of the feminized east. As David Palumbo-Liu notes, "America's 'modernization' called for its penetration into the Pacific region" as part of "a particular strategy of expansion and 'development,' " such that "managing the modern was inseparable from managing Asian America."[12] However, by the mid-fifties, with the cold war in force and with the Korean War having ended in a standoff with Chinese-backed North Korean Communists, it became vital to promote, unrelentingly, the critical importance of democratic expansion to America's security, rather than merely to its development as a modern power. The need to reinforce the myth of American exceptionalism was critical to sustaining the assumption of the naturalness and desirability of American dominance. The proof of America's right to a unique preeminence in the world of charged international relations was often found in the portrayal of a pure and protected American domesticity, guarded by the nurturing maternal forces that were presumed to flower there.

The Hiroshima Maidens Project, which State Department officials tried to ground in 1955, eventually evolved into a wildly successful celebration of just such an America. Despite the fact that the maidens were the victims of an American bombing that devastated their homes, their story of war and struggle was quickly turned into an illustration of American benevolence and of the renaissance of Japanese domesticity. On a deeper level, and one less obvious in narratives of the Hiroshima Maidens Project, the philanthropy of the West was also driven by the profound need to recharge ideals of American femininity and domesticity. In 1959, at the opening of the American National Exhibition in Moscow, Vice President Richard Nixon would draw Nikita Khrushchev into a debate about the relative merits of democracy over communism by comparing and contrasting the modernization of the domestic lives of their respective citizens. His argument, which rested on the assumption that American housewives' greater access to modern gadgets must logically give the nation an edge over the USSR, was dubbed "the kitchen debate" in recognition of the primacy of ideals of middle-class domesticity to cold war politics.[13] In the interest of rehabilitating the damaged domestic potential of the young Japanese female victims in their charge, white American women, and the domestic realm they symbolized, could be reaffirmed as exemplary, not merely to testify to American humanitarianism but on a much deeper level that anticipates Nixon's legendary statement to ensure U.S. supremacy in the cold war with communism. The middle-class American home became the logical site for the regeneration of the feminine capabilities of war-damaged Japanese women. The suppression of the role of Japanese

American women became almost inevitable, as the Hiroshima Maidens Project appeared to work best as a media event that celebrated white, middle-class American mothers.

Healing Mothers, Healing the Nation

Although the women seemingly most in need of regeneration were clearly the young Japanese bomb victims, the underlying and perhaps deeper success of the project was its almost immediate effectiveness in at least temporarily reviving American femininity as a healing rather than a menacing force. Just as he had initially emphasized the desire of the young women to be like "American girls" in his April 1955 report before the Hiroshima Maidens arrived, Norman Cousins continued to highlight the women's positive development toward an American girlhood. His periodic reports on the progress of the project in the *Saturday Review* became both a means of keeping the readers who had supported the venture informed of its success as well as a direct way to ensure that the project was perceived in the popular press as an unquestionable success. In his second report, published on October 15, 1955, Cousins informs his readers that "the girls" were settling in nicely with the Quaker families who had offered to board them at Pendle Hill, a Quaker retreat near Philadelphia, before their scheduled operations.[14] Despite the expected problems of homesickness and differences in food, Cousins depicts the relationships between the women and their assigned families as an immediate bond. "The first week," according to a Wilton, Pennsylvania, Quaker man who volunteered his home, "was too good to be true. The second week was even better. Here it is six weeks and not a single one of the dreadful calamities that had been predicted has come to pass. . . . 'Guests' isn't really the word for it. They're really members of the family" (22). Cousins emphasizes that the patron families were really the American "parents" of the Hiroshima Maidens, and he describes at length the manner in which "the girls have adjusted beautifully to their new 'parents,' towards whom they showed equal devotion" (22). The subsequent decision to "rotate" the women to other interested families in the New England area after their operations was met with resistance on the part of the maidens and the Quaker families alike, some of whom jokingly threatened "to keep the front door locked" if anyone came to take "our girls" away (22).

But what the maidens learned at Pendle Hill had apparently prepared them for contact with other suburban American households by instilling in them an appreciation for the American household as sanctuary. According to the Quaker respondents, although "the girls" had expected to find an American household predominated by "American materialism and gadgets" they discovered instead that "there is much more than this to America" (23). Cousins concluded that the success of the Pendle Hill period was that the girls quickly learned to "share in the family pleasures" (23). The *New York Daily Mirror* reiterated this optimistic view of life in American homes when it published a series of human-interest stories on the Hiroshima Maidens in early 1956.[15] "Living in America has been like a dream," according to Michiyo Zomen, the first woman interviewed by the paper, because "I've learned the American way of running a house."[16] The *New York Journal-American* reported that at least a part of this "way of running a house" involved the greater egalitarianism between the sexes in homes, such that "American men wash dishes, help women around the house, and are otherwise available to run errands" (Naeve 104). The women apparently "liked the change" they encountered in the New England suburbs, as well as liking the American women who were the living embodiments of "an American house" (Naeve 104), and who quickly became the chief players in the drama of the Hiroshima Maidens' feminine recovery.

But conspicuously absent in the media reports on the Hiroshima Maidens Project was the central part played by both Helen Yokoyama and Mary Kochiyama as the women's Japanese American mothers and, in the case of Kochiyama, as their primary link to Japanese American communities. Of course, the growing focus on American maternal influences was, in many ways, simply an extension of Cousins's initial narrative of Quaker "parents" and their Japanese "girls." But the growing visibility of white women as American "mothers" to the project also reshaped the first impression of the Hiroshima Maidens' relationship to American benevolence. The protectors of the women had previously been the legendary "fathers" of the project, Tanimoto and Cousins, but within a few months of arriving in the United States, newspaper and journalistic reports increasingly represented the new guardians of the rehabilitation of the Hiroshima Maidens as their new American mothers, such that it became a narrative of domestic femininity. Thereafter, the public narrative of the healing of the bomb victims from Japan began to merge with the story of the healing effects of white American mothers in anecdotes that were often blatantly maudlin sketches of unbounded devotion.

The relationship of Helen Yokoyama and Mary Kochiyama to the Hiroshima Maidens Project was, on the other hand, rife with troubling questions about the potential or willingness of American domesticity to shelter and safeguard the happiness of all peoples. Although Helen Yokoyama was living in Japan when the war began and was married to a Japanese citizen at the time, she was then and remained throughout her life an American citizen, a Japanese American who had been born and raised in Los Angeles and had received a graduate degree from UCLA. Her knowledge of both American and Japanese cultures and languages made her, in Cousins's eyes, an obvious liaison for the project. But her presence as a Japanese American who because of her race had been barred from returning to her home indirectly invoked the specter of the internment with all of its potential for unraveling the narrative of American beneficence. Mary Kochiyama's history as a Japanese American represented an even more direct affront to the evolving story of American goodwill, because she had endured the war in the United States in an internment camp in Jerome, Arkansas. Born Mary Nakahara in 1921 in San Pedro, California, the daughter of a Japanese immigrant fisherman, Kochiyama, like Yokoyama, later attended college in California and was legally an American citizen by birth. Yet unlike Yokoyama she had become involved in the project by choice rather than by circumstance, by the desire to fight the cruelties of the war waged on both sides of the Pacific. When Norman Cousins asked Helen Yokoyama to accompany the bomb victims to the United States, she hesitated before agreeing to go along. Married to a Japanese national, Yokoyama had resigned herself to living out her life as an exile in Japan. In interviews with Rodney Barker, Yokoyama is reported to have claimed that the thought of "her own two, very lucky daughters" convinced her "that she had no choice but to go."[17] For Mary Kochiyama, however, the decision to become involved in the project was motivated by her growing sense of social responsibility and by a political questioning of her own role in American culture that had been initiated by the violation of internment and that would later be nurtured by the movements of the 1960s. Their distinctly different geopolitical positions as Japanese Americans would necessarily influence their function within the discourse on the mothering miracle of the Hiroshima Maidens Project.

Unlike the attention paid to defusing the overt political implications of aiding the victims of an American bombing, the dilemma of Japanese Americans' participation in a project that, from its conception, was designed to bolster the image of America as a land of compassion was never addressed. The national ignorance of Japanese American history and subjectivity seems remarkable, particularly when one considers that, just a decade before, Japanese Americans were the very visible and primary targets of home front fears during the war. Yet one of the chief paradoxes of Japanese American identity in the years that spanned the 1940s and 1950s is that Japanese American life was marked both by heightened political scrutiny and suspicion as well as by national neglect and, at times, even invisibility.

In the immediate postwar years, Japanese American communities experienced a reversal of the wartime surveillance of their lives and histories, as the national interest in their lives all but disappeared. The War Relocation Authority's plan in the last year of the war to relocate Japanese Americans to Midwestern cities away from their communities on the West Coast largely failed to break up the prewar "Little Tokyos." Dissatisfied with the lack of job opportunities and the relative absence of communal support in cities such as Cleveland and Chicago, many Japanese Americans eventually drifted back to the West Coast, reestablished their old networks, and struggled to restart their lives in the wake of the economic devastation and psychological repercussions of removal and internment. A small minority of Japanese Americans, such as Helen Yokoyama and Nomi's fictional mother in *Obasan*, were trapped in Japan when the war began and were altogether disregarded as what they in fact were, Americans in exile. Whether in the United States or outside it, Japanese American identity in the postwar years was generally characterized by a profound sense of geographical displacement and national effacement.

In the case of Helen Yokoyama, her status as a geographically and nationally displaced Japanese American, as someone existing on the borders between Japan and the United States, in many ways may have encouraged observers of the Hiroshima Maidens Project to overlook the facts of her American identity and history in favor of simply seeing her as another Japanese woman involved in a project about their American salvation. Because Yokoyama's return to the United States occurred in the context of a goodwill mission for women from Japan, her identity as an American citizen was no doubt obscured by the fact of her foreign residence and her seemingly similar Japanese identity. But, in addition, Helen Yokoyama was a woman involved in a project designed to construct women's relations and spaces as removed from the public and political concerns of nations and wars. At least initially, she was cast as the Hiroshima Maidens' first "den mother," one of a series of older women who would be seen as primarily nurturing the development and recovery of the young women in their charge. Although the emphasis on the American mothering of the Hiroshima Maidens would eventually become the exclusive domain of the white women who boarded them, the implication that the project was primarily a private venture taking place in domestic settings had the effect of rendering every woman's involvement, and particularly Yokoyama's, as another part of Norman Cousins's "personal event." In the end, the casting of Yokoyama as both another Japanese woman *and* the original "den mother" of the group allowed for her inclusion in the story of the Hiroshima Maidens Project without the need to cite the wartime evacuation and internment of Japanese Americans that led to her unique position as an eternal exile effectively displaced in both the United States and Japan.

If the focus on the greater healing power of American domesticity and maternal influence was pivotal to the project's avoidance of political controversy, it was also important to veiling the political implications of Japanese Americans' presence in the project. Yokoyama's experience as a Japanese American was secondary to the story of her function as a sort of Japanese maternal figure, one whose ability to shuttle between the two cultures, rather than being the sign of national and political exclusions, was instead used to reinforce the transcendent nature of maternal love and domesticity in the United States. Although the Hiroshima Maidens Project ensured that neither the Russians nor the Japanese could compete with the miracle of the suburban American lifestyle, it was ironically a Japanese American, one excluded from the national privileges extended to the Japanese bomb victims, who would be most instrumental in promoting the Americanness of unconditional love and domestic tranquility.

Mary Kochiyama's function within this national narrative would be less certain. When the Japanese bombed Pearl Harbor, her family was one of a thousand who were immediately detained under suspicion of collaborating with the Japanese military. Kochiyama's father, Seichi Nakahara, was immediately picked up by the FBI and sent to a federal penitentiary on Terminal Island, despite the fact that no proof of the suspicions against him was ever found, and no charges were ever officially made. In prison and separated from his family, Nakahara's health rapidly deteriorated and he was released on January 20, 1942, only to die the next day, at sixty years of age. Mary Kochiyama recalls his funeral, the last gathering of the Nakahara family with their long-time Japanese American friends, as a precursor of the days ahead. The private mourning of a family over the untimely death of a father, who was never able to clear his name, was overcast by the presence of federal officials. The FBI, still suspecting the elder Nakahara of Japanese intelligence connections, informed his family "that anyone who came to the funeral service would be under surveillance."[17] Today Kochiyama recalls that as the crowd of mourners filed into the service, "sure enough, the FBI was right there in front of the funeral parlor" (172). When the Nakahara family was subsequently sent to the Santa Anita assembly center for relocation to the internment camp in Arkansas, they witnessed the death of both their private lives and their expectations of domestic security as American citizens.

At the Jerome, Arkansas, internment camp, Mary Kochiyama quickly lost her youthful assumptions about American democracy and its promise of security for all its citizens. When she and her family arrived at Jerome, they were introduced into a drastically different environment than the homes and communities they left behind them. The camp at Jerome was similar to other inland camps being set up in the United States, with its flimsy construction and crowded conditions set against a dismal and isolated rural landscape. "The government called them relocation centers," Kochiyama recalls, "we called them concentration camps. I felt anger and shock—I couldn't believe America could actually do it. I thought it was a democratic country."[18]

Kochiyama's claim that, for the first time, she was aware of the grim political realities for Japanese Americans during the personal upheaval of internment was common among young Japanese Americans. Faced with the devastation of their domestic lives and the breakup of their families, many Nisei, who previously saw themselves simply as Americans, began to realize the precariousness of their individual security and their civil rights. In Mary Kochiyama's case, it was the harbinger of a life that united marriage and family with politics and activism. Later, in 1960, when Mary and her husband Bill Kochiyama moved to Harlem, she was vaulted into public visibility as a friend and supporter of Malcolm X, quickly becoming an active voice in the antiwar and anti-racism protests of the late 1960s and early 1970s. Although Kochiyama has asserted that moving to Harlem was the act that "changed our lives" by opening her and her husband to daily political life in a thriving and close-knit community, it was the internment that initially exposed her to the contradictions of democratic nationalism for ethnic and racial minorities.[19] Although Mary Kochiyama's social activities in the 1950s were not yet defined by the radical politics to come, her internal questioning of the idyll of American democracy is emblematic of the experience of other Nisei during the immediate postwar years. Her sense of "shock" and "anger" immediately invokes their shared, silent histories as ethnic Americans living an underground life in the first decade after the war.

Clearly the mere presence of these two Japanese American mothers, Mary Kochiyama in particular, had at the very least the potential to undermine the unrelenting optimism of these reports, which depended largely on the overt racial and national differences between the maidens and their American mothers to ensure the moral superiority of white American femininity and, with it, the success of middle-class domesticity. Norman Cousins's reports on the maidens' progress established the tone of future narratives, such as Rodney Barker's. Often the most maudlin stories utilized the concept of the universal goodness of American motherhood to suggest that the nation would be guided by such moral ideals to deploy its future technology for global benefit, rather than to fulfill selfish needs. In an October, 15, 1955, report in the *Saturday Review*, Cousins recounts the story of one white woman, "a parent," who was "bringing her girl to the hospital for a second operation."[20] Asking to meet the doctor who was to perform the difficult skin grafts, the woman "begged him to consider" taking her own skin for the grafts. Against her heartfelt and repeated requests, the doctors explained to the woman that the grafting of skin from one person to another was a medical impossibility. This demonstration and idealization of maternal sacrifice and devotion, which clearly evokes "the kitchen debate's" conflation of moral and technological superiority, became a common feature in stories of the Hiroshima Maidens' experiences in American homes, where their "bitterness, bewilderment and anxieties . . . have disappeared in the warmth and understanding shown them by Americans" (Cousins 23). This subtle narrative gesture had the effect of not only absolving the nation of its past sins at Hiroshima, but also attempted to limit any further concerns by suggesting that the future of American technology would be, like its motivations here, unassailable in the world's view.

In his more recent account of the project, Rodney Barker relies heavily on the motif of the selflessness of American "mothering" as a critical element in the Hiroshima Maidens' rehabilitation.[21] He recounts the story of the "mother" who offered her own skin for "her girl," as well as an anecdote shared by Yoshie Harada, who was staying with a Flushing, New York, couple in 1955. When she approached her American hostess to ask for help with the television, the language barrier was overcome by recourse to the one concept that seemed to provide the solution to all cultural obstacles in the Hiroshima Maidens Project: "She wanted to address her hostess but was at a loss when all of a sudden she recalled a doll that her father has given her as a child that had been made in the United States. When it was stood up its mouth opened and a two-syllable sound came out, 'Mom-mee.' Softly, Yoshie said, 'Mommy?' Her hostess turned, astonished. She was so moved, tears sprang to her eyes as she embraced Yoshie in her arms. Yoshie was not sure what she had done, but she would always remember that incident" (109). Although the passage again clearly promotes the concept of "mommy" as a universalizing concept, leveling all material or cultural differences, in fact the details of the story are rife with evidence of the persistence of those differences.

The doll was exported from the United States during the prewar years when Japan was assiduously remaking itself as the modern, Asian superpower, often in the image of Western industrial capitalism. According to Yukiko Koshiro, the Japanese saw themselves during this period "as the only Asians who could progress to a higher level of civilization along with white Westerners. This identity was extremely important in legitimizing Japan's status as a colonial power."[22] The demand for U.S. consumer goods prompted by the fascination with U.S. culture was high, even despite the Japanese government's futile struggles with the U.S. government during the prewar period to procure favored status for its immigrants. The American-made doll that opens its mouth to say "mommy" is thus much more than a simple example of the appeal of maternality, because it evidences the disturbing historical roots of the identification between Japan and the United States that were based on Japanese emulation of, and later antipathy toward, the modern, imperialist thrust of the nation in the late 1800s and early

1900s. It is also interesting to note that while the American "mommy" is moved to tears by the utterance, Yoshie remains perplexed by her response, indicating that, on the most fundamental level, the leveling of differences was perhaps not so effortlessly or unproblematically achieved by the recourse to maternity.

Yet, these observations notwithstanding, when the Hiroshima Maidens left to return to Japan in June 1956, just a few months after this reported incident, the American press continued to carry the news of their departures in the same overly sentimental or affective framework. The press routinely played up the importance of the maternal bonds the women had developed in America in headlines such as "10 Hiroshima Maidens in Tearful Farewell to 'American Mommies'" and in articles that quoted the girls as saying that leaving was "like saying goodbye to my own parents."[23]

The visit of the Hiroshima Maidens was in every way perceived as a success, despite the fact that the medical venture had proven to be less than successful. "From a strictly surgical point of view," according to Barker, "the results were moderate."[24] But as a "personal event" the visit had been a double success, "something close to a Cinderella story" (151). The formerly withdrawn victims of atomic warfare had reclaimed their femininity through the care of American families and the guidance of American "mothers," or as Barker says of Shigeko Niimito, one of the most popular of the group, the Hiroshima Maiden now "saw herself as the cinder-faced daughter on whose foot the glass slipper had fit" (165). In addition, the power of American domesticity and motherhood was positively reaffirmed in "the Maidens' newfound confidence in the future" (167) and in their acceptance that "a responsibility flowed from the privilege of going to America" (174). The nature of that responsibility was always understood as the imperative to marry and thus reproduce the romance of heterosexual norms they discovered in American suburbs. "For ten years the Maidens had been led to believe that they were sentenced to spinsterhood by the ugliness of their scars," concludes Barker, "but the girls' fears were enough allayed that many had returned with marriage on their minds" (178–79). On the foreign bodies of these young Japanese women, then, the regeneration of domestic capabilities might be written, a flowering of faith in the safety and accessibility of domestic bliss that was discovered in their contact with America.

Only occasionally in the unending litany of feminine successes that seemed to emanate from the maidens' time in America did the myth of American domesticity as an idyllic enclave, an oasis from the anxieties of the cold war, seem to be in jeopardy. For the most part the American press, the State Department, and certainly the organizers of the project were at least superficially able to keep politics at bay, to maintain the appearance of "a personal event." Perhaps the words of an anonymous donor who wrote to Cousins to express his own hopes for the project provides the best analysis of the project's function in the tense environment of cold war politics and postwar uncertainty.[25] The donor's letter unwittingly hints at the underlying blurring of public and private anxieties that was repeatedly overlooked in the interest of depoliticizing the Hiroshima Maidens' story. Although the anonymous letter writer clearly did not intend to criticize the project, his words nonetheless momentarily expose the dubious appeal of the Hiroshima Maidens Project was its potential to reaffirm the strength of American domesticity in the face of mounting postwar troubles. The project, as he inadvertently suggests, had as much to do with assuaging broader, unspoken political anxieties about American domesticity as with rehabilitating the young Japanese bomb victims:

> This program seems to be a fine example of what Americans as individuals rather than as faceless citizens of a powerful nation, can and should do to further the cause of world peace and international understanding. With the Russian satellites in the sky, with America's deep anxiety about her position in the world, with citizens like myself wondering what we or anyone can do to prevent a catastrophic war and feeling helplessly at the mercy of the governing Powers That Be in the United States and Russia, a program such as that undertaken by the Hiroshima Peace Center Associates provides at least a glimmer of hope that man can, if he will try, heal himself rather than destroy himself. (Barker 158)

Coincidentally, although the need to overcome "feeling helplessly at the mercy of the governing Powers that Be," aptly describes the general anxiety over the cold war, it also encompasses the experience of those other Americans connected to the project whose experiences and influences were not as easily contained by the themes of maternal longing and domestic bliss. And, on occasion, one becomes aware of the historical erasures and national fissures on which the success of this formative mission of peace depended.

Rodney Barker describes Yokoyama's chief contribution to the project as "an instinctive ability to grasp the significance of an occasion" and "rescue an immediate emotional reaction from escalating into an ugly conflict, converting it into a detailed illustration of the diversity among people of different backgrounds and orientations—and in such a way as to bring about a respect for those differences."[26] Yokoyama's national and geographical invisibility, then, became enshrined as the necessary position of postwar peacemaking and reconciliation; in addition, her seeming transcendence of national interests and political ideology soon emerged as an instinctive American quality. When early in the project one of the young Japanese women asks Yokoyama to explain the concept of altruism or philanthropy, qualities purportedly alien to the Japanese, Yokoyama's response "that some people have a philosophy of life which enables them to regard all human beings as belonging to a single family" (130) is interpreted by Barker as the unique lesson of American culture. The benevolence of the American family becomes the constant in his account, culminating with the idyllic domestic scene reportedly witnessed by Yokoyama "when she visited them [the Maidens] in their American homes and saw them sitting by the hearth in cashmere sweaters and tweed skirts" (131). Barker clearly suggests that Yokoyama's viewpoint as an unmarked cultural go-between is the most objective source of the "regenerative power of love" (130–31) in American domestic culture. The dubious efficacy of this approach is that it simultaneously recognizes the indeterminacy of Yokoyama's national status, and, by casting it as an eternal characteristic of Americans' greater capacity for cultural understanding, also refuses to acknowledge that her national displacement is rooted in another version of American experience, the evacuation and internment of Japanese Americans. In Barker's history, which is the only in-depth information on Helen Yokoyama now on record, she becomes not simply a nationless presence but a nationless presence whose ability to "grasp the significance of an occasion" and "bring about a respect for differences" ironically describes the American way from which she is barred, and becomes a useful means of promoting Americans as "a people responsive to human suffering" (131).

Helen Yokoyama's explanation that "some people" are able "to regard all human beings as belonging to a single family," might, in retrospect, be seen as damning rather than affirming or describing not a whole nation of people, but merely those few who deviate from the national norm experienced by Yokoyama during the war when Japanese

Americans like herself were clearly not regarded as part of the American family. But by further obscuring Yokoyama's identity as a Japanese American who has been displaced from her home and family, whose personal choices have been dictated by political events, Barker's account relies on solidifying the illusory boundaries between the political and the personal, the public and the private. His retelling of the Hiroshima Maidens' story shares Cousins's initial commitment to keeping this "a personal event" and, in so doing, limits the understanding of the project to evidence that establishes the allure of American domesticity. From the start, the projection of America as a nation of domestic bliss and unbounded maternal love depended on sustaining an ignorance of the contradictions of Yokoyama's participation in the project as a Japanese American.

Still, despite the attention to keeping the project "a personal event," the political contradictions and dilemmas of the postwar period were not altogether dissolved. The repeated emphasis on the apolitical nature of domesticity and motherhood was an indication, by misdirection, of their inherently political, public bases. As the original "den mother" to the Hiroshima Maidens, Helen Yokoyama is, for instance, only apparently unmoored from political struggles and national history.

As even a brief, retrospective reading of the project in terms of Yokoyama's identity as a Japanese American reveals, the avowal of national unity in fact was heavily dependent on her continued suspension between the two cultures, like a living boundary demonstrating the positive difference between "us" and "them" by becoming invisible within that binary logic. The recognition of Yokoyama as a Japanese American and as a representative of the political and legal dispossession of Japanese Americans in the 1940s and 1950s threatened the assumption that generosity was, as Ralph Edwards termed it, "the American way." In order to forestall this recognition, the organizers of the Hiroshima Maidens Project, who were well aware that Yokoyama was an exiled American citizen whose personal life had been limited by political events, insisted that this story of femininity redeemed transcended the flotsam of history and politics. The ultimate result of framing a story of domesticity and motherhood as timeless attributes to national life was that women, as subjects, were denied historical and political significance and agency. But as the broad contours of Yokoyama's postwar history reveals, the need for overlooking the meaning of her nationality in a story about national difference was not merely coincidental, just as the reaffirmation of domestic femininity during the fifties was always historically and politically overdetermined.

Yokoyama's status as a Japanese American—who, like Nomi's mother in *Obasan*, was, oddly enough, a part of the war effort of the Allied nations and a casualty of it as well—meant that she ultimately occupied a liminal space in the already restricted narrative of American maternal benevolence and Japanese feminine healing. Thus, the scrutiny of the narrative liminality of Japanese American subjectivity —as that element of the Hiroshima Maidens' story that most needed screening—becomes for contemporary cultural critics and historians the key to unraveling the myth of the insularity of domesticity and femininity in American culture; the history of Japanese American identity during the postwar years provided irrevocable evidence of the mutually constitutive relationship of the personal and the political in American life.

Although the record of Helen Yokoyama's life both in the United States and in Japan remains overwhelmed by the narrative themes of the Hiroshima Maidens Project both then and now, the political significance of Mary Kochiyama's life as a Japanese American woman deeply involved with the Hiroshima Maidens during their visit to the United States seems more apparent. Mary Kochiyama's presence in the project carried, of course, the more immediate burden of the internment process, which was the problem that always beset the visibility and utility of Japanese Americans in national narratives during the 1950s. Although Yokoyama is granted at least a nominal, enabling part in the original media circus and subsequent retellings of the Hiroshima Maidens story, the significance of Kochiyama's involvement as a Japanese American "mommie" is altogether unremarked. In later decades, Kochiyama's erasure was further ensured by her well-known political activism and radical stands. Recovering even the broad fabric of Kochiyama's life in the wake of internment, just as she was becoming connected to the project, is a piecemeal process because the record of Kochiyama's presence in the story we might tell of cold war America is absent. But resurrecting the remnants of her life as both a reflection of the written record of Japanese American experience and a radical departure from it is essential to fleshing out the complicated history of women's relationships to American domesticity and femininity in the 1950s.

Mary Kochiyama: "From Out of the Ashes" of History

In one instant Hiroshima was ashes. Completely destroyed were 56,000 of its 70,000 buildings and homes. The balance were damaged and uninhabitable. But from out of the ashes and horror came hope.—Bill and Mary Kochiyama, from a preface to their scrapbook on the visit of the Hiroshima Maidens

The process of questioning their status as Americans was, at first, a deeply private one for many Nisei such as Mary Kochiyama and her husband Bill, who simply struggled to find their place in American life after the trauma of internment. Most Nisei left the camps filled with the sense that the future of the Japanese American community's success depended on them, on their acceptance by mainstream white institutions and communities.[27] Although some historians of Japanese American internment and resettlement, such as Michi Weglyn, agree that "there is no question that unexpected good things came out of the Japanese Americans' wartime travails" by "opening up opportunities for them that would never have been possible on the Coast," they are also quick to point out that the psychological costs of these economic opportunities were often extreme.[28] "They had suffered years of infamy," Ronald Takaki concludes, "years they would never forget" as they attempted to fulfill the directives of the War Relocation Authority that closed the camps and dispersed the Nisei away from their West Coast homes and the lingering prejudice that remained there.[29] Although they were free to resume their lives, they were clearly not free to be Japanese Americans. As I pointed out in chapter 1, in John Okada's novel *No-No Boy* his central Nisei character, Ichiro, returns to Seattle after the camps only to find that he is "a foreigner coming to the city for the first time," and is trying "to be grateful to them and prove to them that you can be an American."[30] He witnesses the increasing paranoia of his fellow Nisei as "the young Japanese hates the not-so-young Japanese who is more Japanese than himself, and the not-so-young, in turn, hates the old Japanese who is all Japanese" (136). Under the continued pressure to prove their Americanness, the Seattle Nisei community is torn apart as they wrestle with the need to deny their Japanese heritage in order to be accepted as Americans. Individuals such as Ichiro are left "chasing that faint and elusive insinuation of promise" (251) that, more than anything else, typifies the 1950s for so many of the Nisei.

Evelyn Nakano Glenn's study of the contemporary experiences of Issei and Nisei women finds at least one troubling dilemma at the core of
this successful movement beyond the confines of the West Coast communities: the impossible requirement that the Nisei achieve success
without the support of their families in a society where the ethnic family was often "the one institution that Japanese Americans could turn
to for comfort, affection, and an affirmation of their individuality and
self-worth."[31] But even beyond this potential source of stress and alienation, there was the broader ideological contradiction involved in encouraging Nisei to break away from their families in order to gain entry
into a postwar American culture that was characterized by its glorifica-
tion of the virtues of family and domesticity. Although most Nisei were
reluctant to articulate the undue burden of their unique postwar settlement, the contradictions that defined their status in America were
perhaps too overwhelming to remain concealed for long. Not even the
conformist mood of the 1950s could entirely suppress them, despite
the widespread Nisei insistence on otherwise leaving the past behind
them.

In 1953, Monica Sone published *Nisei Daughter*, an autobiographical
account of her early life as a young girl, which chronicled the negative
impact of evacuation and internment on her sense of self as an American. If as Frank Miyamoto argues in the foreword to the 1979 edition
of *Nisei Daughter*, her autobiography is indeed symbolic of the Nisei
"search for identity," then the search clearly begins in the recognition that the realm of family and home is an effect of the vagaries
and anxieties of national politics.[32] The internment and subsequent
attempts to relocate during the postwar period proved to Japanese
Americans that "the search for better homes outside the central Japanese community was likely to yield bitter experiences of prejudice and
discrimination" (xiii). When the announcement of "E-day," or evacuation day, as General DeWitt termed it, was handed down in April 1942,
the Sones along with others were given a week to dispense with their
business and personal affairs and to choose among their possessions
only those that would fit in the allotted "one seabag and two suitcases
apiece" (166). Sone describes her mother's furious attempts to "resort
a lifetime's accumulation of garments, toys and household goods," and
the ominous scene of "our empty house where our voices echoed
loudly and footsteps clattered woodenly on the bare floor" (166-7). On
the day of evacuation, standing "for the last time" in "a modern bath-

room," Sone inspects her new perm, "given to me by an operator who had never worked on oriental hair before" (167). In a gesture symbolic of the family's coming attempts to deal with the humiliation of family life in government camps, Sone decides "there was nothing to do but cover it with a scarf" (167).

The mass exodus to the new government-assigned apartments marked the final phase of a process of physical and legal displacement that would make Japanese American families prisoners of the state. Sone's descriptions of their arrival via crowded trains at the Puyallup Assembly Center outside of Seattle is representative of the repressive regimentation that would come to define Japanese American existence during the war: "We stumbled out, stunned, dragging our bundles after us. It must have rained the night before in Puyallup, for we sank ankle deep into gray, glutinous mud. The receptionist, a white man, instructed us courteously, 'Now, folks, please stay together as family units and line up. You'll be assigned your apartment'" (173). The scene of masses being transported behind black shades in old train cars then herded into the barbed-wire compound that was now "home" makes the evacuation seem vaguely reminiscent of the removal of Jews during the early days of the Holocaust. Although the internment of Japanese Americans in no manner approaches the savagery of the treatment of European Jews, the imprisonment of citizens primarily on the basis of racial difference irrevocably disrupts any notions of the sanctity of private life and individual freedom and blurs the distinctions between German totalitarianism and American democracy. "Our home," Sone notes, "was one room, about 18 by 20 feet, the size of a living room. There was one small window in the wall opposite the one door. It was bare except for a small, tiny wood-burning stove crouching in the center. The flooring consisted of two by fours laid directly on the earth" (174). Separated from adjoining families by a seven-foot-high partition, through which the residents could hear the conversations of their neighbors, the Sones first few weeks of internment "were filled with quiet desperation" (178). The family's final destination, the Minidoka camp in Idaho, was no less dreary a new home, with its sudden, blinding windstorms and apartments "with thick layers of dust covering the dining tables and benches, and filling teacups and bowls" (192–93). The notion of home as a nurturing cocoon of domesticity suddenly seemed an absurdity.

Feeling that their tie to an American future had been severed in the literal, physical erosion of family privacy and domestic comfort, the Sones tried, like other internees, to reconstruct the appearance, at least, of middle-class respectability. In a vain attempt to recreate the accoutrements of a suburban American home, and perhaps draw a veil of prosperity across the deprivation of camp life, they "confiscated scrap lumber" that was officially off-limits and worked to turn it into "a coffee table, a writing table, a glamorous table" (195). But there was little the Sones could do to distract from the squalor of their surroundings. Although *Nisei Daughter* concludes on a reassuring note, with Sone declaring "I had discovered a deeper, stronger impulse in the American scene" (238), her celebration of American possibilities seems premature, shadowed by the simultaneous knowledge that too many people like her Issei parents continued to live in "their no-man's land" (237). In the end, there was finally no escaping the unremitting sense that "we had drifted farther and farther away from the American scene. We had been set aside, and we had become adjusted to our peripheral existence" (198). Sone's words seem to echo Kochiyama's sense of disillusionment, if not her anger, with the domestic and political dispossession of Japanese Americans.

The lack of closure, or what Lisa Lowe deems the "false ring of the ending," also defines the work of so many other Japanese Americans during this period, including Carlos Bulosan's *America Is in the Heart* (1946) and Mine Okubo's *Citizen 13660* (1946), as well as John Okada's *No-No Boy* (1959) as I have previously pointed out.[33] But the critical difference of Sone's autobiography is her construction of a new type of modern Japanese American womanhood, one that hinges on recognition of what literary critic Traise Yamamoto describes as the fact that the agency of Japanese American women "is not an a priori condition; rather the 'I' self-reflexively confers that agency through the autobiographical act."[34] Thus Nisei women enter the discursive field of autobiography already conscious of themselves as "split subjects" and their efforts are expended to cover or "mask," but not completely obscure, this fact in anticipation of the hostility of the non-Asian American reader. The "ruptures" in Sone's narrative, such as those cited above where her text admits the ambivalence and pessimism that followed Japanese Americans as they left the camps to try to remake their lives, is not a "slip" in the attempt to put a happy face on the ordeal but is instead a carefully controlled performance that allows her "to stage the contradictions and incommensurabilities between juridical, cultural and ideological citizenship" (123). These "contradictions and incommensurabilities" are compounded by Sone's positioning as a gendered and racialized national subject who must negotiate the obstacles posed by both for the speaking, autobiographical subject in the 1950s. Monica Sone's predicament, although muted and even at times problematically repressed, nonetheless provides a window on how the internment further limited the means by which Japanese American women could speak honestly and fully about their lives and still be heard by a nation suffused with anxieties about women no less than racial minorities' rights.

Ironically, less than three years after the publication of Monica Sone's searching account of the ordeal of internment for Japanese Americans, the Hiroshima Maidens would seem to announce the resurrection of domestic security in the wake of overwhelming wartime fears and deprivations. For Mary Kochiyama, as a formerly interned Japanese American now involved in the project, the unfolding public discourse of the generous American impulse to embrace these former "Japanese enemies" by accepting them into their homes and extending to them the full pleasures of middle-class life must have seemed both a positive change as well as an unsettling reminder of her own contrasting experiences in America. As a young Japanese American woman, Kochiyama had not been the recipient of the unbounded generosity that was fabled as "the American way" in media accounts of the success of the Hiroshima Maidens Project. Neither her own nor Helen Yokoyama's experiences of American domesticity easily yielded the halcyon portraits of grateful young women safe "by the hearth in cashmere sweaters and tweed skirts." Theirs was instead the "peripheral existence" that haunts Monica Sone's memories as well. For Yokoyama, of course, the possibility of life in America ended the day Pearl Harbor was bombed and she was caught in Japan, a Japanese American married to the enemy and all but barred from ever returning. For Kochiyama, as for many others, the internment did end, and she was able to return to the national scene in the postwar period, but with a new and disturbing sense of the social dilemmas and domestic contradictions defining American democracy in the cold war years.

As a result, the Kochiyamas' home life in the 1950s became inseparable from their growing social and political engagement, as they opened their house to those who also felt that, in the words of Diane Fujino, they were living "a peripheral existence" in an affluent nation.[35] Mary Kochiyama's participation in the Hiroshima Maidens Project grew out of this period of post-internment involvement, the precursor to her later radical political activities. In a sense, the Hiroshima Maidens Project figured as an important interlude for Mary Kochiyama, a lull between the "shock" of internment and the rising political activism of the 1960s. Her participation in the project thus simultaneously recalls the memory of the unresolved political dilemmas of the 1940s and looks forward to the widespread political rebellions of the 1960s. As another kind of American "mother" to the young women, Kochiyama's presence as a Japanese American still processing the meaning of wartime incarceration placed her in a position to offer the Hiroshima Maidens a very different view of American domestic life and the function of women within America, although, like Sone, she was still constrained by the precariousness of her position in a nation that just a decade earlier had repudiated her status as a citizen.

In May 1955, when Mary Kochiyama became involved in the project, many Japanese Americans who were aware of the bomb victims' visit were reluctant to volunteer "to show America" to the young Japanese citizens. In one of his rare references to Japanese Americans, Rodney Barker notes that Japanese Americans primarily stayed away because "most had put up with hardships and prejudices during the war and were afraid that if something went wrong with the project it would mean more trouble for them."[36] When "it became evident that a success story was in the making," (118), and the fear of reprisals for Japanese Americans was removed, some members of the Nisei community agreed to become involved. Mary and Bill Kochiyama, of course, immediately assumed a leadership position in linking the Hiroshima Maidens to the rest of the Japanese American community and even started a scrapbook of news clippings, letters, and diary entries chronicling the women's visit and subsequent correspondence with their American "parents." The Kochiyamas set up the maidens' first meeting with members of the New York Nisei community in the summer of 1955, at which they reportedly met the Naritas, a family that soon developed a close relationship with several of the women. In their scrapbook, the Kochiyamas cite "Mrs. Narita" as "one of their [the maidens] closest and most helpful friends."[37] When five of the young women opted to spend New Year's Eve with the Naritas, the Kochiyamas journal entry describes it as simply a place "where they can relax and enjoy Japanese food" (116). The depiction of the meeting of Japanese Americans and

Japanese nationals as another heartwarming family event was unquestionably in line with the larger story of the Hiroshima Maidens' visit that Cousins was promoting. But the gradual development of a deeper relationship with Japanese Americans who had experienced the dispossession of American life could also mean much more than a chance to "enjoy Japanese foods" with a kind of surrogate Japanese family.

Because the Kochiyamas had not yet adopted the critical political stance that would define their view of American life in the coming decade, their public comments on the project were, at least for public consumption, overwhelmingly approving. In a Christmas card to friends in 1956, they describe the project in glowing terms as an event that proved "there are forces mightier than the forces of atomic energy."[38] The Kochiyamas' attempts to support the women's recovery meant also supporting the narrative of America as the foundation of a postwar regeneration, despite the contradictions that their own presence made clear. In the end, it was their mere presence as Japanese Americans that opened a window onto another America, where domestic security was not so assured and the private life not so private. Not even the few isolated references to the involvement of Japanese Americans could avoid at least touching on the delicate issue of Japanese American dispossession during the war, just as Sone's autobiography, despite its anticipation of a happy ending for her and her family, could not avoid striking a "false ring" in its optimism.

Rodney Barker acknowledges that in the seemingly unrelenting stream of stories about the maidens, "from time to time it did occur to some of the Maidens that they were looking upon America at its best and only seeing the sunny side of this country."[39] Not surprisingly, the most critical view of American life was often provided by Japanese Americans, according to Barker, who "visited them in the hospital" and ultimately told them "what it had been like living in resettlement camps during the war" (133). Although Barker concedes that the occasional glimpses of racism in American life helped the women "to remember that even in America poverty and wealth lived side by side, and there seemed to be no justice in its distribution" (134), he fails to elaborate on the potential of this recognition of the inequities that continued to plague American culture in the affluent 1950s. Instead, Barker ends his consideration of the sobering events of the maidens' visit with the story of the death of one of the maidens, Tomoko Nakabayashi, after surgery. Although Nakabayashi's death might have undermined the entire project by casting doubts on the proficiency of American medical procedures, even this tragedy was turned to good account by the organizers of the project. Rather than becoming an obstacle to the public promotion of the project as a success, the doctors' vigil and the concern of Cousins during the patient's final hours actually became viewed as proof "that this was not a publicity stunt" (141). Like so much else that had the potential to derail the success of the Hiroshima Maidens Project, the political problems that might have emanated from Nakabayashi's death were never allowed to materialize. Neither did the potentially incendiary presence of Japanese Americans visiting the maidens in the hospital to tell them of the ordeal they had experienced as alienated citizens. Instead the potential subversive meaning of their histories remained unarticulated, however much they now seem critical to having altered our understanding of the Hiroshima Maidens Project.

As cultural critics of the period attempt to retrieve the suppressed histories that were made insignificant in the depoliticized narrative of personal recovery, we are left with only the ashes of the history of the impact of Japanese Americans' participation, sifted in pieces from the celebratory accounts of the Hiroshima Maidens Project. In these ashes, however, are the counter-histories of the postwar American lives of Mary Kochiyama and Helen Yokoyama. Mary Kochiyama, for one, would with her political involvement in the 1960s come to realize more fully her own naïveté in the wake of the internment. Her post-project reflections on the grim realities of life for Japanese Americans provide a powerful addendum to the traditional history of the Hiroshima Maidens Project and to the nostalgic tableau of 1950s domesticity, and as such, her later recollections represent a final rejoinder to the exclusion of Japanese Americans from the public discourse about the project. Mary Kochiyama's subsequent doubts about the redeeming power of American democracy are directed precisely at the fantasy that sustained general interest in the Hiroshima Maidens Project, at the concept of familial unity and private bliss as a uniquely American condition benevolently made available to all. Most important, Kochiyama's later comments testify to the critical potential of Japanese American memory and experience to fracture the meanings of cultural history, in this case by offering an alternative and deeply politicized vision of postwar American womanhood and motherhood. Without the story of Japanese American women's involvement with the Hiroshima Maidens Project, the memory of the project maintains a false faith in domestic tranquility and privilege as facts of American life, which remains imbued with the suprahuman power to redeem and even overturn the wartime damage done to female Japanese bodies. In fact, Mary Kochiyama's redemption as a national subject entailed an ironic rejection of this faith and the idyll of American domesticity that incorporates it. Hers is a national politics increasingly built on a stance of critical otherness that exceeds the popular narrative of the Hiroshima Maidens' American redemption, both ideologically and historically. Yet the history of the Hiroshima Maidens Project is only half told without it.

In 1975, some twenty years after the Hiroshima Maidens Project and long after Malcolm X's assassination in 1965, Mary Kochiyama became the subject of a pamphlet published by the American Committee for Protection of the Foreign Born.[40] The pamphlet was designed to alert Americans to the presence of the Eastland Bill then before Congress. The bill would make "punishable by 10 years imprisonment and $10,000 fine," giving "aid and comfort" to "any foreign nation or armed group which is engaged in open hostilities with the Armed Forces of the United States" (8). Fearing the potential for the bill to create "a police state" in America, the committee was campaigning against it by reminding readers that similar episodes of injustice had, after all, been allowed to unfold in the past. The internment of Japanese Americans, as told through the words of Mary Kochiyama, seemed to provide the best evidence as the heading announced "Mary Kochiyama, Concentration Camps U.S.A. It has happened here. It could happen again, to you!" (1). Mary Kochiyama's account of her life as an American "mother of six children" reads as nothing less than explosive. She presents her story about the treatment of Japanese Americans as the embodiment of American domestic life in many regards. Far from being the exception to the rule in America, the wartime internment of Americans of Japanese descent was represented as an almost logical symptom of uniquely American historical precedents, "for harsh measures against dark-skinned people were commonplace, as manifested by the enslavement of African people brought to this continent" (2).

From the vantage point of the 1970s, Kochiyama comprehends her former view of American society as that of "a naively idealistic, apolitical, provincial twenty-year old" (3). She goes on to tell the story of the cruelty of internment, sparing no opportunity to emphasize, in particular, the erosion of that "twenty-year-old's" expectations of the good life in America. In a section titled "Home in a Horse Stall," Kochiyama graphically describes the "horse stall that became our home" (5) during internment. Recalling the memories of Monica Sone, published some twenty years previous, Kochiyama explains "Army cots and straw-filled mattresses were the only furnishings given to each family. Boxes had to be converted into tables, chairs and dressers" (5).

But the historical changes in the rhetoric of American ethnic self-representation had shifted radically from the accomodationist mode ostensibly adopted by Sone. By 1975, when the pamphlet was published, Kochiyama had already been profoundly influenced by the liberation movements of the 1960s, and in particular by Malcolm X's teachings and the broader discourse of black militancy and revolution. In this regard, Kochiyama's transformation from a figure who in the 1950s was publicly reticent about criticizing the government to one who two decades later vigorously denounced the government in attempting to appeal to voters was representative of a generation of Nisei who experienced a political and personal metamorphosis of sorts. As one observer of the period remembers: "The 'Black is Beautiful' cry among black Americans instilled a new awareness in Asian Americans to be proud of their physical and cultural heritages."[41]

Asian Americans may also have been influenced by the fact that many African American leaders openly protested the war in Vietnam out of sense of solidarity with their "yellow brothers" against white violence. Eldridge Cleaver, the former minister of information for the Black Panthers, for example, asserted from his prison cell that "the relationship between the genocide in Vietnam and the smiles of the white man toward black Americans is a direct relationship."[42] Directly affected by these changes, Kochiyama began to realize the buried potential of her earlier discontent, as she highlights rather than masks, performs, or even internalizes the lingering trauma of Nisei women's alienation. She angrily rejects the illusion of the hearthside idyll so memorable from the portrait of America appearing in the Hiroshima Maidens' coverage in favor of exposing a violent vision of American domesticity undercut by a scene of citizens living in livestock quarters, where, in order to keep warm, "in some blocks, women dragged . . . trees in like teams of horses."[43] "Again coming to the fore," Kochiyama asserts, "is the traditional pattern of dealing with the 'unassimilables' . . . those who have been violated the most—the Black people who know this country as few others do, Indians, Mexican Americans, Puerto Ricans, dissenting youth, militant workers and the foreign born." (6). Her ominous conclusion, "Each of us must answer, what have we become?" (7), frames the internment experience, in particular the Japanese American memory of it, as the other side of Americans' faith in the power of democracy. As a self-proclaimed racial democracy, the United States must, by necessity, assume the primary burden of this urgent question, which by the 1970s it could no longer ignore. In a clever twist on McCarthyism and its familiar patriotic call to arms to citizens against the radical elements of national life, Kochiyama asks: "How strong or weak are we in combating this national congenital disease called racism, whose malignancy has penetrated every fibre of social life?" "It matters not," she concludes, "the name, concentration camps, plantations, reservations, relocation centers or *strategic hamlets*. We must stop the threat" (emphasis added) (7).[44]

The "mother of six" who tells her story in this document, one of the few written accounts of Mary Kochiyama's life, projects a mother's concerns as primarily political ones rather than exclusively private or moral ones. This addendum to the history of Kochiyama's participation in the Hiroshima Maidens Project emphasizes the concept of motherhood as a profoundly political construction, and in turn it reminds us of the historical constructedness of the maternal as a powerful agent for political and social change. Karin Aguilar San-Juan attributes Kochiyama's "constructive and passionate dialogue with Black activists" as "an important counterexample to those individuals who would argue that Asian Americans lack common ground with other people of color."[45] The development and embrace of this "counterexample" also marked the advent of a vital, new rhetorical model for the racialized American subject who would break free of the discursive forms that marked her positioning in the national order.

It should come as no surprise, then, to discover that the most visible if not the most enduring public image of Mary Kochiyama may be her appearance on a 1965 cover of *Life* magazine announcing the assassination of Malcolm X, her friend and mentor. As he lay dying on the floor of the Audubon Ballroom, Malcolm X rests his head in Mary Kochiyama's arms, an image that captures the essence of their mutually nurturing relationship to each other and to a politics of national critique. As one recent observer notes, "as you peer to the top of the photograph, the complete image begins to take on a modern version of Michelangelo's Rondanini Pieta, with a younger Kochiyama cradling the head of the wounded and dying Malcolm X. The classic image of a mother's love, coupled with her mourning a sacrificed leader, was now colored by the complex issues of American identity, class structure, race and other social and politcal agendas."[46] Although the sentimentalized healing image of the mother is sustained in this description of Mary Kochiyama's motherly embrace of the dying Malcolm X, it also marks the difference of Japanese American motherhood as a political and social force. Like many feminists who would come after him, Malcolm X consistently argued for the importance of realizing that the concept of a private life, safe from political or public concerns, was an illusion that hid from racialized Americans in particular the source of their discontent and their liberation. Thus, the awareness of the illusion of the separation of public and private promoted by Malcolm X, and by civil rights leaders in the 1960s, has fueled, perhaps unintentionally, the feminist awareness of the national and political investment in controlling women's private lives and roles.[47] Certainly in the 1950s the relevance of Japanese American women to the recasting of national debates was undeniable. Although the historical discourse on these women was also limited by the political and social pressures of the time, in the voice of Yuri Kochiyama it became a force to be reckoned with, and it continues even now as we remember the ways in which it went unremarked.

FIVE

"Out of an Obscure Place": Japanese War Brides

and Cultural Pluralism in the 1950s

In spring 1954, the American philosopher Horace Kallen was invited to the University of Pennsylvania to deliver a series of lectures on the state of cultural pluralism in American postwar society. The concept of cultural pluralism was Kallen's own invention, an idea of American society first expressed in his 1915 essay "Democracy versus the Melting Pot," in which he defended America's growing racial and ethnic diversity, "the federation or commonwealth of nationalities," that seemed to emerge in the wake of early-twentieth-century immigration as the strength rather than the curse of the nation.[1] Although by 1954 the supposed menace of immigration had long since been checked, most notably by the 1924 Immigration Act that imposed severe restrictions on immigration from Europe and Asia, the diversity Kallen had defended earlier in the century was once more poised to overwhelm the national imagination. As Kallen delivered his lectures that spring, the Supreme Court was hearing the Brown case, the culmination of a stream of compelling legal arguments that contested the notion of "separate but equal" established in 1896 in *Plessy v. Ferguson*. Given the anxiety that racial desegregation provoked in many whites, Kallen and the liberal intellectuals attending his lectures understood the need to reassess and restate the case for cultural pluralism.

It was in the face of the tense public and legal debate over desegregation that Kallen reasserted the promise of pluralism in stirring strains that seemed at times to evoke an almost radiant vision of what Americans might yet achieve. His vision depended on the willingness of white Americans in particular to embrace change. As he put it, "the dogma that we cannot change the past is not an understanding of the process of change but a prejudice of our resistance to it and a static illusion symbolizing our fear of it."[2] The chief effect of his lectures, and the published responses to them, was to affirm that the coming changes in race relations anticipated by the Brown deliberations would be generative rather than enervating: "It is the variety and range of his participations which does in fact distinguish a civilized man from an uncivilized man, a man of faith and reason from an unreasoning fanatic, a democrat from a totalitarian, a man of culture from a barbarian. Such a man obviously orchestrates a growing pluralism of associations into the wholeness of his individuality" (25). In descriptions such as this one, Kallen recasts the threat of integration as a deft "orchestration" of differences that would leave the nation "whole" rather than fractured. But while most Americans might have assumed this orchestration would soon occur through increased interactions between blacks and whites, as indeed it did, there were other, less visible avenues by which public voices sought to orchestrate or imagine the successful transition to racial integration in the mid-1950s.

As one participant in the lecture series, Stewart Cole, observes in his response to Kallen's lectures, the liberal assurance expressed by Kallen grew out of the belief that because "the resurgence of real democracy has redeemed this country" in the past, it could not fail to do so again in the future.[3] But Cole goes one step further to predict that the coming democratic resurgence would more likely emerge "out of unofficial or obscure places" (114). Although the Brown decision clearly established the postwar challenge of cultural pluralism as the integration of African Americans into the opportunities formerly reserved for whites, so much so that it has since become common to view race relations in the 1950s as primarily a black-white struggle, the case for integration also frequently provoked anxieties and shame about racism in America that encompassed the conditions of other racialized groups. In this way, the threat of black-white integration proliferated a range of overlapping and uneven fears about the histories or conditions of race relations that seemed to emerge, almost overnight, "out of unofficial or obscure places" to become a part of the broader discourse on racial integration and cultural pluralism.

Such is the case of Japanese Americans in the postwar period, a group often neglected in considerations of American pluralism and postwar integration despite the fact that the meaning and shape of Japanese American identity was caught in a tremendous crisis. The relocation and internment experience was, of course, the most startling evidence of that crisis. But the postwar dilemma of Japanese Americans as citizen-subjects, although often localized to discussions of the internment experience of the West Coast population, in fact incorporates a range of national experiences and histories, including the resettlement program after the war and the impact of the immigration of Japanese war brides on the meaning of Japanese American citizenship.

Japanese war brides were perhaps the most visible representatives of Japanese American life in the postwar period, and they were further attractive for being seen solely as wives and mothers unfettered by the disturbing public history of internment. Settling into domestic life in the 1950s with little fanfare, as unfamiliar national subjects who had formerly been citizens of an enemy nation Japanese war brides soon became meaningful figures in the discourse on racial integration and cultural pluralism. As white Americans tried to negotiate the threat of black integration, and government programs tried in vain to resettle interned Japanese Americans, Japanese war brides provided at least one "unofficial or obscure place" out of which the redemption of cultural pluralism, as an ideal that stabilized relations rather than disrupted them, would reemerge as a distinct possibility. In significant ways, the postwar popular media's changing view of Japanese war brides projects them as an early form of the Asian American model minority.[4] The 1950s transformation of the Japanese war bride from an opportunistic and ignorant alien seeking to penetrate the suburban affluence of white America to the gracious and hardworking middle-class housewife was an early exemplar for achieving the integrated future in America, a halcyon story of domestic bliss and economic mobility difficult to extract from the stories of long-time racialized citizen-subjects.

Yet the idyllic evolution of Japanese war brides into model minority wives and mothers was also occasionally shadowed by the absence of those other Americanized Japanese subjects, the Japanese Americans who, coming out of the internment camps or returning from war service, were struggling to establish themselves in the American landscape. In contrast to the story of social accommodation and economic mobility celebrated in stories about the Japanese war brides, longtime Japanese Americans' resettlement into American life was a lingering source of frustration characterized by economic devastation or at best economic uncertainty, as well as by a continuing sense of social isolation. Even those who heeded the advice of appointed government sociologists by attempting to gain acceptance from and entry into white American institutions were often struck by a sense of what Dorothy Swaine Thomas called the "spoilage" of the promise of democracy in volume one of her famous two-volume publication of a University of California study of the Japanese American relocation and resettlement.[5] Ironically, then, the narrative of the newly arrived Japanese war bride's successful Americanization, which was initially generated in response to the anxieties over integration, in turn produced its own formidable challenges to the belief in a prosperous pluralism by invoking, if only through silence and indirection, the unrealized inclusion of existing Japanese Americans. The celebration of Japanese war brides' success in postwar America only thinly veiled the broader failures and limits of then contemporary ideas of integration: both the widespread reluctance to grant African Americans fundamental freedoms and the continuing ignorance and neglect of the economic and psychological struggles that Japanese Americans faced in the postinternment years.

The obstacles and frustrations that characterized the histories of African and Japanese Americans in the 1940s and 1950s clearly diminished their potential for "redeeming democracy" or reflecting a national "wholeness." As a narrative of racialized national identity interposed between African and Japanese Americans, the evolving story of the Japanese war brides in America exposes the complicated functioning of racial and national identities, which come together in the mid-1950s at vastly different junctures in their histories in the United States to reflect and reshape race relations in subtle ways. The story of the war brides' passage and settlement in America reveals the manifold layers of racial and national identity implicated in the attempts to represent postwar pluralism. By considering the immigration of Japanese war brides as an answer to the threat of racial integration, which includes the dilemma of Japanese American subjectivity after the war, we compound our understanding of the processes by which the urgent need to redeem democracy was achieved in the postwar period.

An Experiment in Racial Integration:
The WRA Resettlement Project

Various meanings begin to coalesce around the concept of post-World War II integration when we extend the meaning of integration to include attempts to conceive a viable Japanese American citizen-subject. Despite the fact that Japanese Americans were clearly implicated in the national experiment to achieve a stable, racially integrated society, they are rarely if ever examined in connection with the growing national discussions about racial integration. The resettlement of Japanese Americans away from the West Coast after the war was perhaps the earliest organized attempt to achieve racial or cultural integration in the postwar period. Even before the resettlement, the internment itself was conceived as the first step in a program to make Japanese Americans more "American" and thus less alien to non-Asian Americans. The camps were organized as model American communities, complete with a rigorous program of public works, agriculture, and manufacturing motivated, in the words of Dorothy Thomas, by "the continued hope of WRA (War Relocation Authority) officials that the reintroduction of Japanese Americans into normal American life was still possible, despite the public hostility that had halted voluntary evacuation."[6] Although the nature of this government-planned integration of Japanese Americans was unique in many respects, as was the internment itself, it still operated within the context of broader anxieties about racial integration in general.

As the government and the military were preparing the way to relocate Japanese Americans in early 1942, forces from within the Roosevelt administration were paradoxically determined that the war effort be an example of democratic cooperation and opportunity. In June 1941, by Executive Order 8802, President Roosevelt made racial discrimination illegal in the defense industry and set up the Fair Employment Practices Commission to oversee and regulate the integration of African Americans in particular into the ranks of skilled factory laborers and managers. Although the commission held little official authority, even the mostly symbolic attention it offered had the effect of announcing that achieving equality of opportunity was the cornerstone of a democratic society, which the nation was defending in the war abroad.[7] After the war, in 1947, President Truman went further to establish the Commission on Civil Rights. A year later, in 1948, in an attempt to make good on a campaign promise to African American voters, Truman took action to integrate the military, an event that has since been interpreted as opening the way for the *Brown* decision in 1954. Thus, although the *Brown* decision was pivotal, it was by no means a surprising decision or an isolated event.

The announcement of the end of racial segregation in legal and public life had been, in truth, slow in coming, delayed by a litany of limited
presidential programs in the 1940s and by legal decisions in the early
1950s that stopped just short of revoking the doctrine of separate but
equal. When, for instance, the Supreme Court heard the 1951 case of
Bagsby v. Trustees of Pleasant Grove Independent School District involving the district's resistance to the abolishment of Negro elementary
schools in a segregated subdivision of Dallas, the case was viewed as a
very direct challenge to separate but equal education. The Court refused to hear it. In the following year, 1952, in yet another major challenge to segregation, the case of *Briggs v. Elliott*, concerning the inequities between white and "colored" educational facilities in Clarendon
County, South Carolina, was presented to the Court. Their ruling was
equally timid, a cautious plan "along separate but equal lines" for
allowing the original district court to rehear and resolve the case.[8] Yet
the delays in overturning segregation achieved in these pivotal cases
also had the effect of highlighting the weak thread of reasoning bind-
ing segregation as an American institution. When on May 17, 1954, the
Supreme Court decided the case of *Brown v. the Board of Education* by
a vote of 8 to 0, it stated what many Americans no doubt already knew:
segregation was no longer viable in a racial democracy. "The earth
shook," writes Taylor Branch of the immediate aftermath of the *Brown*
decision, "and then again it did not."[9] As if to provide further evidence
of the ends to which American institutions might go to avoid the recognition of racial differences and inequities, the Court would wait a year
before rendering its implementation ruling, and even then would only
advise that integration be achieved "with all deliberate speed."[10]

It was against this uneasy play of symbolic accommodation of and
procedural delay on the issue of racial integration that Japanese American resettlement began to unfold in the final years of the war, some
ten years before the *Brown* decision would officially mark the end of
segregation. As the war ended, the Japanese American resettlement
project was organized in the interest of achieving a controlled and gradual transition to integration, the type of gradualism that would later be
reflected in the polite rhetoric and legislative timidity in pronouncing
on the issue of black-white segregation. In some sense, the WRA, which
initiated the resettlement process, was seeking to reconstitute Japanese Americans as the model minority and strike the first blow in the
fight for a racially integrated postwar nation.

Beginning in March 1943 and lasting through December 1944, the WRA began a process of reviewing Japanese Americans interned in the camps for permanent release into the general population. Prior to 1943, some 250 internees had been granted permission to leave and enter colleges and universities, while another 10,000 were granted leave on temporary work furloughs. Still, none of these "outmigrations," as they were called in official reports, were part of a program of permanent relocation or integration. The requirements for the selection of internees for resettlement or "indefinite leave" were not initiated until the following year, when in early 1943 internees who wished to leave the camps were required to fulfill the following criteria of "loyalty" before being deemed eligible for resettlement: an unqualified affirmative response to the two-part loyalty oath administered in January 1943, which asked for a vow to serve "wherever ordered" in the armed forces and for "unqualified allegiance" to the United States, forswearing "any form of allegiance and obedience" to Japan or any Japanese organization; no evidence of having applied for repatriation to Japan; no evidence of having ever been a Shinto priest; no record as an alien on parole from the Department of Justice internment camp; and no intention to relocate to any of the seaboard states under the Eastern Defense Command. Although most internees met these base requirements, the catch-22 was the added stipulation that one was not eligible for indefinite leave if one was related to any individual deemed "disloyal" for any reason. This last requirement greatly restricted the number of those who were allowed to leave before the camps closed.[11]

The result of the restrictive requirements was that by summer 1944 only 9,177 "loyal" internees had been deemed eligible to be resettled by official means. In November, when the exclusion order was rescinded and the WRA was liquidated, 62,000 of the approximately 100,000 original internees were still in the camps. The draft had actually claimed the bulk of the internees who left the camps, so that those who did not qualify for resettlement and were left behind included "disloyal" Nisei, elderly Issei members, young children or infants, the poor, and the infirm. Those few internees who participated in the resettlement plan at the close of the war were a handpicked segment of the camp population: overwhelmingly younger Nisei men and women from middle-class backgrounds, with some degree of college training, who were willing to go to great lengths to prove their "loyalty" and their willingness to be reformed and relocated. These Nisei members of the

resettlement program were selected to ensure the success of the program and, by implication, to establish the terms for successful racial
integration in American society.[12]

Any potential claims for the openness of American society that the
WRA might hope to make through the resettlement program were compromised from the start, because the program was obviously limited by
the exclusion of older and poorer Japanese Americans, in addition to
those unwilling to accede to the loyalty oaths and the rounds of government review in order to become eligible for either the draft or resettlement, the only two permanent roads out of the camps. The WRA resettlement program, although designated as a means to effect the smooth
integration of Japanese Americans as a group, in accordance with other
attempts to deal with racial inequities in the postwar period actually
delayed the integration of the majority community left in the camps.
The selection process exacerbated the already complex divisions within
the camps, where internees expressed a range of responses to the ordeal of imprisonment and often struggled to find some foothold on the
future. Some internees rebelled, some languished in doubt over how
to respond, some succumbed to the pressures against association with
suspect parties, and still others went even further to disassociate themselves entirely from all things Japanese. Within this setting, the WRA
winnowed out a small sampling of college-educated or skilled laboring
Nisei as those who were "salvageable."

The concept of the resettled Nisei as those worthy of saving reso-
nates in the title of Dorothy Swaine Thomas's second book *The Salvage*,
which was based on the results of a separate University of California
study of the effects of the resettlement program. As Thomas's study reveals, the WRA program of resettlement promoted successful integration as the denial of and separation from the ethnic community in favor of increased association and identification with white middle-class
Americans. As Thomas herself concedes, the resettlement program
was fundamentally designed to erase in the Nisei the threatening consolidation of racial difference perceived in the prewar Japanese American community, so that "the net effect of forced mass migration and
selective resettlement was, therefore, the dispersal beyond the bounds
of segregated ethnocentered communities into areas of wider opportunity of the most highly assimilated segments of the Japanese American
minority" (128). In order to track the achievement of "dispersal" of the
first wave of resettled Nisei, members of the University of California

Evacuation and Resettlement Study, which, in addition to Thomas, included a group of fieldworkers who conducted interviews and reported their findings to her, followed the progress of a group of fifteen Nisei who had "outmigrated" to Chicago in 1943 and 1944. The study is chiefly concerned with tracking the incidence and frequency of interracial contacts with "Caucasians." The official questionnaires delivered to the Nisei respondents frequently request data concerning "whether employers and fellow workers were Japanese or Caucasian," whether friends or romantic interests included Caucasians, and "what were [the individual's] relations with and attitudes toward Caucasians." Under the heading "Mechanism by Which Resettlement was Accomplished" the questionnaire explicitly asks the Nisei informants to track the frequency of "opportunities to break away from minority group; opportunities to break away from family." Subsequent follow-up questions further advise the informant to consider as "positive influences" those who "pulled the individual to his destination" and as "negative influences" those who "pushed" the individual "away from the relocation project." "Parental or group pressures against resettling, and how they were overcome" appear as central to the study's means of evaluating success, with the effect of heightening respondents' awareness of the need to break the perceived chokehold of Japanese difference on Japanese American futures. The study's overwhelming attention to "not only what the resettler does, but *with whom* he does it, with special reference to interracial contacts or limitation to intraracial contacts" evidences the primary importance given to the capacity of the resettling Nisei for securing increased white contacts and the implied future success that such contacts conveyed.

Anthropologist Alexander Leighton, who had spearheaded the study of Japanese behavior and personality in the camps in 1942, also advised Japanese Americans to seek white friends because "it was largely from such white friends—who were in a sense patrons—that the Japanese children acquired their goals and ideals in American life, as well as manners and language."[13] As I point out in chapter 2, the establishment of community analysis projects in each of the ten inland internment camps was an important institutional development that reconstituted the concept of Japanese American citizenship and its place in the national politics of the next two decades. Conclusions drawn from the surveillance and interrogation of internees were not only used as sources of information on Japanese culture but later were also deployed by liberal anthropologists who felt uneasy with their part in internment to argue for the potential of Japanese Americans to assimilate into mainstream white middle-class America. Of course social scientists had been intrigued by the so-called unassimilability of Asian Americans in general since at least the 1920s, when, according to Henry Yu, "the oriental problem" gave rise to a powerful discourse on Asian American identity that affected Asian Americans' perceptions of themselves as modern citizens.[14] In addition, it firmly established the social science expert as the arbiter of future improvements in the lives of Asian Americans. As a result of internment and the massive uprooting that it necessitated, Japanese Americans logically became the focal point of social scientific theories about Asian Americans, and their theories indirectly mirrored the earlier concerns with assimilation into white mainstream culture.

The encouragement of white contacts for racialized minorities as a measurement of minority success was not only one of the unspoken tenets of the WRA's plan to remake the Nisei, it also underlined Kallen's description of American society as a "growing pluralism of associations."[15] He encourages both "interfaith" and "interracial" movements as "conscious ends and conscious means to attain the ends," although he stops short of approving of interracial marriages by clarifying his image of an integrated America as "a lasting intersocial and interpersonal peace *still remoter than words can tell*" (emphasis added) (98–99). Kallen's conditional support of interracial relations as the best route to minority success steers clear of addressing the issue of miscegenation, still the source of many white Americans' deepest fears about racial integration. The conclusion of Gunnar Myrdal's 1944 study *An American Dilemma: The Negro Problem and American Democracy*, that white Americans were not yet prepared to accept "intermarriage and sexual intercourse involving white women," marks the limits of postwar white Americans' conceptions of an integrated society.[16]

Given the high price of integration—that is, the obsession with white approval and the prohibitions built into the program of WRA integration—it is not surprising that most of the fifteen Nisei respondents to the resettlement study often expressed an ambivalent array of feelings about their own positions as American citizens, blending a desire to be accepted by white Americans with a resulting resentment of being seen as Japanese along with a pronounced cynicism regarding the potential for an integrated future. In a very real sense, the Nisei were struggling to reproduce themselves as "whole" Americans, and their own reports on their progress toward integrated success are at once contradictory and disaffected. Their reports of life outside the camps ultimately throw into relief the failed terms of Japanese American integration in the early postwar years.

Seeking a Postwar "Poise": Reports from the Integration Front

In line with the dictates of the resettlement program, most of the Nisei participants in the resettlement were resigned to viewing themselves as exceptional minority figures. As alienated representatives of the possibilities of postwar integration, they were locked in an impossible paradox: although their status as Japanese distinguished them as citizens, their success as citizens depended on an active desire to alter that status. Clearly their reports to the University of California examiners were designed to highlight their progress in moving beyond ethnic identification. However, the testimonies of the Nisei resettlers ironically and perhaps unintentionally provide a portrait of twentieth century Japanese American identity as economically and socially disadvantaged, and in so doing record a longstanding American history of both social and legal racism against Asian immigrants.

Despite the fact that most of the Nisei resettlers had been able to procure varying degrees of college training, the autobiographies collected in the study recall prewar childhoods marked by the dire conditions of rural and urban Japanese home life as a result of the relatively narrow economic opportunities for Japanese Americans to succeed in the industries of the West Coast. Alien land laws in California had made it legally impossible for early Issei immigrants to own land and forced many of them into long-term work as farm laborers or service workers in the cities.[17] Although many of these same Issei were theoretically later able to own land through their children, who by virtue of being born in the United States were citizens with property rights, the difficulty of procuring the funds to do so while also trying to support a growing family and educate older children tended to eliminate all but the most successful laborers, merchants, and those with family money to draw on. The majority of Japanese Americans frequently struggled to earn a living in the early 1940s, many having barely survived the Depression. They continued to struggle to send their children to college, where the Nisei confronted still other circles of white privilege. As a result, a majority of the fifteen Nisei respondents traced their ongoing sense of separateness as Americans to an early and chronic awareness of their lower-class status, even going so far as to suggest that their attraction to the comforts of white middle-class culture was a desire to escape poverty as much as racial discrimination.

The Nisei's memories of their early home and work lives are often punctuated with embarrassment over the deprivations they endured, particularly in comparison to the local whites whose economic opportunities they envied. One young man, who calls himself a "schoolboy" in the interviews in Thomas's study, remembers working "in the California slave pattern which existed at that time, . . . denied all of the things that normal kids had because of our extreme poverty," a situation that, in his terms, "made us feel inferior."[18] Other respondents concur, routinely describing their homes as "not too good" (187), "miserable" (369), or as "barely scraping along" (484). The one respondent who cites an unremarkable home life also acknowledges that prior to moving into "a regular American home," the family had lived in a "rudely constructed farmhouse" that was "not much different from the other Japanese" homes (212). As a young Nisei woman concludes, "most of us felt self-conscious" because "the Japanese were all poor in that area and the Caucasians were in much more comfortable circumstances" (484). The accumulated reports of an early sense of deprivation depict Japanese American culture as synonymous with the entrapment and depression of poverty from which there seemed no immediate escape. "I became more aware of my race," reports the same young Nisei woman, "and I recognized that the Caucasians on the whole were really superior to the Japanese culturally . . . they had a poise which we Nisei lack" (484). "I wanted to get over the border which prevented the Nisei from fully participating," remembers one Nisei man, "but I didn't know how" (215).

Indeed, some of the resettling Nisei felt an inordinate responsibility for figuring out how to "get over the border" that apparently separated Japanese Americans from white Americans. Achieving a college degree was viewed as one means of gaining entry to greater opportunities. The Nisei who did so often felt that the fate of the community was in their hands and some even believed "that if [they] had taken more part in the community life and if they had gotten to know the Caucasians better, such drastic steps [as the internment] would not have been taken" (311). By early 1943, those who chose to endure the qualification process for the WRA resettlement program were prepared to go "along with the attitude that I did not care what happened as long as I got out of the camp" (174). They began to get what was popularly termed "the resettlement fever" (225). In pursuit of what they perceived as the (white middle-class) American "poise," the Nisei who resettled in the Midwest during the closing years of the war were prepared to dissociate themselves from their poorer ethnic communities and to adopt new patterns and social contacts. Although the terms of their integration may now be viewed as regressive, it was not unusual for Nisei resettlers to see themselves as pioneers bravely attempting to transgress privileges denied to them. The price of admittance to white society sometimes required courage, given the lingering anxieties over racial mixing. Although most Nisei report early memories of white schoolmates and friends, by adolescence they had gradually come to understand that "certain taboos" governed their friendships with whites so that they often went "no further than casual friendships" (215). The unspoken taboos against miscegenation, which always carried the threat of physical violence, were only reinforced by the discernible class differences between whites and Japanese Americans, making white acceptance that much more unattainable and, as a result, for some Nisei more attractive. The WRA's resettlement program clearly appealed to the Nisei who registered because it seemed to offer an official means of circumventing the limits and perils that normally distinguished the ambitions of Japanese Americans.

The resettling Nisei struck a difficult bargain that on the one hand seemed to make them sacrificial lambs to the government's tentative experiment in integration. But on the other hand, given their pronounced sense of guilt and frustration over Japanese Americans' wartime ordeal, many Nisei viewed the program as a second chance at achieving American success. Some resettlers speak of the practical benefits of pursuing white acceptance, saying "they have a lot of pull and we have to depend on them for many things" (297). Still others express the hope that resettlement might have positive longstanding implications for all Japanese Americans. Couched in terms of "our great chance" (320) or "a great opportunity to build Utopian communities" (555), the resettlement is explicitly articulated as a redemptive process, both for the Nisei who were participating and, more indirectly, for ideals of American pluralism and democracy that were imperiled by the internment. "I also feel," says one woman who worked as a domestic servant, "that I am contributing something toward the real achievement of democracy" (320). Even those who express cynicism about their experiences continue to believe that "the Nisei do have a future in America" if "a negotiated peace" is reached with whites (376). Yet by the end of 1945, despite their efforts to relocate and their willingness to cut ties to the ethnic community, the resettled Nisei remained adrift in the Midwest. In stark contrast to the initial vision of resettlement as "a great opportunity," a substantial number of Nisei who responded to Thomas's study express increasing doubts about the coming decade.

Although the Nisei had explicitly sought entry into white society, both at work and in leisure pursuits, their reported state of mind was not encouraging. The price of resettlement had been high. Most of the respondents had originally believed that integration would resolve their anxieties about being marked as racially different, but, if anything, working and living with whites seemed to increase their sense of self-consciousness, even for those who were ostensibly more fortunate. In Chicago, a man working as a journalist reports that "on resettling out here, I had a renewal of my race consciousness and I felt very insecure" (230). Although one woman "lucky" enough to be employed as a bookkeeper claims she has "not consciously been trying to break away from the Japanese group," she also admits "I do feel embarrassed when I see them on the streets" and wonders aloud why other Nisei "try to avoid me" (473). Even those who admit to registering for the resettlement program in order "to escape the sight of any Japanese faces," faces that had become "symbolical of all my shattered life hope," also admitted "it would be impossible to ever pick up the pieces again" (500). The notion that "if integration was to be worked out right, we had to lose our group identity" (177) seemed to be furthering rather than diminishing the participants' sense of dispossession. "On the whole," reports a man who had been in Chicago for a year, "the way most Nisei are existing now is not satisfactory to them. They are restless and they have no definite place to go for recreational activities" (340). Although he "most emphatically" does "not want to see a Japanese colony started here," as it "would ruin the whole resettlement program," he also concedes that "it may be that a good adjustment will not come in their [the Nisei] lifetime" (340). Yet another young man working in a defense plant predicts that all Nisei "have to expect a few hard knocks and that nobody is going to hand their future to them on a silver platter, not by a long shot" (455).

Thomas's study, completed on the eve of the postwar period, seems to indicate a grim future for the overwhelming majority of the resettled Nisei. The resettlement reports consistently summarize Japanese Americans' integrated future in America as "indefinite" (180), "uncertain" (263), "disillusioned" (360), and, remarkably enough, "*unsettled*" (504). Even those few who feel that things are better, simultaneously look to their postwar possibilities with a sense of lingering anxiety.[19] The most damning conclusions are perhaps those drawn from a young woman from California who, according to the interviewers, "voluntarily explored personal problems which many Nisei are too sensitive to discuss" (474). After recounting a long-standing history of trying "to acquire some of the better characteristics of the hakujin [whites]," she observes that "the future is fraught with grave uncertainties, though, and we can only hope that some of our ideals will be realized. . . . It's no use trying to hide and get lost in a crowd. That is what I have tried to do ever since I came out here. That is the reason why I left camp. I still will continue to do it. But there is no denying that I am Nihonjin [Japanese]. I might as well accept the fact that I will never be accepted in Caucasian society on an equal basis no matter how hard I try. Very few Nisei will ever be able to do that" (504). According to *The Salvage*, the WRA resettlement program, with its emphasis on the redeeming nature of interracial contacts with whites, had apparently done little to help Japanese Americans acquire the "culturally superior" poise of whites. Instead, the break with the ethnic community and the resulting pursuit of an unmarked racial identity as Americans had only increased the Nisei sense of disillusionment with American society. However seemingly progressive in theory, in practice the resettled population's inclusion as "loyal" Americans was ultimately purchased at the price of their alienation from both the white and Japanese American communities. Precisely because it cast selected Nisei participants as the exceptional "salvage" from the "Japanesy" world of their parents and of the Japan-educated Kibei, the resettlement program initiated in mid-1943 did not work to integrate the majority of Japanese Americans into the opportunities outside the camps, but rather worked to accommodate and assuage the fears of non-Japanese Americans, particularly white Americans, upon whose approval the resettlement was deemed to depend.

The Japanese American resettlement program foreshadowed the

practices of symbolic accommodation and procedural delay that would become common in the late 1940s and early 1950s. The resettlement, as an early experiment in racial integration, was a concerted attempt to reconstitute rather than to include Japanese Americans. Its methods of tracking respondents encouraged them to sever themselves from identification with the "ethnocentered communities" that had sustained them and thus to neglect the powerful critiques embedded in their reported histories as the undesirable burden of racial insularity. The logic of Japanese American resettlement did not fully recognize and thus never really attempted to address the concept of "segregation" as the racist exclusion practiced by American institutions. It instead redefined "segregation" as the inherent provincialism of ethnic or racial communities—the poverty and desperation of prewar life—with the resulting aim of integrating the conscious movement of racialized minorities "beyond the bounds" of those limited and limiting communities.

Most important, though, is the fact that, as the University of California study reveals, the resettlement program failed to produce the desired new postwar Japanese American subject, a racialized citizen no longer burdened by the memory of "a shattered life hope."[20] The frustrations voiced by the selected Nisei, who more often than not floundered in the uncertain postwar world beyond the ethnic communities of the West Coast, fracture the vision of postwar America as "the orchestration of a growing pluralism of associations" into the "wholeness" of the individual (Kallen 25). The resettled community was instead the antithesis of this vision and threatened to bring down the already precarious optimism that marked the early postwar years. By the early 1950s, though, the arrival of the Japanese war brides presented another opportunity to renegotiate the failure of the Japanese American citizen-subject and, with it, the chance to project a benevolent cultural pluralism in America through the salvaged Japanese subject.

"Terra Incognita" on the Home Front

As new national subjects, the Japanese war brides immigrated to the United States beginning in the late 1940s and culminating in the late 1950s. The Soldier Brides Act of July 22, 1947 (Public Law 213), was the first temporary order allowing for the admission of any alien wives

"before 30 days after the enactment of this Act . . . irrespective of race."
Although clearly a short-term and tenuous acceptance of the thousands
of GI marriages that occurred in the wake of peace in Europe and Asia,
the deadline was eventually extended and finally done away with altogether on June 27, 1952, when the McCarran-Walter Act repealed the
1924 Immigration Act. The new law eliminated race as a barrier to naturalization and cleared the way for legal recognition of Asian-GI marriages. The passage of the McCarran-Walter Act had an immediate and
profound effect on immigration patterns from Asia.[21] In the end, Asian
war brides came to represent the single largest migration of Asian
women ever to come to the United States. Between 1947 and 1964, approximately 66,700 Asian women immigrated, of these, 45,853 were
Japanese; 14,435 were Filipino; and 6,423 were Korean.[22] If one considers the numbers of Asian Americans from the same countries already
settled in the United States before the war—approximately 383,650—
the arrival of 66,700 Asian women in just over fifteen years represents
an increase of almost 20 percent in the Asian American population.[23]
Among this group of postwar Asian immigrants, Japanese women
soon became the focus of popular attention.

There were a few immediate reasons for the heightened visibility
and popularity of Japanese war brides during the early 1950s. The most
obvious reason was the sheer number of Japanese war brides, which far
exceeded the numbers for any other Asian war bride group immi-
grating in the period before the Vietnam conflict. When the law was
changed in 1952, the number of Japanese war brides increased from
fewer than 900 prior to 1952 to 4,220 in the year 1952 alone.[24] The
surge of Japanese women entering a country that had, less than a decade earlier, considered them enemy aliens was a phenomenon arguably deserving of the attention it accrued. But a more compelling, although less obvious, explanation for the interest in Japanese war brides
was rooted in the late 1940s rhetoric of partnership between Japan and
the United States in which Japan was viewed as the passive recipient of
American guidance and good will. As their numbers surged, Japanese
war brides came to embody the dangers and the promises of that partnership.

In 1947, in the face of widespread criticism of his first year as leader
of the occupation of Japan, General Douglas MacArthur and his staff
actively began to issue statements and encourage press coverage of the
United States' presence in Japan as a partnership of complementary

opposites.[25] The Japanese woman became a significant figure in this representation, in which the white American soldier was depicted as husbanding the Japanese woman's emancipation from the formerly oppressive Japanese patriarchy.[26] Right away, however, the fraternization between American GIs and Japanese women presented a definite dilemma in light of MacArthur's initial proposal of "a spiritual revolution" in occupied Japan.[27] Given his approval of the Army's attempts to discourage or break up many of these relationships, MacArthur's public comments on the matter were surprisingly qualified. On record, he wisely objected to "an existing widespread promiscuous relationship between members of the occupying forces and *Japanese women of immoral character*" (emphasis added) (147). But he simultaneously conceded that "it would be useless to issue any order banning all social contact with the Japanese people" (148).

MacArthur's unexpectedly cavalier attitude about the relationships was, however, quite reasonable when one considers how vital it was to represent the new Japan as a nation of women and children rather than showing the patriarchal wartime images of generals and soliders. In countless feature stories appearing in popular American magazines, writers observing the occupation began, under the strict codes of publicity enforced by MacArthur's office, to reconstitute the relationships between GIs and Japanese women as an innocent liaison. Edgar Snow dubbed it as proof that Japanese women "were refusing to accept male Japan's verdict" and in their words were only shamed by "having to get our rights from our conquerors."[28] Martin Huberman went even further to assert that "the contagious grins of the big American who learned to say, 'Kunichiwa,' " may have warmed the hearts of Japan's women and children, but the American was always "a friendly gentleman."[29] Framing the political alliance between Japan and the United States as a domestic heterosexual arrangement also had the unintended benefit of rendering MacArthur's mystical description of "a spiritual revolution," which was often parsed in terms too obscure for many observers, more recognizable to politicians and the public alike. The ideological "romance" between the two countries had the added benefit of naturalizing the dominant role of the American presence in Asia as a whole.[30] Tales of schoolgirl crushes and fleeting occupation romances between white American GIs and Japanese women quickly became the literal manifestations of this new partnership, even though they dangerously blurred the line between a mutually beneficial partnership and an illicit, interracial affair. As long as interracial occupation romances remained a distant metaphor for the inevitability of U.S. dominance in Asia, they could serve a stabilizing function by casting the American mission in Japan as benevolent. But regardless of the damage control exercised by MacArthur's press corps, when these romances ended in marriage and the Japanese woman came home, as it were, her presence in America provoked palpable discomfort.

The first feature article on Japanese war brides in the early 1950s embraces the hazards inherent in the idea of a Japan-U.S. partnership imagined by the provisions of heterosexual attraction and domestic cooperation. In its January 19, 1952, edition the *Saturday Evening Post* presented an article titled "They're Bringing Home Japanese Wives."[31] The authors, Janet Wentworth Smith and William Worden, generally forecast a gloomy future for these new "Madame Butterfly's," who were then being trained for the rigors of American domesticity in special Red Cross classes available to foreign wives of American GIS. The tragic suicide of Puccini's eponymous operatic character Madama Butterfly fixes the Japanese war brides as victims doomed by their own desperate attempts to qualify for a middle-class American future. "The great question of how they will fit in and whether they will be welcomed or shunned remains to be answered" (25), the authors begin, as they proceed to assess expert opinions on "the great exodus now underway . . . the great trans-Pacific jump" (25). Although the women's racial differences are clearly the basis for their being "welcomed" or "shunned," the authors largely ignore the racial dread aroused by the influx of Japanese women and focus instead on the dubious class backgrounds of the women in question. Throughout the article Smith and Worden maintain that doubts about the women's suitability for suburban life are less the result of U.S. racism than the war brides' uncertain or lower-class origins. Pointing out that "there are very few highly educated women and virtually no representatives of important Japanese families" (79), the authors describe the Japanese war brides as "all sorts of people," an indeterminate source of future troubles. They are repeatedly depicted as naïve young girls fumbling through the Red Cross classes in cooking and cleaning because they lack the sophistication and aplomb to navigate the rigors of middle-class white suburban domesticity. They are sophomoric "youngsters" who "think having their sleek black hair frizzled into dulled mops" (79) makes them American women. The Japanese war brides are "women stepping into terra incognita" (79), and the implied risk to the nation is their invasion and disruption of the imagined space of white middle-class domesticity.

Although the women themselves were often from many different class backgrounds, from "all sorts of people," their husbands were often from lower- or lower-middle-class backgrounds, with aspirations to bring their wives back to the states in order to live out the American dream of upward mobility. However, in contrast to the popular historical representation of the 1950s as a time of affluence and wild consumerism, in truth the era was rocked by an unstable economic system. The economy did indeed "boom," as Wendy Kozol notes, as a result of the government "pumping vast sums into the economy to ensure the relative stability of the postwar boom."[32] However, even though some experienced increased prosperity with the rise in military-industrial spending and jobs precipitated by the advent of the cold war, the decade was also rocked by wild inflation fluctuations and rising and falling unemployment levels. The GI Bill, which gave newly returning GIs the opportunity to go to college, was actually a response to the tremendous shortage of jobs and the fear that unemployment, especially high on the eve of victory, would be severely affected by the return to work of tens of thousands of military men. In fact, the lack of jobs often meant wives took part-time work to augment the family's income, while their ex-GI husbands went to school. The returning soldier was viewed as an economic liability as well as a war hero; when he returned with a Japanese wife to boot, he necessarily compounded the perception that his entry would disrupt the already tenuous economic and cultural order of the nation.

The upswing in the numbers of Japanese war brides coming to the United States in 1952 also indirectly regenerated memories of an earlier struggle to contain an unpredictable Japanese presence in America. In December 1941, national hostility against the Japanese heightened prejudice against the West Coast Japanese Americans, and the escalating paranoia quickly resulted in their internment. But in 1952, with the war won and the Japanese nation subjected to U.S. occupation, the "concern and skepticism" over this new Japanese presence registered at a far lower pitch and was impacted by a different set of matters, including growing apprehensions about cultural pluralism in America. The Supreme Court was increasingly being asked to decide the fate of segregation in a democratic nation, although the majority of judges were loath to pronounce the end of segregation. The evasions of the Court, and of the lower circuit courts, only put off the inevitable appointment with segregation and the centuries of racism that had supported it, in a manner that threatened to indict America's position as a free and democratic society. The somber "skepticism" over Japanese war brides' futures described in the *Saturday Evening Post* article by Smith and Worden confronts a similar dilemma, as it attempts to balance the pervasive misgivings about the war brides' chances for success in the event of "racial discrimination and an uncertain welcome in the United States" against the national myth of equal opportunity for all.[33] Redefining the major obstacles confronting the women as their own insurmountable class deprivations, rather than focusing on the problem of U.S. racism, provides the authors with one means of negotiating the dilemma. But the final line of the article breaks down, exposing the tenuous nature of their negotiations, as they wonder "if the Americans who meet them on the other side of the ocean will try a fraction as hard to help them along" (80). The question, which remains unanswerable in 1952, turns the spotlight on middle-class white America, on whose shoulders the fate of cultural pluralism once again seems to depend.

Like the Nisei selected for the 1943 resettlement program, the Japanese war brides sought entry into predominantly white national spaces and opportunities, although the terms of their entry were unexpected and unplanned. Although the resettlement officially tried to disperse selected Nisei away from their ethnic communities and encouraged their efforts to penetrate white enclaves, in contrast the war brides' entry into those same enclaves was contested on the grounds that, like the elderly Issei, their national and class differences were simply too great to overcome. To complicate matters even further, the article by Smith and Worden simultaneously projects the Japanese war brides as too eager to "shed everything Japanese in favor of American substitutes as fast as they can," because they prove resistant to advice "that soup served in Japanese lacquer will make a tremendous hit with American guests, and that everybody will wish to see the kimono" (80). In coming to America with the intention of being perfect middle-class housewives, these Japanese women were caught in a predicament: their success as housewives relied on their success in divesting themselves of all that formerly made them appealing to non-Asian Americans—their distinct and *distant* Japaneseness. Unlike the resettled Nisei, who were national subjects and whose Japaneseness was in need of eradication if their challenge to Americanness was to be neutralized, the loss of the war brides' Japanese traditions and their instantaneous adoption of American ways ultimately threatened to expose the illusion of national identity. The risk at the heart of assumptions that Americanness may be learned, particularly from white Americans as in the case of both the Nisei and the war brides, is the potential for the erosion of the myth of American exceptionalism.[34]

But even more troubling for the concept of national identity was, in the words of Smith and Worden, the issue of "the Eurasian children of these marriages."[35] In tow with their mothers, they promised to increase "the Japanese-race population back home" (25). However, the underlying concern of the authors is less that the Japanese American race would be replenished by these immigrant women than that their mixed-race marriages and their "Eurasian children" would eventually erode the distinctions between the white and Japanese races. "The effect of these mixed marriages on American life at home is still to come," conclude the authors, who imagine in mythic terms "the arrival of thousands of dark-skinned, dark-eyed brides in Mississippi cotton hamlets and New Jersey factory cities, on Oregon ranches or in Kansas country towns" where "their bright-eyed children soon will be knocking on school doors in most of the forty-eight states" (25). The probability of mixed-race families living openly in formerly white or non-Asian areas of the nation not only renders these regions unfamiliar, it also disturbs miscegenation anxieties at the root of white resistance to racial integration. Yet Smith and Worden's article only anticipates the problems to be faced by "Eurasian" children whose fathers were white, although many Japanese women married men who were African American, Mexican American, and Japanese American or Nisei soldiers. The perception of "their bright-eyed children . . . knocking on school doors" was even more hostile, particularly in the case of children whose fathers were African American at a time when the threat of black-white integration stoked white resentment and anger in at least every one of the southern states among the forty-eight then in the union. The neglect and invisibility of these biracial children in then contemporary discussions of the Japanese war bride suggests the exclusive, cultural role into which the bride was cast: to rehabilitate white masculine identity.

But the interracial marriages of Japanese war brides did so by dangerously expanding the limits of white-Japanese relations, limits that had been checked in the case of resettled Nisei by the idiom of patronage that defined their contacts with whites. As the war brides began their uncertain "exodus" out of one national context and into another, the notion that white America might become "a terra incognita" to itself was a real if unexpected possibility in the context of the build-up to the Brown decision. Or, as Smith and Worden tellingly define the stateside situation that the Japanese war brides will encounter: "Nothing much but time and bitter experience can overcome great hazards like language difficulty, *racial question marks* and the separation of truth about America from the dream of America" (emphasis added) (79). In less than five years, however, these seemingly insurmountable barriers and the pessimism about war brides' futures in America would undergo a radical reversal, as the terms of the popular discourse on racial integration took yet another turn.

The Making of a Model Minority:
Sachiko Pfeiffer Meets James Michener

Perhaps the pronounced discomfort with the idea of Japanese war brides as American wives and mothers may be attributed to the unwillingness or inability of most non-Asian Americans to reconcile the national maternal or domestic ideal of American femininity with that other feminine ideal, the Asian, or sometimes simply "Asiatic," woman as the sexual delight of the war-weary white soldier. In the 1940s and 1950s, a slew of popular mass-market novels promoted this image of the Asian woman in stories set against a familiar wartime backdrop in which the white GI finds himself uncontrollably drawn into a sexual relationship with a mysterious and nubile Asian girl. By the novel's end, she usually either dies, becomes impossibly unavailable, or otherwise conveniently disappears under the jungle canopy before any question of marriage or of her returning to the states can be entertained. Her space is not the domestic American space, defined exclusively as a white sphere of experience, but the frontier beyond home and hearth, the lush tropical isles or the steaming port cities of the exotic red-light districts of the East. Among the list of those relying on this trope for the West's encounter with the East, Richard Mason, who wrote *The World of Suzy Wong* (1960), and James Michener, who wrote the earlier war story *Tales of the South Pacific* (1946), became the most successful purveyors of this genre of fiction. Michener was the more critically acclaimed of the two authors, winning a Pulitzer Prize for *Tales*, which then went on to win a Pulitzer as a stage musical and later became one of the most successful films of the 1950s. Michener's career was literally founded on the refinement of the story of East-West romance, a story line that was central to the plot of nearly all of his early works, including *Tales of the South Pacific* (1946), *The Fires of Spring* (1949), *Return to Paradise* (1951), *Hawaii* (1959), and *Sayonara* (1953). The last of these, *Sayonara*, became the best-selling literary portrait of Japanese war bride romance and remains arguably the most influential of the genre. Its longevity and cultural visibility, which culminate the popular appeal of the white GI-Asian women romances to a mostly non-Asian American audience, offer some clues as to why and how Japanese war brides became implicated in the popular discourse on racial integration and cultural pluralism in the early 1950s.

When *Sayonara* was published in 1953, it mirrored other early fifties perceptions of the white GI-Japanese woman romance as in the words of Bok-Lim Kim, "a gloomy conflict-ridden intermarriage."[36] But in its passage from novel to film in 1957, *Sayonara*'s narrative of these interracial romances was significantly altered. The 1953 novel version of *Sayonara* tells the story of Major Lloyd Gruver, a young white American officer who has the world by the tail: scion of an aristocratic, old southern family and educated at West Point in the distinguished tradition of his forefathers. When the novel opens he is the Air Force's ace pilot and is engaged to the beautiful debutante daughter of a general.[37] Initially critical of the interracial romances between American GIS and Japanese women, he eventually falls in love with Hana-Ogi, the exotically beautiful star of the all-female theatrical troupe, the Takarazuka. The romance with Hana-Ogi causes him to question his relationship with his white fiancee, Eileen Webster, as well as the conventional middle-class future now looming ominously in front of him. As he struggles with the idea of committing to the relationship with Hana-Ogi, the military intervenes to stop him from "ruining things" (207). In keeping with the plot of other white-Asian romances, the Air Force arranges for Hana-Ogi to be sent into hiding by the Takarazuka. In the final scene, General Webster, Eileen's father, drives a silent, brooding Gruver to the airport where Eileen is waiting for them. Gruver resigns himself to Eileen and the demands of middle-class domesticity by bidding an ambivalent farewell to the romantic island-nation: "And you, Japan, you crowded islands, you tragic land—sayonara, you enemy, you friend" (208). The novel varies little from the typical depiction of war bride marriages as tragic encounters that could not be sustained if the national domestic order were to be reproduced. The film, however, is another matter.

Released in 1957 and starring Marlon Brando and Miiko Taka, the film version of *Sayonara* is mostly faithful to the novel, but with a crucial difference: at the end the lovers stay together and openly imagine a happy domestic life in America. Rather than succumbing to the forces of prejudice and his duty to marry Eileen, Gruver, played by a properly surly Marlon Brando at the height of his popularity as a masculine icon, seems almost menacing in his rejection of conventional racial mores.[38] In the final scene of the film, he storms the Takarazuka compound where Hana-Ogi is hiding. Finding her there in the medieval regalia of a geisha, he convinces her to marry him. After a heart-wrenching discussion of the barriers preventing their union—in which she asks, "But what will our children be?" and to which he responds, "What will they be? Well, they'll be half of you and half of me, they'll be half-yellow and half-white! That's what they'll be!"—they step outside to tell the throngs of reporters, who have been captivated by the story of the romance, that they have decided to marry and return to America. Hana-Ogi, who renders her statement in a halting Japanese, imagines a loving family scene awaiting them, where she will "teach my children and someday my grandchildren to dance." But the final word goes to Gruver. When an American reporter asks him for "a word for your critics back home," his sarcastic retort is "tell 'em we said, sayonara!" The music swells triumphantly and the credits roll while the couple is packed into a cab that recedes amid the bustle of a busy urban street in Japan. Interracial marriages between white American men and Japanese women seem not only nobler in 1957 but also destined to succeed. What happened in the four years separating the publication of the novel in 1953 and the release of the film in 1957 to effect this dramatic reversal in the story of Japanese war bride marriages? What shifts in the postwar politics of racial integration and the crisis of cultural pluralism made it possible, or even necessary, to rewrite the ending of the Japanese war bride story to suggest not just the viability of these marriages but, at least in this case, their virtual idealization?

The question of what happened to change the coverage of Japanese war brides is valid, not the least because the transition from Madama Butterfly to American wife and mother is also reflected in the popular journalistic reports of Japanese war bride marriages. Feature stories in mainstream magazines in the mid-1950s confirm that the turnaround in the film version of *Sayonara* was not isolated. The tragic strains in articles such as that of the *Saturday Evening Post* report from 1952 are repudiated by the coverage that emerges in the mid-1950s. Like the novel-to-film metamorphosis of Michener's novel, the trend of popular press coverage of Japanese war brides was toward greater tolerance and even celebration, as stories appearing in major magazines turned away from forecasting the futility of Japanese war brides' futures in America to embrace the Japanese war bride as a symbol of the realization of the American dream. The Japanese war bride had arrived as perhaps the postwar prototype of the Asian American model minority.

Consonant with the later flowering of the model minority myth of Asian American success, the adulation visited on the Japanese war bride, at least in the pages of magazines and in popular film, gained its immediate momentum from the changing dynamics of black-white relations in America. As Asian American critics of the 1960s model minority narrative have repeatedly pointed out, the narrative is dubious because, in the words of Bob Suzuki, it ultimately serves "to discredit the protests and demands for social justice of other minority groups" by positing the success of Asian Americans as implicit proof of the failure of other racialized groups.[39] As the model minority, Asian Americans' success reaffirms the stability of democratic capitalism and makes a critique of the systemic inequities of Americanism unnecessary.

As David Palumbo-Liu notes in his masterful review of the creation of the modern Asian American subject: "The first articulation of the model minority thesis was made in an article by social demographer, William Petersen, entitled 'Success Story, Japanese American Style.'"[40] According to Palumbo-Liu, Peterson was the first modern voice to use the image of hard-working, patriotic postwar Japanese Americans as a counter to perceptions of African American failure in an attempt to recover the ideal that hard work could still bring success in America despite the criticisms of the limits of democratic capitalism. Five years later, the article motivated a book titled *Japanese Americans: Oppression and Success* (1971), which attempted to detail the arguments put down earlier.[41] But rather than suggesting how such efforts could be repeated with equal success by other disenfranchised groups in America, which might have been the real test of Petersen's claims, instead he attributes the dubious credit for Japanese American success to their unique cultural loyalty to something he terms the "subnation."[42] The subnation is the maintenance of a common biological descent, common territory, and a strong sense of identification with others inside this group; in short, the fact that Japanese Americans are a geographically and culturally segregated group ultimately accounts for their success. Palumbo-Liu further concludes that Petersen's argument "implies that by not accepting their status as separate (and unequal), blacks have signed their own death warrants."[43] Japanese Americans, in contrast, were rendered even more attractive as racialized citizens by such arguments, which assuaged white anxieties about racial or ethnic integration by suggesting that they were safe with Japanese Americans, who by cultural practice would know their place or would stay in their subnations. In the mid-1950s, Japanese American war brides were still "women stepping into terra incognita" (Smith and Worden 79), only now their national and racial difference had the potential to redeem rather than to agitate the fraught racial landscape of America. The Japanese war bride briefly, but significantly, emerged in the mid-1950s as an early form of the model minority Asian American; she was granted the privilege of American identity and even inclusion in the suburban world it inhabited, but for the price of covering and erasing other racial threats and promising not to assert a political voice.

This deft operation of assimilation was no simple matter in the last five years of the 1950s, which seem complexly marked by both change and complacency. It was a period that saw the continuing racial violence against African Americans unfold against a backdrop of apparent middle-class comfort and growing national power. Given the events of 1954, the nation in early 1955 seemed suspended between some sort of action on the issue of segregation, which would dismantle the enormously influential line between black and white in American culture, and the celebration of peacetime affluence, of finally being free of struggles. The Brown decision in May 1954 was immediately perceived as opening up an unprecedented national and legal space from which African Americans could protest prevailing forms of public discrimination and, by implication, force white Americans to acknowledge the pervasiveness of white privilege. Although the Court delayed the ultimate decision on implementation for a full year, until the summer of 1955, the issue of how integration would proceed was, for varying reasons, a major concern of many Americans. In a brutal twist of irony, the implementation decision would be almost immediately followed by the murder of fourteen-year-old Emmett Till at the hands of two white supremacists in late summer 1955, which was followed by widespread press coverage of the kangaroo court in Mississippi, where the murderers were acquitted. The refusal of Rosa Parks to give up her seat on a Montgomery, Alabama, bus in that same year, an act that set off the legendary Montgomery bus boycotts, completed the cataclysmic events following in the wake of the Brown decision. But, for the purposes of this essay, late 1954 and early 1955 represent the period before those struggles erupted, the suspended time when Americans waited anxiously for the issue of racial integration to be decided, and the time when many might still imagine a stable transition to integration. This is the point at which popular representations of Japanese war brides became screens for the imagining of a successful racial integration in postwar life.

When in February 1955 *Life* magazine published "Pursuit of Happiness by a GI and a Japanese" by James Michener, its feature on the phenomenon of GI-Japanese marriages, Emmett Till was still alive and the Montgomery buses were still segregated.[44] Although the magazine had run a story on the Supreme Court decision in 1954, it generally ignored the meaning of the decision. The editors insisted that "most southerners were calm" despite the fact that polls showed that 80 percent of white southerners "vehemently opposed" (21) racial integration. The media also consistently represented blacks as a monolithic, manageable group in photospreads of black children standing in line to be admitted to those few schools that voluntarily agreed to integrate. Moreover, they praised President Eisenhower's early editorial on the decision for "setting a good example," although he had actually refused to endorse the decision and privately held that it was wrong for the federal government to tamper with Jim Crow customs.[45] In the year-long period that followed between the Court's decision and its implementation ruling, *Life*, the most popular and widely distributed magazine in the country, was curiously evasive or silent on the issue of integration, attempting in most instances to downplay white anxiety and resistance to desegregation. Even after the 1955 implementation decision, *Life* prophesied that the impending desegregation of American society would be achieved with relative ease. In a June 13, 1955, article on Thurgood Marshall, who argued the Brown case, the magazine focused on the "kind words" of some southern lawyers for Marshall. In a similarly optimistic July 25, 1955, article on voluntary desegregation in Hoxie, Arkansas, writers played up the "quick acceptance for new pupils" by whites even while several mothers confessed that their children are "always afraid of negroes" (31). In this transitional period of late 1954 and early 1955, *Life*'s coverage of race relations between blacks and whites was defined by the denial of racial hostilities in the United States in favor of imagining a benign and accommodating national landscape, where the rights of racial minorities were at least tolerated by whites who could be depended on to abide by laws.

But there was also an international dilemma that necessitated the reconsideration of racial policies in the United States. The focus on Japanese war brides as "Japanese" women not only skirted the volatile issue of domestic racial tensions, but it also revealed the means by which Japan, as a nation, was implicated in America's attempts to reaffirm its status as a democratic nation to counter Soviet criticisms of its racial caste system. The nation also faced a challenge from abroad in the form of what it perceived as a growing Soviet Communist menace to its international reputation and postwar security by way of a critique of domestic race relations. "The Cold War," as Robert Lee points out, "provided a national security dimension to the 'race problem.' "[46] In 1949, as the Soviet Union exploded its own atomic bomb for the first time, China became a communist nation and suddenly went from being a chief Asian ally in the war against Germany and Japan to being the single biggest threat to democracy in the region. In turn, the need for Japan to become a reformed, democratic partner in Asia was made even more urgent. As early as 1947 the decision was made "to reconstruct Japan's prewar economic machine as a foil to a possible revolutionary China" (156). According to Sucheng Chan, by way of a logical extension of these cold war politics, "while Chinese Americans were intimidated into silence and political inaction, Japanese Americans began their comeback into American society."[47] Their reentry into national favor would situate them as a potential counter to the Soviet and leftist critiques of domestic racism, thus linking the cold war and integration crisis in the changes that affected the discursive representation of Japanese war brides.

A case in point is provided by *Life* magazine's "Pursuit of Happiness by a GI and a Japanese." This article tells the tale of Sachiko Pfeiffer, a Japanese war bride who immigrated to the United States in 1948 after marrying Frank Pfeiffer of Chicago, Illinois. Sachiko Pfeiffer's story has all the elements necessary during the period to project the nation as an ideal of cultural pluralism; it takes up the timely issue of racial integration on the home front, but without the need to address directly the historical abuses of the nation in regard to African and Japanese Americans. By maintaining Sachiko Pfeiffer's status as "a Japanese," the article avoids asking the most urgent questions regarding racial integration. Instead, the famous author of the article, James Michener, chooses to focus attention on the struggles of a Japanese woman trying to become American. Michener, described by the editors as "one of the more sympathetic interpreters of the East" (124), recounts the Americanization of Sachiko Pfeiffer in a manner that foreshadows the sense of sentimentalized triumph that would later distinguish the conclusion of the 1957 film version of Sayonara. Although Michener's 1953 novel about Japanese war brides had previously offered a pessimistic view of the potential for these interracial relationships to survive, and despite the fact that he had researched the novel while working for the State Department in order to help discourage GIs from marrying their Japanese girlfriends, he agreed to spend time with the Pfeiffers at the editors' request, to observe "firsthand the workings of one such family in the U.S." (126). The title of the article, "The Pursuit of Happiness," manifests Michener's approach to the Pfeiffers as a typical American postwar success story, the rise of a young couple steadfastly ascending to middle-class status and finding that racial discrimination in the United States does not impede their rise. If anything, Sachiko's successful struggles against prejudice reinvigorate the notion that a stabilizing cultural pluralism is at the heart of American society. The related fears of returning GI's burden on the postwar economy and of emigrating war brides' disruption of an already tense racial order were answered in this narrative of the rise of a working-class son of a butcher and a Japanese American war bride. As a story of "the growing pluralism of associations" that Kallen observed in 1956, Sachiko Pfeiffer's adjustment to American life renders both her and her white neighbors more "whole" as a result.

   Michener begins his article with a brief synopsis of the Pfeiffers' courtship and marriage in Japan, the "soft-spoken slaughterhouse butcher from the Chicago stockyards" and the hardworking "tiny girl" from Japan with the perennially smiling face, who was lugging a sixty-pound sack of rice when Frank first saw her: "After four speechless dates they knew they were in love" (124). After arriving in the United States, however, they faced their toughest challenge from Frank's mother, Mrs. Esther Pfeiffer, a middle-aged woman who was from the beginning exceedingly apprehensive about the marriage. Although they initially lived with Mrs. Pfeiffer when they arrived in Chicago, in time the presence of a Japanese daughter-in-law proved too disturbing. When Mrs. Pfeiffer "cracked" one night and commanded Sachiko not to speak another word of Japanese in her house, Frank and Sachiko were forced out and into an area of Chicago where they were exposed to the harsh realities of lingering postwar hostilities against the Japanese. In their first apartment, located in the city, the Pfeiffers lived with daily hostility from neighbors because many of them "resented Japanese." "Women began to stand in the street and stare up at the Pfeiffer apartment, talking loudly about 'that dirty Jap'" (129). Describing this period as a time when the Pfeiffers "had practically no money" and were forced to live in a cramped apartment, Michener constructs the neighborhood as a crowded residential area where neighbors were close enough to yell epithets from the street and where "soon there were threats of eviction" and "notes were stuffed in their mailboxes advising them to get out or else face trouble" (129). Sachiko and Frank considered leaving but eventually opted to stay until they could save enough money to buy a house in the suburbs. The rest of the article is built on the melodramatic tale of the Pfeiffers's efforts to find their place in the suburbs of Chicago, their tenacity against overwhelming alienation and economic hard times, and their eventual success in achieving acceptance from neighbors and reuniting the Pfeiffer family as a whole.

Sachiko Pfeiffer's story of assimilation invites parallels with the experience of the resettled Nisei, not the least because the Nisei had also attempted to find acceptance in Chicago less than a decade earlier. In addition, Sachiko's success is depicted as hinging on the whims of white approval, like the resettled Nisei covered in Dorothy Thomas's study who were encouraged to seek and cultivate white contacts. Yet while the Nisei generally reported that they had failed to find a sense of belonging in postwar Chicago, Sachiko's story is a paean to the dramatic potential for American assimilation of racial differences. Unlike the resettled Nisei, Sachiko's Japaneseness is precisely what makes her integration imaginable, because it is the means by which the national racial landscape becomes defamiliarized. When Frank Pfeiffer concludes, "actually, Chicago as a whole is about the best place in America for people like us," because "about 30,000 Japanese were resettled here during the war, and 20,000 stayed on" (130), he unwittingly reflects the unconscious processes of that defamiliarization. Despite the fact that Frank collapses their marriage and Sachiko's recent immigrant status and experience with the history of resettled Nisei, "the people like us," the Pfieffers are ultimately accepted by their white suburban neighbors because they are not people like the Nisei. As a Japanese American, Sachiko's racial and cultural history is seemingly unfettered by the injustice of internment and the failure of resettlement. It is precisely because she is not like the Nisei that she may symbolize the regeneration of cultural pluralism and Japanese American life in America, just as Frank Pfeiffer's whiteness ensures the avoidance of other domestic crises. If Sachiko's American husband had been black or Nisei, *Life* would not have been able to utilize their story to regenerate the notion of America as a racial as well as political democracy. The future of this new cultural pluralism for Japanese Americans seems to reside in the booming and free access to white suburban life, with the suburban terrain as a space in which the tense racial drama of urban Chicago, and other threatening problems of racial and cultural inequities, might be recast or, better yet, forgotten.

Sachiko's entry into the suburbs as an unmarked national subject enriches the suburbs as a means to project racial integration in the United States as the pristine beginnings of an as yet unsullied national history rather than the confrontation with and correction of a tarnished past. As a Japanese woman, Sachiko "had known trouble before" (129) and enduring white discrimination is made to seem a natural extension of her Japanese legacy. "Her mother," according to Michener, "was one of those strong women one meets in Japanese fiction" (129). Sachiko's peculiar Japanese fortitude in the face of undue struggle is further augmented by the nature of the racism she confronts; it is, to use Frank's term, "accidental." "We had the bad luck," Frank concludes, "to move in among a few families who hated Japanese" (129). The "bad luck" that circumscribes their Chicago experiences is represented not as a pervasive problem in the United States but rather as a localized one, confined to the crowded, low-rent parts of the city. The key to their problems proves to be escape from the urban jungle that breeds racist resentment and pressure. When one neighbor begins eviction proceedings against them, they step up their plans. Taking an unexpected leap, they decide to move to the suburbs and build a "shell house," a housing experiment "whereby the builder whips up four outside walls, a sewage system, running water, sub-flooring and a skeleton kitchen" and the owner "undertakes to finish the construction himself" (130). Michener dubs the shell house, "the American miracle" (131), and so it proves to be for the Pfeiffers.

Deciding on a plot in Melrose Park, Illinois (infamous at the time for the violence that had erupted in nearby Oak Park in 1950 when "the brilliant Negro chemist, Dr. Percy L. Julian, moved in") the Pfeiffers face an uncertain racial climate because "tempers in the area were still inflamed" (131). To assuage the fears of white neighbors and prospective buyers, Sachiko is asked by the builder to pass an inspection of sorts, to agree to meet her new neighbors and seek their approval before being approved by the builder. The result is a resounding success, by Michener's accounting, a miracle conversion to go along with the miracle shell house. Although several white neighbors were initially skeptical, some being World War II veterans with a long-simmering hatred of anyone with Japanese blood, or as Michener puts it, "hardly the ones who might be expected to accept a Japanese" (131) Sachiko wins the day. "I walked in," remembers one white woman, "and saw Sachiko for the first time. She was staring at the floor, afraid to look up. She seemed so *clean*, so needing a friend that I started to cry and ran over to her and threw my arm around her shoulder" (emphasis added) (131). Similarly, another white woman recalls "it was the finest time of my life. Such warmth, such love we discovered in one another" (132). Michener encourages his readers to celebrate Sachiko's achievement of white acceptance, concluding that it was then, while embraced in "the love in which her neighbors held her," that "she became an American" (133).

Sachiko Pfeiffer's American success story, as represented by James Michener, is a study in the triumph of racial tolerance in the postwar period and the amazing potential of white middle-class America to forego the legacy of racial prejudice, including, in this case, the very recent violence that had welcomed the arrival of a black doctor some five years earlier. Reborn under the spreading umbrella of shell housing, the white middle-class community opts now to throw its arms, quite literally, around the Japanese war bride who in 1952 it had pre-

Fig. 4 The Pfeiffers of Oak Park, Illinois (*Life*, February 21, 1955).

dicted would fail to adapt to its kind of America. The same white America that the *Saturday Evening Post* had conjectured might not try "a fraction as hard to help them along" now had perhaps a new incentive for seeing the Japanese war bride succeed in America. Certainly Michener, reflecting on the potential for the Pfeiffers' "pursuit of happiness" in white middle-class America, had altered his own narrative framework for the Japanese woman. But Sachiko also remains "one of those strong women one meets in Japanese fiction" (or in Michener's own novels), so that her offer to subject herself to a visual survey by white buyers simultaneously reiterates the war bride as victim. As a result, her ordeals in the United States, which might have provided evidence of the considerable prejudice still gripping white Americans, are instead processed as the necessary vagaries of a Japanese woman's oppression. Her story, in a sense, would not be complete without these hardships. She is the ideal postwar racial subject, one who succors white anxieties about the racial integration to come by reaffirming the power of white middle-class domesticity to absorb and dissolve such anxieties. The "terra incognita" symbolized by the groups of Japanese war brides entering the United States in the early 1950s enables Michener's portrait of a "terra incognita" of cultural pluralism in the suburbs.

As a Japanese woman, Sachiko Pfeiffer becomes a means of approaching the issue of racism in the United States without ever taking up the historical and political threat to white privilege posed by the *Brown* decision. At the same time, however, the moral challenge of African American integration structures the appeal of the Pfeiffer's tale and is cleverly reclaimed in this story of "a marriage surmounting the barriers of language and intolerance" (124). As would subsequently be the case in future narratives of Asian Americans as "the model minority," the Japanese war bride is interposed between black and white to resolve the dilemma of racial hostility in American history. But, in addition, the story of Sachiko Pfeiffer's successful ascendance to white middle-class spaces becomes the means of foregoing the recognition of Japanese Americans' frustrating resettlement in the same city and, perhaps, the very same spaces.

In the way Michener concludes his article, with the story of Sachiko's efforts to reunite Frank with his mother, he effectively constructs the Japanese war bride's desirability on the ashes of the white matriarch, that historically vilified racial figure on whom it may be said the responsibilities for white racism rise and fall. Esther Pfeiffer's racism causes her to fail to be a proper American mother to Sachiko, whom she turns out of her house. An insurgent figure, Esther's racism and her subsequent regret are metonymic of the national struggle of whites to accept the racial Other into formerly segregated spaces. "Desperately lonely," Esther takes to "spying on" the Pfeiffers from a distance, until the day Sachiko packs her two young children, Penny and Dale, into the car and with her husband drives to her mother-in-law's house. Frank knocks at his mother's door and asks, as if replaying the parable of the immigrant seeking entrance at the golden door of opportunity, "Mom, Sachiko wants to know if we can come in" (138). Happily reunited ever since that day, the Pfeiffers reaffirm the potential of Japanese war brides' difference in postwar culture for national redemption. Even the racist white mother is drawn in and reformed by their entry, and the integration of the nation is symbolically completed.

The final irony of this story of successful integration is that its focus, Sachiko Pfeiffer, disappears in the end. The story of a "successful pursuit of happiness" by the racial Other necessitates not only the absence of disturbing racialized figures, such as the resettling Nisei or the African American Dr. Julian, but ultimately the erasure of Sachiko as well, who dissolves under the pressure of a narrative of cultural pluralism that stabilizes the national scene rather than exposes it. When, at the end of the story, Michener asks about the prospects for Sachiko's own daughter in American life, her final words provide an apt description of the costs of her projection as the postwar model minority, as well as a veiled indictment of the mounting pressures of white hostility to racial difference: "Maybe my children want marry pure Japanese. Same-same by me. Maybe they more happy they marry pure Caucasian. I like same-same. I content to lose my Japanese blood stream in America. I gonna die in America. This is my home forever" (139). Although the urgency to recognize a changing racial pluralism without giving up the illusion of national wholeness and security is resolved in Michener's story, the loss to Sachiko is finally encoded in this cryptic closing identification with the nation's repressed desire for homogeneity—"I like same-same"—as well as in her acknowledgment that such an America can not sustain racial difference—"I content to lose my Japanese blood stream in America."

Her words expose her understanding of the limited function of the Japanese American subject in U.S. political discourse, which demands that she cast her merging into the American landscape as a question of cultural hybridity that is not threatening to the white hegemonic economies of the nation, rather than as a question of racial hybridity or mixing. The fears and anxieties of miscegenation and the dilution or erosion of a stable white America that might have been evoked by Sachiko's comments on intermarriage are instead reconfigured to reassure Americans that the losses will be unilaterally sacrificed by the racialized or, in this case, immigrant subject. In the 1950s, then, the unacknowledged political or national urgency to stave off the encounter with the various histories of racism in favor of a redeemed dream of cultural pluralism, along with the deft manipulation of presumed requirements for loss or retention of racial difference or privilege as a precondition for an assimilated America, continued to define the condition of American cultural pluralism and the centrality of the Japanese American subject.

EPILOGUE

Late one evening, during the last stages of my work on this book and in a moment of uncertainty about the relevance of the history of representation I was attempting to piece together, I decided to take a break. I settled down in front of the television fully prepared to be distracted, transported away from the questions raised by my immersion in the post-World War II period and Japanese American history. Instead, within five minutes I sat watching a commercial for the YMCA narrated by an elderly Japanese American man who identified himself as one who had lived in "a detention center" during the war. As his voiceover touched on the internment experience, an old black-and-white photograph of what was either an assembly center or an internment camp was briefly shown. The photograph was a wide shot, depicting a crowd of people assembled in a yard that I could only guess was "the detention center." The YMCA, he quickly added, offered him a helping hand when he left "the detention center," a way to regroup and reenter American society. His testimonial, no longer than sixty seconds, promoted the YMCA as the quintessence of goodwill and tolerance. In the last, lingering image of the commercial, I watched as the man, a smiling, grandfatherly figure, strolled arm in arm with two younger people along a sunny, flower-lined walkway. No doubt, they were all headed to the YMCA. If I ever questioned the enduring relevance of Japanese Americans' "absent presence" in the 1940s and 1950s, then here, it seemed, was evidence to the contrary.

The visible effacement of Japanese American wartime history, to say nothing of the obscuration of their complex postwar struggles, is eerily maintained in the commercial's euphemistic designation of internment camps or, as they were officially called, relocation centers or detention centers, words rarely if ever invoked in the scholarly histories and personal memoirs of the camps. In fact, "detention camps" were officially a short-lived series of centers in which some Japanese Americans were detained before being repatriated, inducted into the military, or relocated to inland internment camps. Interestingly, the YMCA commercial's use of the term "detention center" avoids direct invocation of the more disturbing facts of involuntary "internment" and "relocation." The commercial only briefly mentions the internment camp history, but it does so in accordance with the historical and cultural discourse on internment, which conveys only the vaguest sense of the politics surrounding the removal of a whole population of individuals, briefly glimpsed as grainy, gray figures in a photograph that ironically purports to show us history by showing us nothing and no one. The narrator's sudden shift to his own postwar rescue by the YMCA, the embodiment of white, Christian American charity, merely builds on this rather blatant tactic of avoidance by effectively framing the "detention centers" as but a brief break in the march toward a fuller freedom. The commercial's final focus on the current, happy inclusion of the Japanese American narrator with the help of the YMCA echoes Ansel Adams's verdict in his 1946 collection of photographs *Born Free and Equal*, in which he unselfconsciously described the Manzanar camp as "a detour on the road to citizenship." One cannot help but be struck by how many aspects of the immediate post-World War II discourse on Japanese American internment still remain in this late-twentieth-century commercial, which appears some ten years after the famous 1988 Redress Act, in which the U.S. government publicly admitted violating the rights of Japanese Americans and agreed to pay the Issei survivors restitution for their economic losses. But the legal redress of Japanese Americans' wartime ordeals in the 1980s has not yet resulted in an appreciable shift in the national representation of Japanese American history, to say nothing of a deeper sense of the ideological stakes in maintaining the national ignorance of internment and the questions it raises regarding the functions of national history and memory.

Although in any other circumstance one would be wise to guard against extrapolating too much from a single, nationally televised commercial, the scarcity of Asian Americans on national television inevitably throws the YMCA commercial into bold relief. What might otherwise seem a random encounter suddenly becomes magnified. In fact, it is precisely because this commercial appears so obviously coincidental (imagine the timing!) and negligible (this is, after all, one commercial, probably with limited West Coast play) that it represents an almost perfect extension of the discursive ambivalence of Japanese Americans' representation in post-World War II mass media. I would argue, furthermore, that the unexpected appearance of this YMCA commercial in my own life is typical of the conditions of the visible effacement of Asian American history and memory in general, conditions that may be defined as the recognition of Asian Americans across a disconnected range of isolated moments that are doomed to be forgotten as historical trifles. In retrospect, the historical narrative of the nation most accessible to Americans makes it virtually impossible to do more than glimpse the appearance of Asian Americans on the national scene, as they flare into prominence and then just as quickly recede into oblivion. We believe we know the history of the man saved by the YMCA, but in fact the counter-memory of internment is effectively obscured by the familiar, redemptive narrative of Americanization. So how is it possible for Japanese American counter-memory to be realized against the containment and misrecognition that typified mainstream representations of them, both during and after the war?

In the short story "The Legend of Miss Sasagawara," published in 1950, author Hisaye Yamamoto acknowledges the national ignorance of Japanese American experience and culture and, going further, offers a compelling portrait of the ethnic community's internalization of this ignorance, the way in which, to endure or survive, some internees fall prey to the pressures of a cultural, discursive economy invested in the alienation and suppression of Japanese American counter-memory or history.[1] Yamamoto also provides an illustration of the means by which we may begin to assemble an alternative narrative of history from the elisions and confusions that were maintained by postwar national discourse. No discussion of either U.S. postwar culture or Japanese American experience can be truly complete without accounting for the powerful, "buried" insights in one of Yamamoto's most haunting stories from the period.[2] "The Legend of Miss Sasagawara" is told retrospectively by Kiku, the Nisei narrator, who recalls her time in the Poston, Arizona, camp. In particular, the story of camp life is organized by Kiku's memories of her observations and knowledge of the lonely, alienated figure of Miss Mari Sasagawara, whom most other internees regard as an endless source of rumor and intrigue. Despite Kiku's obvious fascination with Miss Sasagawara, in the course of relating her distant, second-hand knowledge of the "legend," Kiku, like the reader, begins to sense, even if she cannot articulate, the disturbing, silent effects of camp life, which become an unlikely mirror of the larger wartime suspicion of Japanese Americans.

According to King-Kok Cheung, whose 1993 book *Articulate Silences* is regarded as one of the definitive studies of Yamamoto's work, the story operates as an allegory for the nation's willingness "to be swayed by prejudice and hearsay into endorsing the imprisonment of an entire people," as Kiku and her friends participate in their own surveillance of Miss Sasagawara.[3] Kiku's initial interest in Miss Sasagawara's appearance, her impression that the woman must be "a decorative ingredient of some ballet," parallels the fear of racial or cultural difference that also gave rise to the government's relocation of Japanese Americans.[4] In turn, Kiku and her friends become transfixed on their imagined sense of the dangers and mysteries that they believe lie hidden in her past, indeed that are written on her body. Miss Sasagawara is alternately seen as "pretty" (20), "splendid" (22), "crazy" (21), or "scary" (28), although the judgments and evaluations of her fellow residents at Poston are increasingly shrouded in doubt as we move through the story. When Kiku's friend Elsie Kubo, the original source of her information about Miss Sasagawara, provides her with the details of the woman's life as the daughter of a devoted Buddhist minister widowed while in the camps and now apparently completely dependent on his daughter, Kiku momentarily wonders "where had she accumulated all her items? Probably a morsel here and a morsel there, and, anyway, I forgot to ask her sources, because the picture she painted was so distracting" (20).

Kiku's willingness to traffic in the rumors and be influenced by the vague fear of Miss Sasagawara, despite her sense that it was somehow unsubstantiated, allows Yamamoto not only to castigate indirectly the delusional nature of the wartime hostility toward Japanese Americans but also to explore, at the same time, its internalization by the victimized community itself, as King-Kok Cheung points out. Although "political and social constraints imposed by the dominant culture necessitated textual constraints" for Yamamoto in approaching the issues of group fear and surveillance of perceived cultural difference, her "muted" critique of the government's irrational suspicion of Japanese Americans simultaneously allowed her the opportunity to comment on the ways in which the targets of this atmosphere of surveillance become slowly invested in its exercise.[5] Although Japanese Americans in the camps should have been sensitive to Miss Sasagawara's need for privacy, because they too "least wanted to call attention to themselves," Kiku and her friends at Poston ultimately seem fated to "watch" Miss Sasagawara.[6] The congestion and poor housing at camp provided the physical proximity that allowed for seeing into others' private lives, just as the daily surveillance and questioning of internees often "turned nikkei into mutual informers."[7] In effect, the internees began "to connect the 'internal state'" to the "external environment," as the material conditions of internment reconfigure the perceptions and preoccupations of the internees (65). Kiku is inevitably drawn into adopting the ritual norms of surveillance that dominated camp life, and her increasingly unsteady narrative subtly comes to reflect Miss Sasagawara's situation, "what unremitting surveillance may do to mental balance" (62). The lines between the sanctioned and the maligned, between the state and its objects of scorn, begin to blur. What do the young Nisei internees really know of Miss Sasagawara after all? As the story ends, Kiku discovers that "my words made me uneasy by their glibness, and I began to wonder seriously about Miss Sasagawara for the first time."[8]

Although she claims that this is "the first time" she has questioned the nature of her fascination with Miss Sasagawara, in fact the story is burdened throughout with Kiku's repressed knowledge that the internees' suspicions and stories betray a wealth of denied or unspoken desires. From her initial sense that Elsie's "items" of gossip are so many scraps gathered from "here" and "there" (20), and extending to her admission that she and Elsie often talked "jealously of the scintillating life Miss Sasagawara had led until now" (21) and to her observation that the gossip "helped along the monotonous days" (22), Kiku comes to sense a dawning discomfort with the others' evaluations of Miss Sasagawara. But perhaps most revealing is the memory invoked by Kiku's mother's revelation that their family had known Miss Sasagawara before the war—"a sweeter, kindlier woman there never was" (23)—and that Kiku herself had met her when the Reverend Sasagawara had read the sutras at Kiku's grandfather's funeral. When asked if she remembers the meeting, Kiku flatly responds, "I could not say that I did. I barely remembered Grandfather, my mother's father" (23). At once a sign of the passing of the immigrant generation and the maintenance of Japanese cultural traditions, the funeral is framed by "the nausea" that overwhelmed her throughout, "the only thing that came back with clarity" (23). But Kiku's claims contradict the narrative that follows, in which she proceeds to remember everything, describing in painstaking detail the surreal events of the service. The memory of the funeral, where "there had been tears and tears and here and there a sob," is paradoxically remembered both in "murky" hues and as a familiar event in which she had been "severely coached" (23) as a child. In the intervening years, in fact, far from being lost to time, that memory had recurred many times, "each time, in fact, that I had crossed again the actual scent or suspicion of burning incense" (23). The inconsistencies in Kiku's representation of her memory of this event suggest that her desire to forget it is perhaps equally conflicted. While her "nausea" is arguably another manifestation of her internalized dread of an archaic, Japanese tradition, one that is subtly linked to Miss Sasagawara here, Kiku also admits being drawn to the three men in black robes whose chanting of "a strange, mellifluous language in unison" (23) seems to have something to say to her. Her recollection of this buried memory of the funeral at which she first met Miss Sasagawara suddenly stirs her sympathy for the Sasagawaras, including the father whom she initially found so much "less spectacular" (21) than his daughter: "So one of those men had been Miss Sasagawara's father. . . . This information brought him closer to me" (23).

But the information provided by the narrator's memory is necessarily compromised by her refusal to recognize her conflicted relationship to it. The information, which is the symbolic scene of her grandfather's funeral, functions as a metonym for the counter-memory of Japanese American loss and suffering, and Kiku's unwitting revelation of what is, in effect, her failure to forget it, to wipe it out, as the self-loathing subject must. It also momentarily opens a window to the crossed lines of history and memory for the young Japanese American narrator, as well as for the reader, for whom, at this point in the narrative, no piece of "information," no memory, is beyond questioning in a cultural milieu that promotes the self-denial of the Japanese American subject who would be heard, who would be accounted for. "The legend" of Miss Sasagawara, patched together from a string of second-hand stories, rumors, and innuendos, more clearly begins to emerge as the haunting presence of a part of the Self, which Kiku and her friends try in vain to forget, to misrecognize, to cast off as Other. Kiku and Elsie desperately seek approval, and their longing is motivated both by racial and gender pressures. As young women faced with the specter of Miss Sasagawara, the thirty-nine-year-old spinster once beautiful and not simply "crazy," their craving for acceptance is predictably formulated as a dream of a middle-class, heteronormative future in which these pressures dissolve as racial or gender comformity: "But we ended up as we always did, agreeing that our mission in life, pushing twenty as we were, was first to finish college somewhere when and if the war ever ended and we were free again, and then to find good jobs and two nice, clean young men, preferably handsome, preferably rich, who would cherish us forever and a day" (21). The community's past, figured in the patriarch's surreal funeral, merges with their present, symbolized by Miss Sasagawara's tragic rejection by the community as a figure too alien to be trusted. Ironically, we discover that she, no less than Kiku and Elsie, yearns for recognition when she begs them: "Don't be afraid of me. I won't hurt you" (28). The "legend" of Miss Sasagawara and the funeral of the Japanese immigrant-patriarch comment on the failure of the community to avoid memory's language of signs, even as they struggle to imagine another, future scene in which they will become absolved of their difference, content to be "an absent presence."

However, Yamamoto insists that neither the memory of the voices at her grandfather's funeral, the "strange, mellifluous language in unison," nor the disturbing specter of Miss Sasagawara will so easily be denied. Some, like Kiku, are drawn to the unspeakable "language" of the past in spite of their internalized self-doubts, while others react with panic at even the fleeting confrontation with the "legend" of Miss Sasagawara. When one young man in the camps awakens at night to find her "sitting there on his apple crate, her hair all undone and flowing about her" like a proverbial ghostly presence, "he could not help it, he . . . sat up and screamed" (31). But Kiku tries, at least, to find Miss Sasagawara behind the "legend" that others would make of her life, an act that gestures toward the reader's own responsibility to listen to what King-Kok Cheung has famously defined as the "rhetorical silences" that pervade Yamamoto's stories, "the layers of emotion embedded in her ellipses."[9] Kiku concludes her account of Miss Sasagawara by recalling a poem of hers that she happened to run across in "the last issue of a small poetry magazine that had suspended publication midway through the war."[10] She feels "a thrill" at this "last word from Miss Sasagawara herself, making her strange legend as complete as I, at any rate, would probably ever know it" (32).

"It was," Kiku tells us, "a tour de force, erratically brilliant and, through the first readings, tantalizingly obscure" (32). The poem described a man, Kiku relates, "whose lifelong aim had been to achieve Nirvana, that saintly state of moral purity and universal wisdom" despite his "handicaps" (33). The man, the poem informs us, is "beyond censure," and yet the poet, the feared Miss Sasagawara, proceeds to question anyway the "purity" of his presence and his effect in the world. According to Kiku, the poet asks:

> Was it not likely that the saint, blissfully bent on cleansing from his already radiant soul the last imperceptible blemishes (for being perfect, would he not humbly suspect his own flawlessness?) would be deaf and blind to the human passions rising, subsiding, and again rising, perhaps in anguished silence, within the selfsame room? The poet could not speak for others, of course; she could only speak for herself. But she would describe this man's devotion as a sort of madness, the monstrous sort which, pure of itself, might possibly bring troublous, scented scenes to recur in the other's sleep. (33)

Once more, revealingly, Miss Sasagawara is not allowed to speak for herself, but is instead paraphrased by Kiku. And yet, at the same time, Kiku's burgeoning consciousness of another level or frequency of memory, a lost tributary of history, is simultaneously expressed as a critical juncture, an opening up to an alternative to the sanctioned representation of Miss Sasagawara and the larger community she both represents and is alienated from.[11]

The "pure" and "devout" man, for instance, seems at once to represent both the patriarchal constraints of the Reverend Sasagawara, who perhaps does remain "blind" to his daughter's suffering even as he shares it, and the U.S. government's simultaneous paternal censure of its Japanese American subjects. Because the poem is "obscure," Kiku is forced to put it into words her listener may understand, which can again only imprecisely and incompletely represent the complexity of Miss Sasagawara's articulation of a memory still "embedded in the ellipses." The poem's meanings seem to proliferate beyond the capacity of Kiku, or of the reader, to contain them or cohere them, just as the counter-memory that is expressed there remains, in some sense, only partially heard. Here, in this moving conclusion to the story of Miss Sasagawara, both an outcast and a representative of her community and the nation's historical memory, Hisaye Yamamoto suggests that the retrieval of Japanese Americans' "absence presence" remains limited so long as we cling, like the irreproachable monk, to a blind "devotion" to the "purity" of historical and national forms, which Yamamoto mockingly indicts as the ambition "to concentrate on that serene, eight-fold path of highest understanding, highest mindedness, highest speech, highest action, highest livelihood, highest recollectedness, highest endeavor, and highest meditation" (33). "The Legend of Miss Sasagawara" stands as perhaps an exemplar of the meta-narrative that, layer by layer, peels away the myth that narrative exhausts meaning. Even in her story, we may glimpse only a glimmer of the counter-history and memory buried there. In some sense, we find ourselves back in the alley at the end of John Okada's *No-No Boy*, the novel that opened my discussion, in which the narrator dimly sees the "faint and elusive insinuation of promise."

Some may argue, and rightly so, that the construction of Japanese Americans as an "absent presence" in post-World War II popular culture may be merely a manifestation of a historical phenomenon that continues to structure the representation of Asian Americans in general, although certainly the distinctly uneven relationships of Asian American groups to the national body at any point in history make it imperative to locate and qualify the shifting meaning of Asian Americans as an "absent presence." This book is but one sounding of the varying depths of Asian Americans' contradictory presence in the national imaginary. It represents a meager beginning of sorts, rather than an attempt to close down by securing, once and for all, the ultimate meaning of the function of Japanese American identity or memory in popular discourses. In the analyses of selected moments of Japanese American "visibility" included in the preceding pages, I have tried to capture and hold those instances meant to be distractions, I have tried to take seriously those events that were meant to be disregarded. I have tried, as I understand it, to undertake the remembering of pasts still forgotten, the salvaging of meanings not yet comprehended. At the same time, however, I am acutely aware that we may still remain, in the reckoning of Miss Sasagawara, "deaf and blind to the human passions rising, subsiding, and again rising" only to "bring troublous, scented scenes to recur in the other's sleep" (33).

NOTES

INTRODUCTION

1 See William Wei, *The Asian American Movement* (Philadelphia: Temple University Press, 1994) for a complete history of the rise of Asian American politics as organized resistance to and critique of government policies of the past.

2 See Monica Sone, *Nisei Daughter* (Boston: Little, Brown, 1953); John Okada, *No-No Boy* (1957; Seattle: University of Washington, 1995); Michi Weglyn, *Years of Infamy: The Untold Story of America's Concentration Camps* (New York: Morrow, Quill, 1976); Richard Nishimoto, *Inside an American Concentration Camp: Japanese American Resistance at Poston* (Tucson: University of Arizona Press, 1995); Peter Irons, *Justice Delayed: The Record of the Japanese American Internment Cases* (Middleton, Conn.: Wesleyan University Press, 1989); Roger Daniels, *Concentration Camps, U.S.A.: Japanese Americans and World War II* (New York: Holt, Rinehart and Winston, 1970); and Hisaye Yamamoto, *Seventeen Syllables and Other Stories* (Latham, N.Y.: Kitchen Table and Women of Color Press, 1988).

3 Michel Foucault, *The History of Sexuality, Volume I: An Introduction* (New York: Vintage Books, 1980), 11–12.

4 In conceding that "the discourse on sex has been multiplied rather than rarefied," Foucault also points out that "by speaking about it so much, by discovering it multiplied, partitioned off, and specified precisely where one had placed it, what one was seeking essentially was simply to conceal sex: a screen-discourse, a dispersion-avoidance . . . the discourse on sex—the discourse of scholars and theoreticians—never ceased to hide the thing it was speaking about" (53).

5 Marita Sturken, "Absent Images of Memory: Remembering and Reenacting the Japanese Internment," *positions* 5, no. 3 (winter 1997): 693.

6 Walter Benjamin, *Illuminations: Essays and Reflections* (1955; New York: Schocken Books, 1969), 257, 263.

7   Michel de Certeau, *The Writing of History*, trans. Tom Conley (New York: Columbia University Press, 1988), 6.

8   Andreas Huyssen, quoted in Sturken, "Absent Images of Memory," 690.

9   Etienne Balibar, "Racism and Nationalism," in *Race, Nation, Class: Ambiguous Identities*, eds. Etienne Balibar and Immanuel Wallerstein (New York: Verso, 1991), 49–50.

10 Andreas Huyssen, *Twilight Memories: Marking Time in a Culture of Amnesia* (New York: Routledge, 1995), 2.

11 Shoshana Felman points out that "the very concept of history" is constituted by "what it excludes (and fails to grasp). History (to sum up) is thus inhabited by a historical unconscious." See Felman, "Benjamin's Silence," *Critical Inquiry* 25, no. 2 (winter 1999): 213.

12 See, for instance, Gar Alperovitz, *Atomic Diplomacy* (New York: Vintage, 1967) and William Appleman Williams, *The Tragedy of American Diplomacy* (New York: Dell, 1972) for pioneering works of revisionist historians of the war and the postwar era. In *The Cycles of American History* (Boston: Houghton Mifflin, 1986) Arthur Schlesinger Jr. points out that these revisionist historians were instrumental to reviewing the cold war in terms of American imperialism and ideological manipulation, although he also believes that their failure to credit America's rejection of the totalitarian regimes of Nazi Germany and Stalinist Russia was "a great omission" (187). Perhaps the culmination of their efforts may be witnessed in the popular uses of Howard Zinn's indispensable *The Twentieth Century: A People's History* (New York: Harper, 1984).

13 Elaine Tyler May, *Homeward Bound: American Families in the Cold War Era* (New York: Basic Books, 1988); Joanne Meyerowitz, ed., *Not June Cleaver: Women and Gender in Postwar America, 1945–1960* (Philadelphia: Temple University Press, 1994); and Wendy Kozol, *Life's America: Family and Nation in Postwar Photojournalism* (Philadelphia: Temple University Press, 1994).

O N E   "That Faint and Elusive Insinuation"

1   "Statement of United States Citizenship of Japanese Ancestry." (Selective Service Form 304A. RG210, National Archives.) This form is also available in Weglyn, *Years of Infamy*, 136–37.

2   In *Years of Infamy*, Michi Weglyn points out that questions 27 and 28 on the loyalty questionnaires were generally perceived as problems by the younger population, although number 28, the longer question, was especially deemed "a trick question" or "a possible trap" because "a 'yes' vote [on number 28] could well be interpreted as an admission of prior allegiance to Japan and the Japanese Emperor; a 'no,' an open admission of disloyalty to America" (137–38).

3 "Victory Celebrations," *Life*, August 27, 1945: 21–33.

4 Sturken, "Absent Images of Memory," 694.

5 George Lipsitz, *Time Passages: Collective Memory and American Popular Culture* (Minneapolis: University of Minnesota Press, 1990), 213.

6 Lipsitz quotes from Foucault's *Language, Counter-Memory, Practice: Selected Essays and Interviews*, ed. Donald F. Bouchard, trans. Sherry Simon (Ithaca: Cornell University Press, 1980), 139.

7 David Palumbo-Liu, *Asian/American: Historical Crossings of a Racial Frontier* (Stanford: Stanford University Press, 1999), 321–22.

8 Lipsitz, *Time Passages*, 215.

9 Ann Laura Stoler, *Race and the Education of Desire: Foucault's* History of Sexuality *and the Colonial Order of Things* (Durham, N.C.: Duke University Press, 1995), 91.

10 See Balibar, "Racism and Nationalism," in Balibar and Wallerstein, 49–50.

11 Stoler, *Race and the Education of Desire*, 61.

12 Michel Foucault, "College de France Lecture" in *Culture, Power, History: A Reader in Contemporary Social Theory*, eds. Nicholas B. Dirks, Geoff Eley, and Sherry P. Ortner (Princeton: Princeton University Press, 1994).

13 See Kaja Silverman, *Male Subjectivity at the Margins* (New York: Routledge, 1992).

14 Sturken, "Absent Images of Memory," 697–98.

15 "Victory Celebrations," 23, 26.

16 Benjamin, *Illuminations*, 263.

17 Lisa Lowe, *Immigrant Acts: On Asian American Cultural Politics* (Durham, N.C.: Duke University Press, 1996), 9.

18 Lowe, *Immigrant Acts*, 6, 9. Lowe also acknowledges a central debt to Lipsitz's theories of counter-memory when she asserts that texts such as Theresa Hak Kyung Cha's *Dictee* and Jessica Hagedorn's *Dogeaters* represent "counter-histories" (100–1).

19 For an extended analysis of the role of the Freudian uncanny in narrative attempts to reimagine national identity, see Priscilla Wald, *Constituting Americans: Cultural Anxiety and Narrative Form* (Durham, N.C.: Duke University Press, 1995).

20 Robert G. Lee, *Orientals: Asian Americans in Popular Culture* (Philadelphia: Temple University Press, 1999), 163. See also Sucheng Chan's *Asian Americans: An Interpretive History* (New York: Twayne Publishers, 1991), in which she argues that the United States even went so far as to liberalize select parts of its immigration policy to "open its doors a crack" in order to compete with the Communist bloc countries for global influence (141).

21 Carl Mydans, "Tule Lake," *Life*, March 20, 1944, 25–35.

22 In her superb analysis of the political aesthetics of photographic records of internment, Judith Fryer Davidov emphasizes how the photographs of Toyo Miyatake, who was imprisoned at Manzanar when Dorothea Lange

arrived to photograph daily life there, differed from those of outside pho-
tographers. Miyatake's representations, Davidov argues, "flatten sentiment" about the interned by depicting the drudgery of the camps and the
daily survival of subjects who were "neither objects of pity nor heroes." The
"emotion-laden visual content" of most representations of internment—
whether as a noble struggle, as Ansel Adams depicted it, or as an extraordinary experience of injustice, as Lange depicted it—miss recording
the numbness and alienation that characterized internees' experiences.
See " 'The Color of My Skin, the Shape of My Eyes': Photographs of the
Japanese-American Internment by Dorothea Lange, Ansel Adams, and
Toyo Miyatake," *The Yale Journal of Criticism* 9, no. 2 (1996): 239.

23 For an excellent historical analysis of *Life* magazine's part in pioneering
and promoting photojournalism as a technology for narrating the nation,
see Wendy Kozol's excellent *Life's America*.

24 Marianne Hirsch, "Family Pictures: *Maus*, Mourning, and Post-Memory,"
Discourse 15, no. 2 (winter 1992–93): 10–11.

25 Foucault, *Language, Counter-Memory, Practice*, 148.

26 Mine Okubo, *Citizen 13660* (1946; Seattle: University of Washington
Press, 1983).

27 Jeanne Wakatsuki Houston, *Farewell to Manzanar* (New York: Bantam
Books, 1973); and Daniel I. Okimoto, *American in Disguise* (New York:
Walker/Weatherhill, 1971). Although Houston's account is more critical of
the effects of the war years on her self-esteem, both of these 1970s autobiographies approach the engagement with the story of the internment as an
exercise in assimilating the demands of national history, which seems to
entail at least the performance of a repression or "forgetting." In contrast,
Mine Okubo's depiction of such "performances" of normalcy in the camps
purposefully highlights the undeniable enervating and alienating half-life
of internment.

28 Balibar, "The Nation Form: History and Ideology," in Balibar and Wallerstein, 103.

29 Felman, "Benjamin's Silence," 219.

30 Ansel Adams, *Born Free and Equal: Photographs of the Loyal Japanese-
Americans at Manzanar Relocation Center, Inyo County, California* (New
York: Public Information, 1944), 24. See also Davidov, " 'The Color of My
Skin.' "

31 See, for instance, the discussions of these recorded abuses by War Relocation Authority officials in Weglyn's *Years of Infamy*, and especially in Nishimoto's *Inside an American Concentration Camp*.

32 The wealth of studies of the frontier in American culture is evidence of the
continuing power of this metaphor for national identity. See, for example,
Frederick Jackson Turner, *The Frontier in American History* (1894; New

York: Dover); Henry Nash Smith, *Virgin Land: The American West as Symbol and Myth* (Boston: Harvard University Press, 1971); Annette Kolodny, *The Lay of the Land: Metaphor as Experience and History in American Life and Letters* (Chapel Hill, N.C.: University of North Carolina Press, 1984); Richard Slotkin, *The Fatal Environment: The Myth of the Frontier in the Age of Industrialization, 1800–1890* (1985; Tulsa, Okla.: University of Oklahoma Press, 1998); and Patricia Nelson Limerick, *The Legacy of Conquest: The Unbroken Past of the American West* (New York: Norton, 1988).

33 Foucault, *Culture, Power, History*, 206.

TWO The Internment of Anthropology

1 John Dower, *War without Mercy: Race and Power in the Pacific War* (New York: Pantheon Books, 1986), 79.

2 Johannes Fabian, *Time and the Other: How Anthropology Makes Its Objects* (New York: Columbia University Press, 1983), xi.

3 See Alexander Leighton, *The Governing of Men: General Principles and Recommendations Based on Experiences at a Japanese Relocation Camp* (Princeton, N.J.: Princeton University Press, 1946); see especially p. 373.

4 The list of camp analysts and their respective camps included, most notably: Alexander Leighton (Poston); Conrad Arensberg (Poston); G. Gordon Brown (Gila); Weston LaBarre (Topaz); Marvin K. Opler (Tule Lake); Morris E. Opler (Manzanar); Edward H. Spicer (Poston); and Rosalie H. Wax (Gila and Tule Lake).

5 For descriptions of the duties of camp analysts and the expectations of administrators, see Leighton, *The Governing of Men*, 247; and G. Gordon Brown, "WRA Gila River Project, Arizona Community Analysis Section Final Report," *Applied Anthropology* 4, no. 4 (1945): 1–52.

6 Dower, *War without Mercy*, 131.

7 This essay proceeds from the foundations laid by both Peter Suzuki and Orin Starn in work published during the 1980s. The critical analyses of the camp analysis project begins with Peter Suzuki's "A Retrospective Analysis of a Wartime 'National Character' Study," *Dialectical Anthropology* 5, no. 1 (1980): 33–46, and "Anthropologists in the Wartime Camps for Japanese Americans: A Documentary Study," *Dialectical Anthropology* 6, no. 1 (1981): 23–60; and culminates with Orin Starn's "Engineering Internment: Anthropologists and the War Relocation Authority," *American Ethnologist* 21 (1986): 700–20.

8 Peter Suzuki, "When Black Was White: Misapplied Anthropology in Wartime America," *Man and Life* 12, nos. 1 and 2 (1986): 10. See also "A Retrospective Analysis" and "Anthropologists in the Wartime Camps" for Suzuki's earlier arguments about camp analysis. Suzuki leveled a number of

charges, most notably that since the war anthropology has been run by well-placed former members of the wra project who have joined together to suppress discussions of the cas. He cited as proof his own difficulty in publishing articles critical of the wra.

9 Yuji Ichioka, ed., *Views from Within: The Japanese American Evacuation and Resettlement Study* (Los Angeles: Asian American Studies Center at ucla, 1989). Although I do not intend to make a thorough critique of *Views from Within*, the reminiscences and recollected incidents of Japanese American assistants to the anthropologists are an invaluable source of information about the intertwined administrative and personal problems they faced.

10 The best-known firsthand accounts of the experience of internment include Okada, *No-No Boy*; Houston, *Farewell to Manzanar*; Sone, *Nisei Daughter*; Joy Kogawa, *Obasan* (Boston: David Godine, 1982); and Milton Murayama, *All I Asking For Is My Body* (San Francisco: Supa Press, 1975). For comprehensive historical analyses of the internment period, consult Irons, *Justice Delayed*; Daniels, *Concentration Camps, USA*; and Ronald Takaki, *Strangers from a Different Shore: A History of Asian Americans* (New York: Penguin Books, 1989).

11 Robert E. Park, "Human Migration and the Marginal Man," in *Race and Culture, Volume 1* (Glencoe, Ill.: The Free Press, 1950), 345–56.

12 Weglyn, *Years of Infamy*, 45; see pp. 33–75 for a detailed discussion of the processes of evacuation leading to internment.

13 Ronald Takaki, *Strangers from a Different Shore*, 392.

14 Quoted in Weglyn, *Years of Infamy*, 43.

15 Leighton, *The Governing of Men*, 373.

16 J. L. DeWitt, Memorandum to Chief of Staff (October 5, 1942), asw 014.311 wdc Segregation: Japs, rg 107, *National Archives*, Washington, D.C.

17 Franz Boas, "The Occurrence of Similar Interventions in Areas Widely Apart," *Science* 9 (1887): 485–86.

18 Franz Boas, *The Mind of Primitive Man* (New York: Macmillan, 1913), 24; Franz Boas, "What the Negro Has Done in Africa," *The Ethical Record* 5 (1904): 106.

19 John Embree, "Community Analysis—An Example of Anthropology in Government," *American Anthropologist* 46, no. 3 (July–September 1944): 278, 287.

20 The unrest at Poston is legendary by now. See Nishimoto, *Inside an American Concentration Camp*, for an account of the riots and protests precipitated by administrative hostility and miscommunication.

21 Henry Yu, "The 'Oriental Problem' in America, 1920–1960: Linking the Identities of Chinese American and Japanese American Intellectuals," in *Claiming America: Constructing Chinese American Identities during the Exclusion Era*, eds. K. Scott Wong and Sucheng Chan (Philadelphia: Temple University Press, 1998), 195.

22 Park, "Human Migration and the Marginal Man," 355.

23 Yu, "The 'Oriental Problem' in America," 195.

24 Embree confirms the formative influence of the Poston project on the establishment of later camp analysis projects in "Community Analysis," 278–79.

25 Alexander Leighton, "Training Social Scientists for Post-War Conditions," Applied Anthropology (July-August-September 1942): 25–30.

26 Alexander Leighton, "Assessing Public Opinion in a Dislocated Community," Public Opinion Quarterly 7 (winter 1943): 652–67.

27 Embree, "Community Analysis," 279.

28 See Nishimoto, Inside an American Concentration Camp; and Weglyn, Years of Infamy, 303, n. 37.

29 Leighton, "Assessing Public Opinion," 652.

30 United States Immigration Commission (1907–11). "Changes in Bodily Form of Descendants of Immigrants," Government Printing Office (GPO), 1908.

31 Abstracts of Reports of the Immigration Commission, Volume 2, 505 1908. See also Palumbo-Liu, Asian/American, for an insightful discussion of the commission's influence on Park, who also relied on using "racial phenotypology" to "cast Asians into the realm of ideology" (86).

32 Leighton, "Assessing Public Opinion," 653.

33 Fabion, Time and the Other, 111–12.

34 Leighton, "Assessing Public Opinion," 663.

35 Henry Yu, "Constructing the 'Oriental Problem' in American Thought, 1920–1960," in Multicultural Education, Transformative Knowledge, and Action: Historical and Contemporary Perspectives, ed. James A. Banks (New York: Teachers College Press, 1996), 156–75. Although this essay is only a slightly revised version of the one that appears in Claiming America, eds. Wong and Chan, it seems to emphasize the institutional effects of the "oriental problem" more than does the 1998 version.

36 Park, "Human Migration and the Marginal Man," 351.

37 Yu, "Constructing the 'Oriental Problem' in American Thought."

38 Palumbo-Lin, Asian/American, 83.

39 Park, "Human Migration and the Marginal Man," 353.

40 Robert E. Park and Herbert Miller, Old World Traits Transplanted (New York: Harper and Brothers, 1921), 273.

41 Conrad Arensberg, "Report on a Developing Community: Poston, Arizona," Applied Anthropology 2, no. 1 (1942): 12.

42 Starn, "Engineering Internment," 706.

43 Alexander Leighton, "Then and Now: Some Notes on the Interaction of Person and Social Environment," Human Organization 43, no. 3 (1984): 192.

44 For discussions of the influence of British functionalism on the develop-

ment of American anthropology, see Virginia Yans-McLaughlin, "Science, Democracy, and Ethics: Mobilizing Culture and Personality for World War II," in *Malinowski, Rivers, Benedict, and Others: Essays on Culture and Personality*, History of Anthropology, Volume 4 (Madison: University of Wisconsin Press, 1986), 188–94; George W. Stocking Jr., "Ideas and Institutions in American Anthropology: Thoughts Toward a History of the Interwar Years," *Selected Papers from the American Anthropologist, 1921–1945* (Washington D. C.: GPO 1976); and George W. Stocking Jr. ed., *Functionalism Historicized: Essays on British Social Anthropology*, History of Anthropology, Volume 2 (Madison: University of Wisconsin Press, 1984).

45 Arensberg, "Report on a Developing Community," 12.

46 Yans-McLaughlin, "Science, Democracy, Ethics," 205–6.

47 Embree, "Community Analysis," 278.

48 Fabian, *Time and the Other*, 39.

49 Geoffrey Gorer, "Themes in Japanese Culture," in *Personal Character and Cultural Milieu*, ed. Douglas G. Harding (Syracuse, N.Y.: Syracuse University Press, 1948), 272.

50 Geoffrey Gorer, "Themes in Japanese Culture," in *Personal Character and Cultural Milieu*, ed. Douglas G. Harding (Syracuse, N.Y.: Syracuse University Press, 1948), 272–91.

51 For more on the implications of Boas's commitment to fighting race-based theories of cultural difference, see George W. Stocking Jr., *A Franz Boas Reader: The Shaping of American Anthropology, 1883–1911* (Chicago: University of Chicago Press, 1974); and Vernon J. Williams Jr., *Rethinking Race: Franz Boas and His Contemporaries* (Lexington: University of Kentucky Press, 1996).

52 Ruth Benedict, *The Chrysanthemum and the Sword: Patterns of Japanese Culture* (1946; New York: New American Library, 1974).

53 For excellent overviews of the development of the culture and personality school, see Richard Handler's "Boasnian Anthropology and the Critique of American Culture," *American Quarterly* 42 (June 1990): 266–80, and his "Vigorous Male and Aspiring Female: Poetry, Personality, and Culture in Edward Sapir and Ruth Benedict," *History of Anthropology* 4 (1986): 152; as well as Yans-McLaughlin, "Science, Democracy, and Ethics."

54 Leighton, "Assessing Public Opinion," 655. In addition to citations of Gorer's work in *The Chrysanthemum and the Sword*, Judith Schacter Modell, Benedict's biographer, states that "it was from Geoffrey Gorer that she borrowed material on Japanese child-rearing practices." See Modell, *Ruth Benedict: Patterns of a Life* (Philadelphia: University of Pennsylvania Press, 1983), 269, 283.

55 Weston LaBarre, "Some Observations on Character Structure in the Orient: The Japanese," *Psychiatry* 8 (1945): 319–42.

56 Weston LaBarre, *Culture in Context: Writings of Weston LaBarre* (Durham, N.C.: Duke University Press, 1980): 23–24.

57 Starn, "Engineering Internment," 713.

58 Arensberg, "Report on a Developing Community," 9.

59 Edward T. Spicer, "The Use of Social Scientists by the War Relocation Authority," *Applied Anthropology* (spring 1946): 16–36.

60 Arensberg, "Report on a Developing Community," 9.

61 Park and Miller, *Old World Traits Transplanted.*

62 Spicer, "The Use of Social Scientists," 26.

63 Gorer, "Themes in Japanese Culture," 286.

64 Park, *Old World Traits Transplanted*, 280.

65 Arensberg, "Report on a Developing Community," 9.

66 Spicer, "The Use of Social Scientists," 26.

67 Asael T. Hansen, "Community Analysis at Heart Mountain Relocation Center," *Applied Anthropology* (summer 1946): 15–25; see p. 18 in particular.

68 Spicer, "The Use of Social Scientists," 26.

69 Hansen, "Community Analysis at Heart Mountain," 19.

70 Alexander Leighton and Morris Opler, "Psychological Warfare and the Japanese Emperor," in *Personalities and Cultures: Readings in Psychological Anthropology*, ed. Robert Hunt (New York: Natural History Press, 1967), 251–60.

71 Leighton, "Then and Now," see especially p. 191.

72 Benedict, *The Chrysanthemum*, 91.

73 Leighton, "The Japanese Family in America," 151.

74 Alexander Leighton, "The Japanese Family in America," *Annals of the American Academy of Politics and Science* 229 (September 1943): 150–56.

75 See Starn, "Engineering Internment," 713–14, for a brief synopsis of the origins of acculturationist theory.

76 Yu, "The 'Oriental Problem' in America," 199.

77 Henry Yu points out that for Park's early Asian American students "there was also the threat of the scholars becoming so identified with the knowledge they possessed that they became 'professional Orientals' . . . the academic equivalent of bit actors consigned to playing only small 'Oriental' roles in Hollywood movies." See Yu, "Constructing the 'Oriental Problem' in American Thought," 170.

78 Quoted in Weglyn, *Years of Infamy*, 255.

79 Leighton, "The Japanese Family in America," 152.

80 Benedict, *The Chrysanthemum*, 306.

81 Quoted in Benedict, *The Chrysanthemum*, 302.

82 Leighton, "The Japanese Family in America," 156.

83 Benedict, *The Chrysanthemum*, 13.

84 Leighton, *The Governing of Men*, 315.

85 See Christopher Shannon, "A World Made Safe for Differences: Ruth Bene-
    dict's *The Chrysanthemum and the Sword*," *American Quarterly* 47 (Decem-
    ber 1995): 659–80.

THREE   How Rose Becomes Red

1 "Who is Tokyo Rose?" *New York Times*, September 1, 1945.
2 See Masayo Duus, *Tokyo Rose, Orphan of the Pacific* (New York: Kodansha
   International, 1979), 3–39.
3 *Los Angeles Examiner*, September 3, 1945.
4 Mark Gayn, "Tokyo Rose Jailed, but May Never Be Tried," *San Francisco
   Chronicle*, May 6, 1946.
5 Alan Nadel, *Containment Culture: American Narratives, Postmodernism,
   and the Atomic Age* (Durham, N.C.: Duke University Press, 1995), 8.
6 Duus, *Tokyo Rose*, 184–85.
7 Yukiko Koshiro recalls the widespread criticism of the Tokyo War Trials
   even in the 1940s when Senator Taft "commented on its 'spirit of ven-
   geance,'" which he pointed out was "seldom justice." See Koshiro, *Trans-
   Pacific Racisms and the U.S. Occupation of Japan* (New York: Columbia University Press, 1999), 19.
8 Andrew Ross, *No Respect: Intellectuals and Popular Culture* (New York:
   Routledge, 1989), 18. Ross uses the recollections of Michael Meeropol, the
   Rosenberg's son, to animate his point about the mediazation of political
   discourse in the 1950s. Meeropol's memory that his family was listening
   to *The Lone Ranger* on the radio at the time of his father's arrest, and Julius's
   later assertion that the charges against him and Ethel were "something like
   kids hear over the television on the Lone Ranger program" (18) seem to
   support Ross's argument. Other critics of cold war culture, including Marjorie Garber and Victor Navasky agree.
9 Nadel, *Containment Culture*, 2.
10 Russell Warren Howe, *The Hunt for Tokyo Rose* (New York: Madison
   Books, 1990).
11 Duus, *Tokyo Rose*, 141.
12 Ellen Schrecker, "Before the Rosenbergs: Espionage Scenarios in the Early
   Cold War," in *Secret Agents: The Rosenberg Case, McCarthyrsm, and Fifties
   America*, eds. Marjorie Garber and Rebecca L. Walkowitz (New York: Routledge, 1995).
13 See Blanche Wiesen Cook, "The Rosenbergs and the Crimes of a Century,"
   25, and David Suchoff, "The Rosenberg Case and the New York Intellectuals," 156, both in Garber and Walkowitz.
14 Victor Navasky, *Naming Names* (New York: Penguin, 1980), 20.
15 Joan Kelly summarizes many feminist scholars' sentiments when she
   states "women's place is not a separate sphere or domain of existence but

a position within social existence in general." See Kelly, "The Doubled Vision of Feminist Theory: A Postscript to the 'Woman and Power' Conference," in *Women, History, and Theory* (Chicago: University of Chicago Press, 1984), 57. See also Linda Nicholson, *Gender and History: The Limits of Social Theory in the Age of the Family* (New York: Columbia University Press, 1986); and, of course, Nancy Armstrong's influential study of domesticity, *Desire and Domestic Fiction: A Political History of the Novel* (New York: Oxford University Press, 1987).

16 Kozol, *Life's America*, 110–11.

17 Ronald Radosh and Joyce Milton, *The Rosenberg File: A Search for the Truth* (New York: Holt, 1983). Radosh and Milton cite a memo by J. Edgar Hoover in which the former FBI director asserts that "proceeding against his [Julius Rosenberg's] wife might serve as a lever in this matter." The authors conclude "from the very first, the government's interest in Ethel was based less on her own alleged complicity than on the possibility that the threat of prosecuting her could be used to pressure her husband into a full confession" (98–99).

18 Joyce Antler, "A Bond of Sisterhood: Ethel Rosenberg, Molly Goldberg, and Radical Jewish Women of the 1950s," in Garber and Walkowitz, 205–6.

19 Carol Hurd Green, "The Suffering Body: Ethel Rosenberg in the Hands of Writers," in Garber and Walkowitz, 187.

20 *The Unquiet Death of Julius and Ethel Rosenberg*, Alvin Goldstein (producer), Facets Multimedia, Chicago, 1988.

21 See May, *Homeward Bound*.

22 Jay Walz, "Arrest of 'Tokyo Rose' Ordered: San Francisco Jury to Sift Case," *New York Times*, August 17, 1948.

23 Gayn, "Tokyo Rose Jailed, but May Never Be Tried," *San Francisco Chronicle*, May 6, 1946.

24 Duus, *Tokyo Rose*, 21.

25 Ibid., 30.

26 Howe, *The Hunt for Tokyo Rose*, 76.

27 Ross, *No Respect*, 16.

28 Navasky, *Naming Names*, 5.

29 Duus, *Tokyo Rose*, 111.

30 "No Happy Birthday!" *San Francisco Chronicle*, July 5, 1949.

31 Duus, *Tokyo Rose*, 116.

32 In 1976, both George Mitsushio and Kenkichi Oki, two Nisei who worked at NHK with d'Aquino and who sometimes wrote scripts along with the Allied POWs, admitted they had been threatened with treason trials of their own if they did not provide testimony against d'Aquino. Their subsequent testimony was repeatedly rehearsed with them, some of it even developed by prosecutors to ensure that it matched that of other witnesses. See Howe, *The Hunt for Tokyo Rose*, 335–41, in which he reprints the original sworn

testimony, indicating where changes were made to alter or "doctor" the severity of the witnesses' statements.

33 Howe, *The Hunt for Tokyo Rose*, 267–68.

34 Duus, *Tokyo Rose*, 169.

35 Howe, *The Hunt for Tokyo Rose*, 289.

36 Duus, *Tokyo Rose*, 40.

37 *Los Angeles Times*, December 18, 1941.

38 Letter from Henry L. Stimson to Cordell Hull, February 5, 1942, Department of State File 740.00115 Pacific War-153, National Archives, Washington, D.C.

39 Weglyn, *Years of Infamy*, 230, 159.

40 Sucheng Chan, *Asian Americans: An Interpretive History* (New York: Twayne Publishers, 1991), 141.

41 Lee, *Orientals*, 159.

42 Quoted in Duus, *Tokyo Rose*, 227–28.

43 Even for those Japanese Americans who assisted the government in its treason case the result was often less than heroic, as both George Mitsushio and Kenkichi Oki discovered. Key witnesses against d'Aquino, as well as fellow Nisei living in Japan during the war, Mitsushio and Oki had submitted to pressure to sign their family registers during the war. As soon as the war ended, they, like many others, regretted their decisions and the legal hazards that could accrue from their acts. Using the evidence of their registration against them, government attorneys pressed them to identify d'Aquino as a traitor in exchange for ignoring their wartime registration. Although Oki and Mitsushio might have been hailed as *good* Japanese Americans—as certainly the journalists Clark Lee and Harry Brundidge were for concocting testimony—the prosecution made few attempts to shield them from Collins's cross-examination, in which he questioned both their motives and their patriotism. In an uncharacteristic move, Judge Roche gave Collins plenty of latitude to impugn Oki and Mitsushio, sustaining few of the prosecution's objections. "It was almost as if," Masayo Duus concludes, "he wanted to see Oki and Mitsushio punished a bit" (*Tokyo Rose*, 177). Ironically, it was only at this point in the trial, when Japanese Americans still vulnerable to the charge of disloyalty were pitted against each other in a futile show of patriotism, that d'Aquino herself elicited any perceived public sympathy. In the end, however, none of the contestants was to benefit from the drama; regardless of their political obedience, and in an age that celebrated the likes of Joseph McCarthy and J. Edgar Hoover, it seemed that Japanese Americans were not yet eligible for celebration. Thus, what Duus characterizes as Japanese Americans' "formidable attachment to invisibility" (177) during this period was perhaps driven by an appreciation for the potential of invisibility as a safeguard from the rigors of

life in a racist society, such that the lower frequencies or silences of Japanese Americans' postwar existence may be now understood as veiled indictments of democratic possibilities in cold war America.

44 Nadel, *Containment Culture*, 42.

45 Michel de Certeau, *The Writing of History*, trans. Tom Conley (New York: Columbia University Press, 1988), 3.

46 Duus, *Tokyo Rose*, 81.

47 Kaja Silverman, *The Acoustic Mirror: The Female Voice in Psychoanalysis and Cinema* (Bloomington: Indiana University Press, 1988), 48–51, 61. For more on the origins of this phenomenon in Western film, see Mary Ann Doane, "The Voice in Cinema: The Articulation of Body and Space" in *Theory and Practice of Film Sound*, eds., Elizabeth Weis and John Belton (New York: Columbia University Press, 1985), 162–77; and Amy Lawrence, *Echo and Narcissus: Women's Voices in Classical Hollywood Cinema* (Berkeley: University of California Press, 1991). Robert Corber also renders an excellent analysis of the impact of these studies of women's filmic representations and voices in his book *In the Name of National Security: Hitchcock, Homophobia, and the Political Construction of Gender in Postwar America* (Durham, N.C.: Duke University Press, 1993).

48 Corber, *In the Name of National Security*, 119.

49 Koshiro, *Trans-Pacific Racisms*, 58.

50 Quoted in ibid., 58–59.

51 Koshiro notes that "toward the end of 1948, when the growing emphasis on the danger of Communism altered the relationship between the Americans and the Japanese, a series of programs quickly emerged which removed the previous anti-fraternization policies and instead furthered a symbolic friendship" (70). D'Aquino's trial, however, was too early to reap the potential benefits of this shift in relations between the two countries, which might have permitted the defense to strengthen the necessity of her friendships with the Allied POWs as in the interests of the nation.

52 "Tokyo Rose on Trial," *San Francisco Chronicle*, August 4, 1949.

53 Duus, *Tokyo Rose*, 81.

54 Howe, *The Hunt for Tokyo Rose*, 140.

55 Quoted from *Argus*, August 26, 1946, in Duus, *Tokyo Rose*, 146.

56 Howe, *The Hunt for Tokyo Rose*, 48.

57 Duus, *Tokyo Rose*, 57.

58 Quoted in Howe, *The Hunt for Tokyo Rose*, 114–15.

59 Ibid., 132.

60 Duus, *Tokyo Rose*, 223.

FOUR   "A Mutual Brokenness"

1   Joy Kogawa, *Obasan* (Boston: David Godine, 1982).

2   Rodney Barker, *The Hiroshima Maidens: A Story of Courage, Compassion, and Survival* (New York: Viking, 1985), 12.

3   See May, *Homeward Bound*, 76. Tyler points out that "three-fourths of the women who had been employed in war industries were still employed in 1946," although "90 percent of them were earning less than they had during the war" (76). She concludes that these narrowing economic opportunities for women reflected the belief that keeping women "in their place" (77) preserved a larger place for men.

4   Sturken, "Absent Images of Memory," 704.

5   Rodney Barker, *The Hiroshima Maidens*.

6   Norman Cousins, "The Maidens are Coming," *Saturday Review*, April 9, 1955: 24–25.

7   In her memoirs *Young, White, and Miserable: Growing Up Female in the Fifties* (Boston: Beacon, 1992), Wini Breines argues that scapegoating white women was "one facet of the story of middle-class, white women in the 1950s" (41).

8   See May, *Homeward Bound*.

9   See Philip Wylie, *A Generation of Vipers* (New York: Farrar & Rinehart, 1942); Helene Deutsch, *The Psychology of Women* (New York: Grune and Stratton, 1944–1945); Edward Strecker, *Their Mothers' Sons: The Psychiatrist Examines an American Problem* (Philadelphia: J. B. Lippincott, 1946); and Ferdinand Lundberg and Marynia F. Farnham, *Modern Woman: The Lost Sex* (New York: Grosset & Dunlap, 1947).

10 See, for instance, Thorstein Veblen, *Theory of the Leisure Class* (1899; New York: Penguin, 1994); Charlotte Perkins Gilman, *Women and Economics: A Study of the Economic Relations between Men and Women as a Factor in Social Evolution* (1901; Boston: Dover, 1998); Henry James, *Daisy Miller* (1878; New York: Penguin, 1988); Theodore Dreiser, *Sister Carrie* (1901; New York: Modern Library, 1999); and Edith Wharton, *House of Mirth* (1905; New York: Modern Library, 1999).

11 For a more specific analysis of the function of Japanese and Japanese American women in this dynamic, see chapter 1 in Traise Yamamoto, *Masking Selves, Making Subjects: Japanese American Women, Identity, and the Body* (Berkeley: University of California Press, 1998). For understanding the significance of normative heterosexuality in a colonial context, see Lisa Lowe, *Critical Terrains: French and British Orientalisms* (Ithaca, N.Y.: Cornell University Press, 1991); and Anne McClintock, *Imperial Leather: Race, Gender, and Sexuality in the Colonial Contest* (New York: Routledge, 1995). Although McClintock is more overtly concerned with instances of sexual and

racial transgression or resistance, chapter 6 in her book provides some useful insights into the way in which the control of women's sexuality regenerated patriarchal arrangements, while chapter 3 offers some related discussions of the power of domesticity to imagine the national polity as one.

12 See Palumbo-Liu, *Asian/American*, 17. Palumbo-Liu also points out that although this concept of Asia "was a particular test of its [America's] self-conception," it would be wrong to assume it never changes shape, because after the 1930s "events in East Asia required the United States to engage in a new set of negotiations of its national destiny in a new global political economy" (18).

13 See May, *Homeward Bound*, 16–21; and Kozol, *Life's America*, 3–5. Kozol concludes "Nixon's reliance on a language of domesticity points to the centrality of cultural ideals in political discourses. Indeed, cultural values are entwined with political structures and ideas as much as power relations are embedded in cultural spaces" (5).

14 Norman Cousins, "Interim Report on the Maidens," *Saturday Review*, October 15, 1955: 22–23.

15 Barker, *The Hiroshima Maidens*, 79–80.

16 Quoted in Virginia Naeve, *Friends of the Hibakusha* (Denver: Allan Swallow, 1964), 104.

17 For a brief history of Mary "Yuri" Kochiyama's life, see Diane C. Fujino, "Revolutions from the Heart: The Making of an Asian American Women Activist, Yuri Kochiyama," in *Dragon Ladies: Asian American Feminists Breathe Fire*, ed. Sonia Shah (Boston: South End Press, 1997), 169–81. Although Fujino points out that Mary Kochiyama now prefers to be known by her given Japanese name, Yuri, in the interest of avoiding confusion I will use the name by which she was known during the years in question in this essay.

18 Katie Wang, " 'U' Opens Asian American Lounge," *Michigan Daily Online*, February 4, 1997.

19 Fujino, "Revolution from the Heart," 174.

20 Cousins, "Interim Report on the Maidens," 22–23.

21 Barker, *The Hiroshima Maidens*, 109.

22 Koshiro, *Trans-Pacific Racisms*, 10.

23 Ibid., 123. The headline is taken from the June 12, 1956, edition of the *New York Journal-American*, while the quote comes from an article in the June 12, 1956, edition of the *New York Post*.

24 Barker, *The Hiroshima Maidens*, 151.

25 Ibid., 158.

26 Ibid., 130–31.

27 See my previous comments in chapters 1 and 2 on the relocation program for Nisei, in which I point out that WRA officials promoted the measure-

ment of Nisei success by the number and frequency of white contacts and white approval.

28 Weglyn, *Years of Infamy*, 268.

29 Takaki, *Strangers from a Different Shore*, 405.

30 Okada, *No-No Boy*, 6, 96.

31 Evelyn Nakano Glenn, *Issei, Nisei, War Bride: Three Generations of Japanese American Women in Domestic Service* (Philadelphia: Temple University Press, 1986), 199.

32 Sone, *Nisei Daughter* (1953; Seattle: University of Washington Press, 1979), foreword by Frank S. Miyamoto.

33 Lowe, *Immigrant Acts*, 48–50.

34 Yamamoto, *Masking Selves, Making Subjects*, 113, 119.

35 Fujino, "Revolutions from the Heart," 178.

36 Barker, *The Hiroshima Maidens*, 118.

37 Quoted in Naeve, *Friends of the Hibakusha*, 114.

38 Ibid., 117.

39 Barker, *The Hiroshima Maidens*, 133.

40 American Committee for Protection of the Foreign Born, "Concentration Camps, USA: It has happened here, it could happen again—to you!" New York: 1969.

41 Amy Uyematsu in *Roots: An Asian American Reader* (Los Angeles: Asian American Studies Center, UCLA, 1971), 10.

42 Eldridge Cleaver, *Soul on Ice* (New York: Dell, 1968), 123. Cleaver argued further that for the black man to fight the war in Vietnam would be to ensure widespread Asian hatred of African Americans, a danger that they could not afford at a time when "black Americans will need the help and support of their brothers, friends and *natural* allies from around the world" (emphasis added) (127).

43 American Committee for Proection of Foreign Born, 5–6.

44 It is difficult to overestimate the impact of the liberation movements on the development of racial identity and race relations in the United States. The rise of protest movements of all kinds in the late 1960s unequivocally marked the closing of an era of articulation for the racialized subject. As a result, according to Michael Omi and Howard Winant, "organizationally, the minority movements of the 1950s and the 1960s nearly ceased to exist" as they gave way to "intense campaigns for racial equality and democracy" caused largely "by the transformed character of 'blackness,' 'whiteness,' and all other racial identities that the movements had initiated." See Michael Omi and Howard Winant, *Racial Formation in the United States: From the 1960s to the 1980s* (New York: Routledge, 1986), 108.

45 Karin Aguilar San-Juan, "Linking the Issues: From Identity to Activism," in *The State of Asian American Activism and Resisitance in the 1990s*, ed. Karin Aguilar San-Juan (Boston: South End Press, 1994), 2.

46 Elaine Calderon, "Speaker Challenges Students to Act," *The Bucknellian On-line*, 1999.

47 I allude here to the by now well-known sexism of many of the male leaders of the early civil rights movements, which often relegated women to secondary or sexualized roles as office aides or "girlfriends" to the cause. Howard Zinn quotes Ella Baker, a member of the Student Nonviolent Coordinating Committee, who recalls that as a woman "there was no place for me to have come into a leadership role." But along with their struggles, many women in the early movements used what they learned there to initiate a call for women's rights as part of the selfsame commitment to nonviolence and equality that characterized civil rights. See Elaine Brown's memoir of her days in the Black Panthers, *Taste of Power: A Black Woman's Story* (New York: Anchor, 1994), in which she presents a similar portrait of the group's sexism. For a broader view of these dilemmas, consult Howard Zinn, *A People's History of the United States* (New York: Harper, 1980), quoted on p. 494. See also pp. 485–504.

FIVE   "Out of an Obscure Place"

1 Horace Kallen, "Democracy versus the Melting Pot," *Nation*, February 19 and 25, 1915, 190–94, 217–20. This essay has been cited remarked by numerous scholars as pivotal to the conception of a racial democracy in the twentieth century.

2 Horace Kallen, "Of Meanings of Culture," in *Cultural Pluralism and the American Idea: An Essay in Social Philosophy* (Philadelphia: University of Pennsylvania Press, 1956), 24.

3 Stewart G. Cole, "A Reaction to Kallen's Essay" in Horace Kallen, *Cultural Pluralism and the American Idea: An Essay in Social Philosophy* (Philadelphia: University of Pennsylvania Press, 1956): 113–15.

4 As a recent study by Paul Wong and others of the emergence and progress of the model minority stereotype of Asian Americans points out, the stereotype is commonly cited as originating in the "middle 1960s," when the general public "perceived Asian Americans as a model minority on the basis of their educational attainment." See Paul Wong, Chienping Faith Lai, Richard Nagasawa, and Tieming Lin, "Asian Americans as a Model Minority: Self Perceptions by Other Racial Groups," *Sociological Perspectives* 14, no. 1 (1998): 96–118.

5 See Dorothy Swaine Thomas, *The Spoilage: Japanese American Evacuation and Resettlement* (Berkeley: University of California Press, 1946), and *The Salvage: Japanese American Evacuation and Resettlement* (Berkeley: University of California Press, 1952).

6 Thomas, *The Spoilage*, 25.

7 See Eileen Boris, "'You Wouldn't Want One of 'Em Dancing with Your

Wife': Racialized Bodies on the Job in World War II," *The American Quarterly* 50, no. 1 (March 1998): 77–108. See especially pages 82–84 for a discussion of the political significance of the FEPC to the wartime promotion of America as a racial democracy.

8   Stephen L. Wasby, Anthony A. D'Amato, and Rosemary Metrailer, *Desegregation from Brown to Alexander: An Exploration of Supreme Court Strategies* (Carbondale: Southern Illinois University Press, 1977), 58–67.

9   Taylor Branch, *Parting the Waters: America in The King Years, 1954–1963* (New York: Simon and Schuster, 1988): 112.

10 Wesby, D'Amato, and Metrailer, *Desegregation from Brown to Alexander*, 108–30.

11 See Thomas, *The Salvage*, 91, 105–12.

12 Thomas remarks that "in general, the college-educated Christian-secular nonagricultural Nisei not only showed the greatest willingness to leave camp and to reenter 'American life,' but they also, initially, had less difficulty than other classes in obtaining 'leave clearance'" (*The Salvage*, 125).

13 Alexander Leighton, "The Japanese Family in America," *Annals of the American Academy of Politics and Social Science* 229 (September 1943): 153.

14 Henry Yu, "The 'Oriental Problem' in America." See especially his claim that "without recovering the ways in which Chinese American and Japanese American identities were affected by these old theories and definitions, we cannot fully map the terrain on which Asian American consciousness arose" (210–11).

15 Kallen, *Cultural Pluralism*, 25.

16 Gunnar Myrdal, *An American Dilemma: The Negro Problem and American Democracy* (New York: Harper, 1944), 60.

17 Takaki, *Strangers From a Different Shore*, 203–8. As Takaki points out, the tightening of anti-Asian laws in California resulted in "a drop in Japanese landholdings" after 1925, which meant losses for Issei parents in the years leading up to the Depression era. Yuji Ichioka's *The Issei: The World of the First Generation Japanese Immigrants, 1885–1924* (New York: Free Press, 1988) explains that the early hopes of the Issei as settlers in America were founded on the dream of farmland development and ownership (148). Taking the possibility of land ownership away, alien land laws hit at the heart of the immigrants' claims to American identity.

18 Thomas, *The Salvage*, 153.

19 A young female bookkeeper, described as an "exceptional personality," concludes "the Nisei may complain about not getting the best jobs out here but I think they are better off than in California. . . . I know that in Los Angeles the Japanese only get to be domestic workers, fruit stand workers, and the rest were students" (Thomas, *The Salvage*, 474). A young man who worked as an "errand boy" and "welder" and often highlighted his sexual

adventures, reports "I haven't met any discrimination out here yet." Later, however, he states "there's no sense hating the Caucasians." And when offering his opinion of his situation in Chicago, further offers, "I don't know if I'm better off now than I was before evacuation. I think that maybe I am" (296–97).

20 Thomas, *The Salvage*, 504.

21 Elfrieda Shukert and Barbara Scibetta, *War Brides of World War II* (Novato, Calif.: Presidio Press, 1988), 209.

22 Figures are taken from "Table 6: Asian Women Immigrants Admitted to the U.S. as Wives of American Citizens," in *Annual Reports, 1947–75*, a report compiled by the U.S. Commissioner of Immigration and Naturalization. The statistical evidence offered in the report is considered conservative. In the most recent demographic reports on Asian war brides, which include the ten-year period between 1964–1975, the numbers are listed as 66,681 Japanese, 51,747 Filipino, 28,205 Korean, 11,166 Thai, and 8,040 Vietnamese war brides. See Bok-Lim C. Kim, "Asian Wives of U.S. Servicemen: Women in the Shadows," *Amerasia Journal* 4 (1977): 91–115; and Rogelio Saenz, Sean-Shong Hwang, and Benigno E. Aguirre, "In Search of Asian War Brides," *Demography* 31, no. 3 (Aug. 94): 549–59.

23 See Roger Daniels, *Coming to America: A History of Immigration and Ethnicity in American Life* (Princeton, N.J.: HarperCollins, 1990), 351.

24 Shukert and Scibetta, *War Brides of World War II*, 216.

25 According to Eleanor M. Hadley, *Antitrust in Japan* (Princeton, N.J.: Princeton University Press, 1970), MacArthur's administration is widely perceived as having launched a massive campaign in 1946 to redefine the situation in occupied Japan as one of friendly cooperation rather than guarded coexistence. Michael Schaller, historian and MacArthur biographer, argues that MacArthur's own political ambitions in the United States as well as problems in the Japanese economy were the foundations of this campaign. See Schaller, *Douglas MacArthur: The Far Eastern General* (New York: Oxford University Press, 1989), 145–52.

26 See Edgar Snow, "What the Jap is Thinking Now," *Saturday Evening Post*, May 1946. In this article Snow notes that the hospitality of Japanese women to American soldiers announced that Japanese women were "refusing to accept male Japan's verdict" in order to "get our rights from our new conquerors." See also Arthur Behrstock, "Japan Goes American," *American Magazine*, May 1947, in which he touts Japanese women's cordial relations with GIs "as evidence of Japan's growing attraction for American democracy." In addition, see John Ashmead, "Japs Look at Yanks," *Atlantic Monthly*, April 1947; Martin A. Huberman, "Backwoods Japan during the American Occupation," *National Geographic*, April 1947; Lindsey Parrott, "Now a Japanese Woman Can Be a Cop," *New York Times Magazine*, June 2, 1946; and Noel F. Busch, "Tokyo Geisha," *Life*, March 17, 1947.

27 Michael Schaller, *Douglas MacArthur*, 145.

28 Snow, "A Town Never Occupied by American Troops," 10.

29 Huberman, "Backwoods Japan during the American Occupation," 511.

30 William P. Woodard, *The Allied Occupation of Japan, 1945–52, and Japanese Religions* (Leiden: E. J. Brill 1972), 14–18.

31 J. E. Smith and William L. Worden, "They're Bringing Home Japanese Wives," *Saturday Evening Post*, January 19, 1952, 25, 79–81.

32 See Kozol, *Life's America*, 86–87. Kozol further points out that "the government subsidized these remarkable postwar consumer habits through federally financed loan programs such as those offered by the FHA and the GI Bill, which enabled more than 7.6 million veterans to go to college and 1.3 million to secure home loans" (86).

33 Smith and Worden, "They're Bringing Home Japanese Wives," 79.

34 The notion that American society represents a unique civilization and society is still contested. See Michael Kammen, "The Problem of American Exceptionalism: A Reconsideration," *The American Quarterly* 45, no. 1 (1993): 1–43.

35 Smith and Worden, "They're Bringing Home Japanese Wives," 25.

36 Kim, "Asian Wives of U.S. Servicemen," 96. See also Paul Spickard's problematic study of mixed-race identity, *Mixed Blood: Intermarriage and Ethnic Identity in Twentieth-Century America* (Madison: University of Wisconsin Press, 1989). Spickard's portrait of Asian war brides is characterized by stereotypical views remarkable for their presentation as scholarly research.

37 James Michener, *Sayonara* (New York: Fawcett Crest, 1953).

38 In 1956, less than a year before this film, audiences saw Brando in *The Teahouse of the August Moon*, a comedy based on John Patrick's 1954 adaptation of Vern Sneider's novel. It had been a big hit on Broadway, but the casting of Brando in the role of Sakini, the Okinawan narrator, was unexpected. Brando, however, chose to play Sakini as a distant relation to the African American stereotypes of Step'n Fetchit and Sambo, as his wide-eyed pleas of ignorance in order to avoid work and duty while under the occupation of the United States belie his underlying laziness and cagey manipulation of his "boss." The character required Brando to tape his lids in order to approximate "oriental" eyes, and to adopt a Japanese accent in English. In obvious ways, Lloyd Gruver was the opposite of Sakini—the serious, brooding representative of the postwar white male conscience that would reconsider and recast his formerly "hard" relationship to the East and, symbolically, to figures like Sakini.

39 Bob H. Suzuki, "Asian-American as the Model Minority," *Change* (November 1989): 13–19. See also the work of Keith Osajima, "Asian Americans as the Model Minority: An Analysis of the Popular Press Image in the 1960s and 1980s," in *Reflections on Shattered Windows* (Pullman: Washington State University Press, 1988), 165–74; and Arthur Hu, "Asian

Americans: Model Minority or Double Minority?" *Amerasia Journal* 15 (1989): 243–57.

40 Palumbo-Liu, *Asian/American*, 174.

41 William Petersen, *Japanese Americans: Oppression and Success* (New York: Random House, 1971).

42 William Petersen, *"Success Story,* Japanese American Style." *Saturday Evening Post* (January 9, 1966): 105–6, 122–25.

43 Palumbo-Liu, Asian/American, 178.

44 James A. Michener, "Pursuit of Happiness by a GI and a Japanese," *Life,* February 21, 1955, 124–26, 129–39.

45 See "Historic Decision for Equality," *Life,* May 31, 1955.

46 Lee, *Orientals,* 157.

47 Chan, *Asian Americans,* 141.

EPILOGUE

1 Hisaye Yamamoto, "The Legend of Miss Sasagawara," in *Seventeen Syllables and Other Stories* (Latham, N. Y.: Kitchen Table and Women of Color Press, 1988), 20–33. The story was originally published in the *Kenyon Review* 12, no. 1 (1950): 99–115.

2 In an early essay on Yamamoto's work, Stan Yogi points out the importance of reading for "buried plots" in her stories, an observation of the silences that permeate many feminist works before the liberation movements of the 1960s. I go on to discuss the implications of this concept for my argument about Japanese Americans and postwar culture. See Stan Yogi, "Legacies Revealed: Uncovering Buried Plots in the Stories of Hisaye Yamamoto," *Studies in American Fiction* 17, no. 2 (1989): 169–81.

3 King-Kok Cheung, *Articulate Silences: Hisaye Yamamoto, Maxine Hong Kingston, Joy Kogawa* (Ithaca, N. Y.: Cornell University Press, 1993), 65.

4 Yamamoto, "The Legend of Miss Sasagawara," 20.

5 Cheung, *Articulate Silences,* 30.

6 Yamamoto, "The Legend of Miss Sasagawara," 59.

7 Cheung, *Articulate Silences,* 65, 67.

8 Yamamoto, "The Legend of Miss Sasagawara," 32.

9 Cheung, *Articulate Silences,* 73.

10 Yamamoto, "The Legend of Miss Sasagawara," 32.

11 It is interesting to note that Kiku's use of the word "scented" in her description of Miss Sasagawara's poem evokes the scene of her grandfather's funeral, which she previously cited as recurring in the presence of "the actual scent or suspicion of burning incense" (23). One might argue that this further ties that scene of memory reconstructed to the attempt to construct an accurate image of Miss Sasagawara, both of which, indeed, "bring troublous, scented scenes to recur" (33).

BIBLIOGRAPHY

Abstracts of Reports of the Immigration Commission. Vol. 2. Washington, D.C.: GPO, 1908.

Adams, Ansel. *Born Free and Equal: Photographs of the Loyal Japanese-Americans at Manzanar Relocation Center, Inyo County, California.* New York: Public Information, 1944.

Alperovitz, Gar. *Atomic Diplomacy.* New York: Vintage, 1967.

American Committee for the Protection of the Foreign Born. "Concentration Camps, USA: 'It has happened here before, it could happen again—to you!' " New York, 1969.

Arensberg, Conrad. "Report on a Developing Community: Poston, Arizona." *Applied Anthropology* 2, no. 1 (1942): 1–21.

Armstrong, Nancy. *Desire and Domestic Fiction: A Political History of the Novel.* New York: Oxford University Press, 1987.

Ashmead, John, Lt. USNR. "Japs Look at Yanks." *Atlantic Monthly,* April 1947: 52–55.

Balibar, Etienne, and Immanuel Wallerstein, eds. *Race, Nation, Class: Ambiguous Identities.* New York: Verso, 1991.

Barker, Rodney. *The Hiroshima Maidens: A Story of Courage, Compassion, and Survival.* New York: Viking, 1985.

Behrstock, Arthur. "Japan Goes America." *American Magazine,* May 1947: 12–16.

Benedict, Ruth. *The Chrysanthemum and the Sword: Patterns of Japanese Culture.* 1946. New York: New American Library, 1974.

Benjamin, Walter. *Illuminations: Essays and Reflections.* 1955. New York: Schocken Books, 1969.

Boas, Franz. *The Mind of Primitive Man.* New York: Macmillan, 1913.

———. "The Occurrence of Similar Interventions in Areas Widely Apart." *Science* 9 (1887): 485–86.

———. "What the Negro Has Done in Africa." *The Ethical Record* 5 (1904): 106–9.

Boris, Eileen. " 'You Wouldn't Want One of 'Em Dancing with Your Wife': Racialized Bodies on the Job in World War II." *American Quarterly* 50, no. 1 (March 1998): 77–108.

Breines, Wini. *Young, White, and Miserable: Growing Up Female in the Fifties.* Boston: Beacon Press, 1992.

Brown, Elaine. *A Taste of Power: A Black Woman's Story.* New York: Anchor Books, 1994.

Brown, Gordon. "WRA Gila River Project, Arizona Community Analysis Section Final Report." *Applied Anthropology* 4, no. 4 (1945): 1–52.

Busch, Noel. "Tokyo Geisha." *Life* (March 17, 1947): 36–42, 56.

Calderon, Elaine. "Speaker Challenges Students to Act." *The Bucknellian Online.*

Chan, Sucheng. *Asian Americans: An Interpretive History.* New York: Twayne Publishers, 1991.

Cheung, King-Kok. *Articulate Silences: Hisaye Yamamoto, Maxine Hong Kingston, and Joy Kogawa.* Ithaca, N.Y.: Cornell University Press, 1993.

Cleaver, Eldridge. *Soul on Ice.* New York: Dell, 1968.

Corber, Robert. *In the Name of National Security: Hitchcock, Homophobia, and the Political Construction of Gender in Postwar America.* Durham, N.C.: Duke University Press, 1993.

Cousins, Norman. "Interim Report on the Maidens." *The Saturday Review,* October 15, 1955.

———. "The Maidens are Coming." *The Saturday Review.* April 9, 1955.

Daniels, Roger. *Coming to America: A History of Immigration and Ethnicity in American Life.* Princeton, N.J.: HarperCollins, 1990.

———. *Concentration Camps, U.S.A.: Japanese Americans and World War II.* New York: Holt, Rinehart and Winston, 1970.

Davidov, Judith Fryer. " 'The Color of My Skin, the Shape of My Eyes': Photographs of the Japanese-American Internment by Dorothea Lange, Ansel Adams, and Toyo Miyatake." *The Yale Journal of Criticism* 9, no. 2 (1996): 223–44.

de Certeau, Michel. *The Writing of History.* Trans. Tom Conley. New York: Columbia University Press, 1988.

Deutsch, Helene. *The Psychology of Women.* New York: Grune and Stratton, 1944.

DeWitt, J. L. Memorandum to Chief of Staff, October 5, 1942. ASW 014.311 WDC Segregation: Japs. RG 107. National Archives, Washington, D.C.

Doane, Mary Ann. "The Voice in Cinema: The Articulation of Body in Space." In Elizabeth Weis and John Belton, eds., *Theory and Practice of Film Sound.* New York: Columbia University Press, 1985.

Dower, John. *War without Mercy: Race and Power in the Pacific War.* New York: Pantheon Books, 1986.

Dreiser, Theodore. *Sister Carrie.* 1901. New York, Modern Library, 1999.

Duus, Masayo. *Tokyo Rose, Orphan of the Pacific*. New York: Kodansha International, 1979.

Embree, John. "Community Analysis—An Example of Anthropology in Government." *American Anthropologist* 46, no. 3 (July–September 1944): 277–91.

Fabian, Johannes. *Time and the Other: How Anthropology Makes Its Objects*. New York: Columbia University Press, 1983.

Farnham, Marynia F. *Modern Woman: The Lost Sex*. New York: Grosset & Dunlap, 1947.

Felman, Shoshana. "Benjamin's Silence." *Critical Inquiry* 25, no. 2 (winter 1999): 201–34.

Foucault, Michel. "College de France Lecture." In *Culture, Power, History: A Reader in Contemporary Social Theory*, eds. Nicholas B. Dirks, Geoff Eley, and Sherry P. Ortner. Princeton, N.J.: Princeton University Press, 1994.

———. *The History of Sexuality. Volume I: An Introduction*. New York: Vintage Books, 1980.

———. *Language, Counter-Memory, Practice: Selected Essays and Interviews*. Ed. Donald F. Bouchard. Trans. Sherry Simon. Ithaca: Cornell University Press, 1980.

Fujino, Diane. "Revolutions from the Heart: The Making of an Asian American Women Activist." In Sonia Shah, ed., *Dragon Ladies: Asian American Feminists Breathe Fire*. Boston: South End Press, 1997.

Garber, Marjorie, and Rebecca L. Walkowitz, eds. *Secret Agents: The Rosenberg Case, McCarthyism, and Fifties America*. New York: Routledge, 1995.

Gayn, Mark. "Tokyo Rose Jailed, But May Never Be Tried." *San Francisco Chronicle*, May 6, 1946.

Gilman, Charlotte Perkins. *Women and Economics: A Study of the Economic Relations between Men and Women as a Factor in Social Evolution*. 1901. Boston: Dover, 1998.

Glenn, Evelyn Nakano. *Issei, Nisei, War Bride: Three Generations of Japanese American Women in Domestic Service*. Philadelphia: Temple University Press, 1986.

Gorer, Geoffrey. "Themes in Japanese Culture." In *Personal Character and Cultural Milieu*, ed. Douglas G. Harding, 272–91. Syracuse, N.Y.: Syracuse University Press, 1948.

Hadley, Eleanor. *Antitrust in Japan*. Princeton, N.J.: Princeton University Press, 1970.

Handler, Richard. "Boasnian Anthropology and the Critique of American Culture." *American Quarterly* 42, no. 1 (June 1990): 266–80.

———. "Vigorous Male and Aspiring Female: Poetry, Personality and Culture in Edward Sapir and Ruth Benedict." *History of Anthropology* 4 (1986): 152–69.

Hansen, Asael. "Community Analysis at Heart Mountain Reloation Center." *Applied Anthropology* (Summer 1946): 15–25.

Harding, Douglas, ed. *Personal Character and Cultural Milieu*. Syracuse, N.Y.: Syracuse University Press, 1948.

Hirsch, Marianne. "Family Pictures: *Maus*, Mourning, and Post-Memory." *Discourse* 15, no. 2 (winter 1992–93): 3–29.

"Historic Decision for Equality." *Life*. May 31, 1955.

Houston, Jeanne Wakatsuki. *Farewell to Manzanar*. New York: Bantam Books, 1973.

Howe, Russell Warren. *The Hunt for Tokyo Rose*. New York: Madison Books, 1990.

Hu, Arthur. "Asian Americans: Model Minority or Double Minority?" *Amerasia Journal* 15 (1989): 243–57.

Huberman, Martin. "Backwoods Japan During the American Occupation." *National Geographic*, April 1947, 491–58.

Huyssen, Andreas. *Twilight Memories: Marking Time in a Culture of Amnesia*. New York: Routledge, 1995.

Ichioka, Yuji. *The Issei: The World of the First Generation Japanese Immigrants, 1885–1924*. New York: Free Press, 1988.

———, ed. *Views from Within: The Japanese American Evacuation and Resettlement Study*. Los Angeles: Asian American Studies Center at UCLA, 1989.

Irons, Peter. *Justice Delayed: The Record of the Japanese American Internment Cases*. Middleton, Conn.: Wesleyan University Press, 1989.

James, Henry. *Daisy Miller*. 1878. New York: Penguin, 1988.

Kallen, Horace. "Democracy versus the Melting Pot." *Nation*, February 19 and 25, 1915, 190–94, 217–20.

———. "Of Meanings of Culture." *Cultural Pluralism and the American Idea: An Essay in Social Philosophy*. Philadelphia: University of Pennsylvania Press, 1956.

Kammen, Michael. "The Problem of American Exceptionalism: A Reconsideration." *American Quarterly* 45, no. 1 (1993): 1–43.

Kelly, Joan, ed. *Women, History and Theory: The Essays of Joan Kelly*. Chicago: University of Chicago Press, 1984.

Kim, Bok-Lim C. "Asian Wives of U.S. Servicemen: Women in the Shadows." *Amerasia Journal* 4 (1977): 91–115.

Kogawa, Joy. *Obasan*. Boston: David Godine, 1982.

Kolodny, Annette. *The Lay of the Land: Metaphor as Experience and History in American Life and Letters*. Chapel Hill: University of North Carolina Press, 1984.

Koshiro, Yukiko. *Trans-Pacific Racisms and the U.S. Occupation of Japan*. New York: Columbia University Press, 1999.

Kozol, Wendy. *Life's America: Family and Nation in Postwar Photojournalism.* Philadelphia: Temple University Press, 1994.

LaBarre, Weston. *Culture in Context: Writings of Weston LaBarre.* Durham, N.C.: Duke University Press, 1980.

——. "Some Observations on Character Structure in the Orient: The Japanese." *Psychiatry* 8 (1945): 319–42.

Lawrence, Amy. *Echo and Narcissus: Women's Voices in Classical Hollywood Cinema.* Berkeley: University of California Press, 1991.

Lee, Robert. *Orientals: Asian Americans in Popular Culture.* Philadelphia: Temple University Press, 1999.

Leighton, Alexander. "Assessing Public Opinion in a Dislocated Community." *Public Opinion Quarterly* 7 (winter 1943): 652–67.

——. *The Governing of Men: General Principles and Recommendations Based on Experiences at a Japanese Relocation Camp.* Princeton, N.J.: Princeton University Press, 1946.

——. "The Japanese Family in America." *Annals of the American Academy of Politics and Science* 229 (September 1943): 150–56.

——. "Then and Now: Some Notes on the Interaction of Person and Social Environment." *Human Organization* 43, no. 3 (1984): 189–96.

——. "Training Social Scientists for Post-War Conditions." *Applied Anthropology* (July-August-September 1942): 25–30.

Leighton, Alexander, and Morris Opler. "Psychological Warfare and the Japanese Emperor." In *Personalities and Cultures: Readings in Psychological Anthropology,* ed. Robert Hunt, 251–60. New York: Natural History Press, 1967.

"Letter from Henry L. Stimson to Cordell Hull." February 5, 1942. Department of State File 740. 00015. Pacific War-153. National Archives, Washington, D.C.

Limerick, Patricia Nelson *The Legacy of Conquest: The Unbroken Past of the American West.* New York: Norton, 1988.

Lipsitz, George. *Time Passages: Collective Memory and American Popular Culture.* Minneapolis: University of Minnesota Press, 1990.

Lowe, Lisa. *Critical Terrains: French and British Orientalisms.* Ithaca, N.Y.: Cornell University Press, 1991.

——. *Immigrant Acts: On Asian American Cultural Politics.* Durham, N.C.: Duke University Press, 1996.

Lundberg, Ferdinand, and Marynia F. Farnham. *Modern Woman: The Lost Sex.* New York: Grosset and Dunlap, 1947.

May, Elaine Tyler. *Homeward Bound: American Families in the Cold War Era.* New York: Basic Books, 1988.

McClintock, Anne. *Imperial Leather: Race, Gender, and Sexuality in the Colonial Conquest.* New York: Routledge, 1995.

Meyerowitz, Joanne, ed. *Not June Cleaver: Women and Gender in Postwar America, 1945–1960*. Philadelphia: Temple University Press, 1994.

Michener, James. "Pursuit of Happiness by a GI and a Japanese." *Life*, February 21, 1955, 124–26, 129–39.

———. *Sayonara*. New York: Fawcett Crest, 1953.

Modell, Judith Schacter. *Ruth Benedict: Patterns of a Life*. Philadelphia: University of Pennsylvania Press, 1983.

Murayama, Milton. *All I Asking For is My Body*. 1977. Honolulu: University of Hawaii Press, 1988.

Mydans, Carl. "Tule Lake." *Life*, March 20, 1944, 25–35.

Myrdal, Gunnar. *An American Dilemma: The Negro Problem and American Democracy*. New York: Harper, 1944.

Nadel, Alan. *Containment Culture: American Narratives, Postmodernism, and the Atomic Age*. Durham, N.C.: Duke University Press, 1995.

Naeve, Virginia. *Friends of the Hibakusha*. Denver: Allan Swallow, 1964.

Navasky, Victor. *Naming Names*. New York: Penguin, 1980.

Nicholson, Linda. *Gender and History: The Limits of Social Theory in the Age of the Family*. New York: Columbia University Press, 1986.

Nishimoto, Richard. *Inside an American Concentration Camp: Japanese American Resistance at Poston*. Tucson: University of Arizona Press, 1995.

"No Happy Birthday!" *San Francisco Chronicle*, July 5, 1949: A-1.

Okada, John. *No-No Boy*. 1957. Seattle: University of Washington, 1995.

Okimoto, Daniel I. *American in Disguise*. New York: Walker/Weatherhill, 1971.

Okubo, Mine. *Citizen 13660*. 1946. Seattle: University of Washington Press, 1983.

Omi, Michael, and Howard Winant. *Racial Formation in the United States: From the 1960s to the 1980s*. New York: Routledge, 1986.

Osajima, Keith. "Asian Americans as the Model Minority: An Analysis of the Popular Press Image in the 1960s and 1980s." *Reflections on Shattered Windows*. Pullman: Washington State University Press, 1988.

Palumbo-Liu, David. *Asian/American: Historical Crossings of a Racial Frontier*. Stanford: Stanford University Press, 1999.

Park, Robert. "Human Migration and the Marginal Man." *Race and Culture*, Vol. 1. Glencoe, Ill.: The Free Press, 1950.

Park, Robert, and Herbert Miller. *Old World Traits Transplanted*. New York: Harper and Brothers, 1921.

Parrott, Lindsey. "Now a Japanese Woman Can Be a Cop." *New York Times Magazine*, June 2, 1946: 59.

Petersen, William. *Japanese Americans: Oppression and Success*. New York: Random House, 1971.

———. "Success Story, Japanese American Style." *Saturday Evening Post*, January 9, 1966: 105–6; 122–25.

Radosh, Ronald, and Joyce Milton. *The Rosenberg File: A Search for the Truth.* New York: Holt, 1983.

Roots: An Asian American Reader. Los Angeles: Asian American Studies Center at UCLA, 1971.

Ross, Andrew. *No Respect: Intellectuals and Popular Culture.* New York: Routledge, 1989.

Saenz, Rogelio, Sean-Shong Hwang, and Benigno E. Aguirre. "In Search of Asian War Brides." *Demography* 31, no. 3 (Aug. 1994): 549–59.

San-Juan, Karin Aguilar, ed. *The State of Asian American Activism and Resistance in the 1990s.* Boston: South End Press, 1994.

Schaller, Michael. *Douglas MacArthur: The Far Eastern General.* New York: Oxford University Press, 1989.

Schlesinger, Arthur, Jr. *The Cycles of American History.* Boston: Houghton Mifflin, 1986.

Shannon, Christopher. "A World Made Safe for Differences: Ruth Benedict's *The Chrysanthemum and the Sword.*" *American Quarterly* 47 (December 1995): 659–80.

Shukert, Elfrieda, and Barbara Scibetta. *War Brides of World War II.* Novato, Calif.: Presidio Press, 1988.

Silverman, Kaja. *The Acoustic Mirror: The Female Voice in Psychoanalysis and Cinema.* Bloomington: Indiana University Press, 1988.

———. *Male Subjectivity at the Margins.* New York: Routledge, 1992.

Slotkin, Richard. *The Fatal Environment: The Myth of the Frontier in the Age of Industrialization, 1800–1890.* Tulsa: University of Oklahoma Press, 1985.

Smith, Henry Nash. *Virgin Land: The American West as Symbol and Myth.* Cambridge: Harvard University Press, 1985.

Smith J. E., and William L. Worden. "They're Bringing Home Japanese Wives." *Saturday Evening Post,* January 19, 1952, 25, 79–81.

Snow, Edgar. "What the Jap is Thinking Now." *Saturday Evening Post,* May, 1946: 9–11; 36; 39.

Sone, Monica. *Nisei Daughter.* Boston: Little, Brown, 1953.

Spicer, Edward. "The Use of Social Scientists by the War Relocation Authority." *Applied Anthropology* (spring 1946): 16–36.

Spickard, Paul. *Mixed Blood: Intermarriage and Ethnic Identity in Twentieth-Century America.* Madison: University of Wisconsin Press, 1989.

Starn, Orin. "Engineering Internment: Anthropologists and the War Relocation Authority." *American Ethnologist* (1986): 700–20.

Stimson, Henry L. Letter to Cordell Hull. February 5, 1942. Department of State File 740.00115 Pacific War-153, National Archives, Washington, D.C.

Stocking, George W., Jr., ed. *A Franz Boas Reader: The Shaping of American Anthropology, 1883–1911.* Chicago: University of Chicago Press, 1974.

———. *Functionalism Historicized: Essays on British Social Anthropology,* History of Anthropology Series, Volume 2. Madison: University of Wisconsin Press, 1984.

———. "Ideas and Institutions in American Anthropology: Thoughts toward a History of the Interwar Years," *Selected Papers from the American Anthropologist, 1921–1945.* Washington D. C.: GPO, 1976.

———, ed. *Malinowski, Rivers, Benedict and Other Essays on Culture and Personality.* History of Anthropology Series, Volume 4. Madison: University of Wisconsin Press, 1986.

Stoler, Ann Laura. *Race and the Education of Desire: Foucault's History of Sexuality and the Colonial Order of Things.* Durham, N.C.: Duke University Press, 1996.

Strecker, Edward. *Their Mothers' Sons: The Psychiatrist Examines an American Problem.* Philadelphia: J. B. Lippincott, 1946.

Sturken, Marita. "Absent Images of Memory: Remembering and Reenacting the Japanese Internment." *positions* 5, no. 3 (winter 1997): 687–707.

Suzuki, Bob. "Asian-American as the Model Minority." *Change* (November 1989): 13–19.

Suzuki, Peter. "Anthropologists in the Wartime Camps for Japanese Americans: A Documentary Study." *Dialectical Anthropology* 6, no. 1 (1981): 23–60.

———. "A Retrospective Analysis of a Wartime 'National Character' Study." *Dialectical Anthropology* 5, no. 1 (1980): 33–46.

———. "When Black Was White: Misapplied Anthropology in Wartime America." *Man and Life* 12, nos. 1–2 (1986): 10–12.

Takaki, Ronald. *Strangers from a Different Shore: A History of Asian Americans.* New York: Penguin Books, 1989.

Thomas, Dorothy Swaine. *The Salvage: Japanese American Evacuation and Resettlement.* Berkeley: University of California Press, 1952.

———. *The Spoilage: Japanese American Evacuation and Resettlement.* Berkeley: University of California Press, 1946.

"Tokyo Rose on Trial." *San Francisco Chronicle,* August 4, 1949.

"Traitor's Pay." *Los Angeles Examiner,* September 3, 1945.

Turner, Frederick Jackson. *The Frontier in American History.* 1894. New York: Dover, 1996.

United States Commissioner of Immigration and Naturalization. "Table 6: Asian Women Immigrants Admitted to the U.S. as Wives of American Citizens." In *Annual Reports, 1947–75.* Washington, D.C.: GPO, 1975.

United States Immigration Commission (1907–11). "Changes in Bodily Form of Descendents of Immigrants." Government Printing Office (GPO), 1908.

The Unquiet Death of Julius and Ethel Rosenberg, Alvin Goldstein, producer. Chicago: Facets Multimedia, 1988.

Veblen, Thorstein. *Theory of the Leisure Class.* 1899. New York: Penguin, 1994.

"Victory Celebrations," *Life*, August 27, 1945, 21–33.

Wald, Priscilla. *Constituting Americans: Cultural Anxiety and Narrative Form.* Durham N.C.: Duke University Press, 1995.

Walz, Jay. "Arrest of 'Tokyo Rose' Ordered: San Francisco Jury to Sift Case." *New York Times*, August 17, 1948.

Wang, Katie. "'U' Opens Asian American Lounge." *Michigan Daily Online*, February 4, 1997.

Wasby, Stephen, Anthony D'Amato, and Rosemary Metrailer. *Desegregation from Brown to Alexander: An Exploration of Supreme Court Strategies.* Carbondale: Southern Illinois University Press, 1977.

Weglyn, Michi. *Years of Infamy: The Untold Story of America's Concentration Camps.* New York: Morrow, Quill, 1976.

Wei, William. *The Asian American Movement.* Philadelphia: Temple University Press, 1994.

Wharton, Edith. *House of Mirth.* 1905. New York: Modern Library, 1999.

"Who Is Tokyo Rose?" *New York Times*, September 1, 1945, A1.

Williams, Vernon. *Re-thinking Race: Franz Boas and His Contemporaries.* Lexington: University of Kentucky Press, 1996.

Williams, William Appleman. *The Tragedy of American Diplomacy.* New York: Dell, 1972.

Wong, Paul, Chienping Faith Lai, Richard Nagasawa, and Tieming Lin. "Asian Americans as a Model Minority: Self Perceptions by Other Racial Groups." *Sociological Perspectives* 14, no. 1 (1998): 96–118.

Woodard, William P. *The Allied Occupation of Japan, 1945–52, and Japanese Religions.* Leiden: E. J. Brill, 1972.

Wylie, Philip. *A Generation of Vipers.* New York: Farrar & Rinehart, 1942.

Yamamoto, Hisaye. *Seventeen Syllables and Other Stories.* Latham, N.Y.: Kitchen Table and Women of Color Press, 1988.

Yamamoto, Traise. *Masking Selves, Making Subjects: Japanese American Women, Identity, and the Body.* Berkeley: University of California, 1998.

Yans-McLaughlin, Virginia. "Science, Democracy, and Ethics: Mobilizing Culture and Personality for World War II." In *Malinowski, Rivers, Benedict, and Others: Essays on Culture and Personality*, ed. George W. Stocking Jr. History of Anthropology series, Vol. 4. Madison: University of Wisconsin Press, 1986.

Yogi, Stan. "Legacies Revealed: Uncovering Buried Plots in the Stories of Hisaye Yamamoto." *Studies in American Fiction* 17, no. 2 (1989): 169–81.

Yu, Henry. "Constructing the 'Oriental Problem' in American Thought, 1920–1960." In *Multicultural Education, Transformative Knowledge, and Action: Historical and Contemporary Perspectives*, ed. James A. Banks, 156–75. New York: Teachers College Press, 1996.

———. "The 'Oriental Problem' in America, 1920–1960: Linking the Identities of Chinese American and Japanese American Intellectuals." In *Claiming America: Constructing Chinese American Identities during the Exclusion Era*, ed. K. Scott Wong and Sucheng Chan, 194–214. Philadelphia: Temple University Press, 1998.

Zinn, Howard. *A People's History of the United States*. New York: Harper, 1980.

———. *The Twentieth Century: A People's History*. New York: Harper, 1984.

INDEX

Caroline Chung Simpson is Assistant Professor of English
at the University of Washington.

Library of Congress Cataloging-in-Publication Data
Simpson, Caroline Chung.
An absent presence : Japanese Americans in postwar American culture,
1945–1960 / Caroline Chung Simpson.
p. cm.—(New Americanists)
Includes bibliographical references and index.
ISBN 0-8223-2756-2 (cloth : alk. paper)—ISBN 0-8223-2746-5 (pbk. : alk. paper)
1. Japanese Americans—Government relations. 2. Japanese Americans—Social
conditions—20th century. 3. Cold War—Social aspects—United States. 4. United
States—Social conditions—1945– 5. United States—Ethnic relations. 6. Japanese
Americans—Evacuation and relocation, 1942–1945. I. Series.
E184.J3 S55 2001
305.895'6073—dc21   2001040213